ARABELLA BOXER'S GARDEN COOKBOOK

D1421305

Also by Arabella Boxer and available from Sphere

CHRISTMAS FOOD AND DRINK

Arabella Boxer's Garden Cookbook

SPHERE BOOKS LIMITED
30/32 Gray's Inn Road, London WC1X 8JP

First published in Great Britain by Weidenfeld & Nicolson Ltd 1974
Copyright © 1974 Arabella Boxer
Published by Sphere Books 1977

Set in Monotype Baskerville

Printed in Great Britain by
Hazell Watson & Viney Ltd
Aylesbury, Bucks

Contents

Introduction

My preference for vegetables, both for cooking and eating, has grown steadily over the past four or five years. As there are several contributory factors, I cannot help thinking there must be many others who feel as I do. I believe the main reason is that they make such beautiful material with which to work, whether gathered from one's own garden, or selected with care from the shops. In this they differ from meat and fish, both of which slightly disgust me in their raw state. There is also the pleasure of choosing vegetables, seeing each week what has newly come into season, and rejecting what has passed its best. Unlike the butcher's shop, where the produce varies little according to season, the greengrocer is a constant reminder of the passing months, and as each new root, leaf and fruit makes its appearance, so a dish that is relevant to that particular moment suggests itself.

As meat grows ever more expensive, my enthusiasm for it has waned still further. Contrary to the general propaganda, urging us to experiment with cheaper cuts and learn to make them into sustaining meals, I find that I have done the opposite, and now think of meat as a luxury. I resent the time spent on transforming unattractive pieces of flesh into edible dishes, and am only prepared to make this sort of effort during the bleakest winter months. During the rest of the year I prefer to buy the best meat, which requires only grilling or roasting, once or twice a week in small quantities, rather than make a time-consuming economical meat dish each day.

I have come to think of fish in the same way. Except for the occasional dish of kedgeree or smoked haddock, I prefer from time to time to buy halibut or turbot, salmon trout or bass without resenting the price, rather than cod or haddock two or three times a week.

Poultry is one of the few foods that has come down in price, and this I buy more often, partly because chicken combines so well with vegetable dishes, and partly because I

7

rely on a regular supply of good chicken stock.

The rest of the time I live on dishes made from combinations of vegetables with pastry, rice, noodles, cheese or eggs, gnocchi or pancakes. I do not always save time or money by eating in this way, for accumulating a varied selection of vegetables is not always cheap, and there is quite a lot of work involved, but the preparation is pleasant, does not smell and provides a series of dishes that are tempting and never monotonous.

I am by no means a strict vegetarian. Many of the dishes in this book contain a small amount of meat, but it is the proportion that is different: the meat is used as an accessory rather than the focal point of the meal. A stuffed cabbage may have some minced meat in the farce, a dish of string beans may be garnished with chopped bacon, while *risi e bisi*, the Italian vegetable risotto, is much improved by a handful of chopped *prosciutto*. A ham bone gives added flavour and nourishment to a soup of dried peas, while duck fat or beef dripping give an excellent flavour and improved texture to a dish of dried lentils or haricot beans. I like to make most vegetable soups with chicken or veal stock, but vegetable stock can be substituted if preferred. There is even a reasonably good vegetable stock cube now available in health food shops.

By writing this book I have hoped to encourage more people to experiment in the realms of vegetable cookery, and to extend their range of vegetable dishes. I am convinced that more and more people in England will be forced, for a variety of reasons, to cut down their average consumption of meat, and compensate with vegetables.

Our knowledge and use of vegetables and herbs is very limited, and has diminished rather than grown over the last three or four hundred years. In *The English Hus-wife* by Gervase Markham, published in 1615, the list of salad vegetables and herbs is impressively long, and includes asparagus, coleworts (collards), spinach, lettuce, parsnips, radishes, chives, garlic, borage, bugloss, chervil, coriander, gourds, cress, marjoram, purslane, rocket, rosemary, sorrel, marigolds, thyme, anise, beetroot, skirrets, succory (chicory), fennel, parsley, cabbage, white and green cole (kale), cucumbers, hartshorn, onions, burnet, leeks, 'apples of love' (tomatoes), artichokes, basil, samphire, gilly-flowers, hyssop, savory, sage, orache, and oreganum. There are also many others with lovely names, such as blessed-thistle, holy-thistle, white-poppy, palma-christi, spike, flower-gentil, larks-heel, which no longer mean anything to us. If one considers the numbers of vegetables that were formerly grown and are now forgotten or rarely seen, the recent introductions seem comparatively few.

The English custom of serving vegetables as an accompaniment to meat has resulted in their unimaginative treatment. If considered merely as an accessory there is little point in taking much trouble over them; a complementary sauce, for instance, would only clash with the gravy. The French custom, where vegetables have always been served as a course on their own, usually following the meat, has resulted in a range of 'vegetable dishes' as opposed to simply 'cooked vegetables'.

In the last ten or fifteen years French eating habits in the home have gradually changed, and a meatless meal is now a usual event. Meat is rarely eaten more than once a day in the average house, while the other meals are carefully planned combinations of vegetables with eggs, cheese, rice or pastry. These little meals, planned and cooked with loving care, usually consisting of two or three courses, are an admirable example of what can be done with imagination in this field. If one studies a suggested week's menus in any popular French magazine, such as *Elle* or *Marie-Claire*, one is surprised by the small amounts of meat consumed, and by the ingenuity of the meals.

In the American home vegetables have always been treated with more respect than in the average English household. The enormous range of salads alone is proof of the respect given to vegetables, both cooked and raw. (I am convinced that the American passion for salads sprang from the first English settlers, as salads were held in high esteem in England at that time. Indeed an English cookery book of the period starts with a chapter on salads as they are rated 'of the first importance'.)

I would simply like to alter the emphasis of our meals; to bring them closer to the Chinese meal, for example, where a dish of meat or fish is included among a selection of other foods, or where a small quantity of meat is cooked with a vegetable, such as strips of rump steak with green peppers or snow peas. Another thing that appeals to me about Chinese cuisine is the way in which each food is treated as of equal importance – a dish of bamboo sprouts that have probably been grown in the kitchen is given the same amount of care as one of sweet-and-sour lobster balls. In recent years our own cookery has become too imbued with snobbery and certain foods are thought 'less good' than others: 'all right for the family', as someone once remarked about my first cookery book, 'but not good enough for dinner parties'. This is a bad way of thinking that has been fostered by journalism and the endless fuss that has gone on about entertaining. As Boulestin, my hero among cookery writers, once said: 'When entertaining one's friends, one should have the same sort of food one has all the time, only more of it.' Even the assumption that one would automatically be entertaining one's friends might seem surprising nowadays.

All foods are equal; some are more expensive than others, some more nutritious, and naturally we all have our individual preferences, but it is ludicrous to think in terms of 'A-foods' and 'B-foods'. In fact I think it is very important to be sure of our own preferences, and to be certain that they are not affected by irrelevant values. Many expensive foods are only good when eaten rarely anyway; to me at any rate, asparagus would quickly become a bore if eaten every day, but occasionally it is truly delicious. Luckily the cheaper foods seem more conducive to daily consumption: I can't imagine growing tired of potatoes and onions, leeks and tomatoes, so long as they are cooked with care and imagination.

It is hard to make vegetables monotonous; they are so versatile and their flavour varies continually, depending on the weather. Many of them can be eaten raw as well as cooked: as juices, salads, soups, purées, casseroles, fritters, pancakes, soufflés, timbales, mousses, flans, etc. Vegetable dishes complement each other, and benefit by being served in combinations of two or three. After each recipe I have suggested suitable dishes to serve at the same time, for those wishing to make a whole meal of vegetables. At the end of the book there are twenty suggested menus for winter and summer meals. The possibilities are truly endless, and in writing this book I have merely hoped to enlarge our range slightly, and to encourage others to take it still further.

Vegetable cookery is one of the few spheres where the amateur has the advantage over the professional. I have long felt defeated by the superior advantages of the restaurateur over the housewife in the field of meat, both in the marketing, hanging and cutting, to say nothing of the huge charcoal grills for cooking. I could never hope to produce as good a steak, except by luck, as the best restaurant, but in the case of vegetables it should be an easy victory for the amateur. The preparation alone makes fresh vegetables uneconomic on a large scale, and the fact that the average restaurant menu is dedicated to the old-fashioned style of eating – meat or fish as a main course with vegetable accompaniments – means that not nearly enough care is given to their treatment. Few restaurants bother to devote much thought or imagination to vegetables; apart from the occasional soufflé in the list of first courses, they are simply considered as side dishes, and treated as such.

I remember seeing, in a simple restaurant in a poor district of Naples, a huge tray, straight from the oven, of tomatoes and aubergines cooked in a delicious oily gratin and spiked with garlic and herbs – a thing one would never find in restaurants of any calibre in England or the United States. Even the vegetarian restaurants offer little in the way of vegetables *tous simples*; they are almost always weighed down with grain or starch in some form.

So it is only in our own homes that we can enjoy vegetables at their best, and in an ideal world this would also include growing them in our own gardens. There can be few things more satisfying than feeding one's family and friends with food that one has prepared, literally, 'from scratch', but alas this is seldom possible. However once one has acknowledged the emotional satisfaction of growing one's own food, even the addition of a handful of herbs grown on the kitchen window-sill can add an individual touch to a dish.

ARABELLA BOXER
1974

Materials and Utensils

When preparing vegetables I find the actual cooking materials of the utmost importance. Perhaps because of the fragility of the vegetable flavour, the choice of other ingredients seems to be vital. Anyone who has ever tried to make a green salad in a rented house, as I have, with *Crosse and Blackwell* olive oil and malt vinegar, will know what I mean. I am constantly experimenting with different varieties of oils, fats and dairy products, and changing my mind about the relative virtues of, say, sunflower-seed oil over arachide oil; but this in itself seems to have a certain value, as it prevents monotony.

FATS AND OILS

I use unsalted butter, despite the cost. I find margarine perfectly adequate for cooking, and I use it sometimes for reasons of diet or economy, but for me nothing can replace the taste of uncooked butter melting over a dish of plainly boiled or steamed vegetables. Animal fats are excellent for certain purposes. I use beef dripping in the winter for dishes of root vegetables and dried vegetables; goose fat is invaluable for hearty vegetable soups, while chicken and duck fat are also good, especially for frying potatoes.

I like to have a range of oils for different purposes, although the two I use most are olive oil and sunflower-seed oil. I use olive oil for salads and for cooking, when I often mix it half and half with butter – the addition of oil stops the butter burning, while the butter gives a good flavour. Sunflower-seed oil I use for salads and for sautéing; it gives a lighter taste than olive oil and seems to suit certain foods better. Arachide (or nut) oil is a good substitute for sunflower-seed oil; they are both light and almost tasteless. For deep frying I use a mixture of arachide oil and sunflower-seed oil; *Rakusen's* make a good combination oil. I buy these in large quantities, but there are other oils I like to have in small amounts: sesame oil, for adding to certain Middle Eastern dishes such as *homus*, or *aubergine mesa*; while *tahini*, the paste made from sesame seeds, is indispensable for both these dishes. Almond oil I use occasionally in salads, while walnut oil is delicious in certain salads, particularly one of chicory, endive and watercress, with a few sliced walnuts added. It is a very rich oil, and I prefer to mix it half and half with a light oil rather than use it alone. Corn oil is one I can do without; I can find no reason for using it except economy, and that does not seem good enough.

I use white wine vinegar almost always, occasionally adding tarragon vinegar for a herby flavour. Red wine vinegar I use for meat dishes; malt vinegar never.

DAIRY PRODUCTS

Apart from butter there are several other dairy products which are invaluable in vegetable cookery. I find the whole range of creams, sour creams, yoghurts, smetanas and buttermilk extremely useful, especially for summer dishes such as cold soups and uncooked sauces and dressings. When eating a lot of salads one needs to vary the dressings; anyone familiar with the hors-d'oeuvre tray in a moderate restaurant will know the monotony of a number of dishes dressed with the identical *vinaigrette*. With both raw salads and *salades composées* (those made with cooked vegetables), it is easy to make numerous variations with mixtures of yoghurt, sour cream, olive oil, etc. When presenting several dishes of this sort at one meal, I also like to have one with practically no dressing at all – just a sprinkling of lemon juice. I find it a relief to the palate to eat one dish with no oil or cream.

I use yoghurt a lot in uncooked dishes; in cooking it must first be treated in some way to prevent it separating and spoiling the appearance of the dish. The easiest way to do this is to mix a carton of yoghurt to a smooth paste with a teaspoonful of flour before adding it to the dish. In many of the dishes in this book, yoghurt, cream and sour cream are interchangeable, depending on your taste and the required degree of richness. Buttermilk is hard to find in England, which is sad as I use it a lot in cold soups. A reasonable substitute can be made by mixing milk with sour cream and a little lemon juice. Smetana is another useful product that

14

is fairly hard to find; it comes in two degrees of richness, and is like a cross between buttermilk and cream. All these products go well with vegetables; they seem to add a degree of richness and creamyness, without the weight produced by quantities of cream. They are also healthier and much less fattening than pure cream, and have a pleasant tartness. They give to cold dishes what butter gives to hot dishes: a certain smoothness of texture, and they seem to bring out the individual flavour of the vegetable itself. It is surprising, for instance, how much buttermilk one can add to a cold soup without killing its own flavour, something the same amount of cream would inevitably do.

SEASONING

As for seasonings, I use sea salt and freshly ground black peppercorns without exception. Even when making a pale sauce, when technically one should use white pepper for the sake of appearance, I usually use black pepper as I much prefer the taste, and don't mind the little black flecks. I sometimes use celery salt for flavouring, and I like experimenting with different mixtures of pepper. At the moment I am very fond of a mixture of coarsely ground red peppers which a friend brought back from Japan, but the name is indecipherable to Western eyes. Except for nutmeg and mace, I find little use for spices in cooking vegetables. These two I use interchangeably in cheese sauces, white sauces and some soups.

Lemons are constantly in evidence in my kitchen; I also use orange juice and lime juice (fresh of course), for light summer salads. During the summer, when fresh herbs are available, there is little need for much else in the way of added flavours; I have a prejudice against dried herbs and, with the exception of bay leaves, I rarely use them.

UTENSILS

There are a few utensils that I find absolutely essential in vegetable cookery, for both the preparation and the cooking. Firstly, a double sink with a waste disposal unit in one side; secondly, a large wooden chopping surface, preferably teak, plus an extra chopping board, and two really good French steel knives, one very small, and one long one. Then for the cooking: two or three large steel saucepans with heavy bases; one very deep pot for making vegetable stocks; one large round cast iron casserole – for cooking dishes like *sauerkraut* in large quantities; one lidded sauté pan which is invaluable for braising and stewing vegetables, and a skillet for frying. *Le Creuset* make a useful combination of a sauté pan and skillet with an interchangeable lid. A steamer is very useful, especially for potatoes and fragile vegetables such as broccoli and cauliflower, but can be improvised by using a colander or strainer inside a saucepan. Then a few luxuries, well worth buying but not essential: a tall narrow pan for sauces, so one can really beat them without splashing, and a small china bowl to fit in the top, for making delicate egg-based sauces like *hollandaise*; and one or two small white china saucepans with lids, for cooking or serving sauces, or small amounts of vegetables.

Next, a vital piece of equipment: the vegetable mill or *mouli-légumes*. I find the largest size far the most useful; the French 'mouli-légumes' which is sold throughout England is excellent, with three removable discs of varying fineness. Since discovering the vegetable mill, I have rarely used a sieve, but I think every kitchen should possess one, either of hair or nylon, and a pair of strainers, one round with a coarse mesh, and one conical with a very fine mesh. An electric blender is extremely useful for puréeing vegetables and for making smooth soups like *vichysoisse*, but I use the vegetable mill far more often as I much prefer some texture to my food to the inevitable smoothness of the blended soup. A juice extractor is a total luxury, at least in my kitchen, considering the price in relation to the amount of use it gets. But it is a lovely thing to have; nothing is better than fresh tomato, apple or carrot juice when these foods are at their cheapest and most plentiful. It is also useful for feeding invalids and sick children as even small amounts of pure vegetable juice are extremely nourishing and appetising.

A gadget that many people find invaluable is the mandoline, or 'waefa' grater. I cut my knuckles badly the first time I tried to use it and have avoided it ever since. I slice my cucumbers on a ham slicer, or by hand. The *Moulinex* electric shredder and grater works well, while there is a

Swiss version, worked by hand rather than electricity which is just as effective and less expensive. The Swiss, who are very keen on raw foods and vegetable diets, make excellent equipment, including a far better potato peeler than any I have seen in England. It has a swivel-type cutting blade at right angles to the handle, and is extremely quick and pleasant to use.

For the most part, however, I dislike assembling and cleaning machines, and resent the storage space they take; I really prefer to do most things like slicing and chopping vegetables and herbs by hand. I cut potatoes and onions in half lengthways, then lay the cut surface flat on the board, and slice them as evenly as possible. I chop parsley on a flat surface with a long sharp knife, holding it with both hands, one at each end, and swivelling the blade round at angles to the point. Chives should always be cut with scissors, as chopping bruises them and they turn black at the edges.

As for serving vegetables, I have an austere passion for pure white china. The vegetables are so colourful, and make such attractive combinations, that I find any decoration on the china merely detracts from the appearance of the dish. The only coloured china I like is the French range of earthenware dishes, rectangular or oval, with brown exteriors and yellow glazed interiors.

Soups

Bean Soup

½ lb dried haricot beans (medium-sized
    soissons beans)
2 carrots
2 leeks
2 stalks celery
½ lb tomatoes
4 Tbs olive oil
1½ pt bean stock
salt and black pepper
chopped parsley

Soak the dried beans for 2 hours, then cook them gently in simmering water until tender, adding salt only towards the end of the cooking time. Drain the beans, reserving the liquid. (Alternatively use ½ lb beans left over from another dish, with 1½ pt of their cooking stock.) Chop the carrots, leeks, celery and peeled tomatoes separately. Heat the oil in a heavy pan and brown the leeks in it, adding the carrots, celery and tomatoes at intervals of about 3 minutes. When all are slightly softened and golden, pour in the re-heated stock. Bring to boiling point and cook until the vegetables are tender (about 20 minutes). Stir in the beans and re-heat. Season to taste with plenty of salt and coarsely ground black pepper. Sprinkle with chopped parsley, or have a bowl of it on the table. Serves 6. This makes a very substantial soup for cold weather; for a less thick soup use ¼ lb beans.

Bortsch

1 large onion
2 large beetroot
2–3 carrots, depending on size
2 stalks celery
2 cloves garlic (optional)
4 large tomatoes
1½ oz butter
3½ pt stock: good beef, duck *or* beef and
    chicken, i.e. the remains of a *pot-au-feu*
salt and black pepper
1 bunch parsley, including the root
2 cloves
1 bay leaf
1–2 Tbs lemon juice
¼ pt sour cream

Chop the onion, cut the beetroot and carrots *en julienne* (like matchsticks), slice the celery, mince the garlic, skin and chop the tomatoes. Melt the butter in a large deep soup pot and cook the onion until it starts to soften and colour. Add the beetroot, carrots and celery. Cook gently for 10 minutes, stirring now and then. Add the tomatoes and garlic and cook another 5 minutes, then pour on the heated stock. Bring to the boil, lower the heat, and add salt and black pepper, parsley, cloves and bay leaf. Simmer gently for 1½ hours. Remove the herbs, add more salt and black pepper, a pinch of sugar, and lemon juice to taste. Serve in a tureen or in individual bowls with sour cream handed separately. Serves 6–8. Alternatively strain the soup and re-heat, adding extra seasonings. Serve in white bowls with sour cream. For a cold bortsch, strain and chill overnight in the refrigerator. Serve with sour cream, as with ICED BEETROOT SOUP.

Celeriac Soup

1 celeriac, weighing about 1 lb
½ lb potatoes
2 oz butter *or* beef dripping
1½ pt beef *or* chicken stock
salt and black pepper
½ gill cream
chopped parsley

Peel the celeriac and cut in cubes. Peel the potatoes and cut in thin slices. Melt the butter in a heavy saucepan and cook the celeriac in it for 5 minutes. Add the sliced potatoes, stir around until well mixed, and pour on the heated stock. Bring to the boil, cover the pan and simmer until both vegetables are soft, about 30 minutes. Put through the medium mesh of the vegetable mill and return to the cleaned pan. Re-heat, stir in the cream and add salt and black pepper to taste. Serve with a bowl of chopped parsley on the table, or sprinkle a little in each bowl. Serves 4–6. Celeriac contains more iron than almost any other food, so this is an extremely nourishing soup, particularly suitable for anaemic children.

Celeriac and Carrot Soup

1 celeriac, weighing about 1 lb
½ lb carrots
light chicken stock, as available (up to 2 pt)
salt and black pepper
1½ oz butter
½ gill cream
chopped parsley

Cut the celeriac in pieces and cover with light chicken stock or water. Scrape and slice the carrots thickly, and treat likewise in a separate pan. (If you have plenty of chicken stock, cook the vegetables in it; otherwise reserve it and cook the vegetables in lightly salted water.) When both the vegetables are tender – about 20 minutes – drain them and reserve the stock or water in which they were cooked. Push both celeriac and carrots through the medium mesh of the vegetable mill and return to the clean pan. Make what chicken stock you have up to 1½ pt by adding some of the water the vegetables cooked in, or if you have no stock, dissolve a little chicken stock powder, or ½ a cube, in 1½ pt of the cooking liquid. Add it to the puréed vegetables (you can use some to help push them through the mill) and re-heat. Add plenty of salt and black pepper, and stir in the butter and cream. Serve in bowls sprinkled with chopped parsley, or have a bowl of it on the table. Serves 6.

Chervil Soup

1½ pt well-flavoured chicken stock
¾ oz butter
1 Tbs flour
1 bunch chervil (2–3 sprigs)
1 egg yolk
1 Tbs lemon juice
salt and black pepper

Heat the stock. Melt the butter, stir in the flour and pour on the heated stock. Stir until blended and simmer gently for about 3 minutes. Put in the bunch of chervil. Leave covered by the side of the fire to infuse for about 30 minutes. Beat the egg yolk in a small bowl with the lemon juice. Remove the chervil from the stock and re-heat to boiling point – if there are any bits of chervil floating about it should be poured through a strainer. Pour a couple of tablespoonfuls of the boiling stock into the egg and lemon mixture, then return the bowlful to the rest of the stock. Stir over very gentle heat for a few minutes without allowing it to reach boiling point. Serves 4. If the stock is strong and good this delicately flavoured soup can be really delicious. It can also be made with tarragon.

Corn Chowder

6 ears corn-on-the-cob
1 large onion
1 leek
2 oz salt pork (e.g. belly of pork) *or* fat bacon
1½ pt milk
1 pt chicken stock
¼ pt thin cream
chopped parsley
water biscuits *or* matzos (optional)
black pepper

Cut the corn off the cobs with a small sharp knife, holding them downwards on a chopping board. For those people who seem resigned to buying corn in tins, this is not nearly so difficult as it sounds. Chop the onion and slice the leek. Dice the salt pork and fry gently until crisp in a heavy casserole. When it has rendered enough fat, add the chopped onion and stir around for a minute or two. Add the leek and continue to cook gently for another 2–3 minutes. Add the corn and stir around till well coated with fat. Heat the stock and the milk together and pour them on. Bring just to boiling point, taste for seasoning – it will probably only need pepper because of the salt pork – and leave to simmer for 20 minutes. Add the cream, sprinkle with chopped parsley, and serve. Broken-up water biscuits or matzos can be scattered over the top of each bowl. Serves 8–10. This delicious soup can be made even more substantial by adding 2 diced potatoes at the same time as the corn, but I personally like it better without.

Fennel Soup

1 head fennel
1½ pt chicken stock
1 Tbs white wine vinegar
salt and white pepper
1 oz coarsely ground almonds (optional)

Wash and trim the fennel, reserving any of the feathery leaves. Slice it and put in a pan with the stock and the vinegar. Bring to the boil and simmer until the fennel is soft. For a delicious clear consommé simmer for 30 minutes, then simply strain the soup and re-heat it, tasting for seasoning. Sharpen with a drop of extra vinegar if it seems too bland. Chop the reserved leaves and use as a garnish. For a slightly thicker soup, simmer for 20 minutes only, then cool slightly. Put in the blender, return to the cleaned pan and re-heat, adding salt and pepper to taste. Some coarsely ground almonds can be added at this stage to add texture. Sprinkle with the finely chopped leaves. Serves 4–6. This soup freezes well, without the garnish.

Garlic Soup

5 cloves garlic
2 oz butter
1½ Tbs flour
1¾ pt chicken stock
salt, 6 black peppercorns
½ bay leaf, ¼ tsp mace, 3 cloves
1 egg yolk
1 Tbs olive oil
3 Tbs finely chopped parsley

Mince the garlic and cook gently in the butter until soft, about 4 minutes. On no account allow it to burn. Stir in the flour, and cook for another 3 minutes, stirring most of the time. Heat the stock and pour on. Bring to the boil, then lower the heat. Put in some salt, peppercorns, cloves, bay leaf and a pinch of mace. Simmer for 25 minutes. Pour through a strainer. Beat the egg yolk in a hot tureen. Stir in the oil gradually. When amalgamated, pour on the almost boiling soup. Stir till smooth, add the chopped parsley and serve. Serves 3–4. An unusual soup with a subtle flavour that is not liked by everyone, but well worth trying.

Gazpacho

1 lb tomatoes
1 medium onion
1 green pepper
½ cucumber
2 cloves garlic
2 slices Hovis *or* other brown bread
¼ pt tomato juice
½ pt chicken stock *or* water
½ gill olive oil
2 Tbs wine vinegar
salt and black pepper
ice cubes

Skin the tomatoes and chop finely, discarding seeds and juice. Chop the onion finely. Remove the pith and seeds from the pepper and chop. Peel the cucumber and cut in small dice. Mince the garlic. Remove the crusts from the bread, and dice. Put all in a large bowl and pour over the tomato juice, stock or water, oil and vinegar. Mix and season with salt and black pepper. Chill for several hours, or overnight, in the refrigerator. Thin with ice cubes and iced water to the desired consistency before serving. Serves 8. For a smooth version, the same soup can be put in the blender, but I prefer the hand-chopped method although it is more work. If made in the blender, have small bowls of very finely chopped cucumber, tomato, green pepper and hard-boiled egg as garnishes. With the unblended soup there is no point.

Cold Lentil Soup

¼ lb brown lentils
¼ lb spinach
1 onion
1 clove garlic
2 Tbs sunflower-seed oil
salt and black pepper
approximately ¾ pt buttermilk
½ lemon

Wash the lentils carefully and cover with cold water. Bring to the boil and cook gently until almost tender, about 45 minutes. Wash and slice the spinach. Add the spinach to the lentils and cook for another 15 minutes, or until both vegetables are tender. Chop the onion and garlic and sauté in the oil. (Add the garlic about 5 minutes after the onion.) When golden, add with the oil to the rest of the soup. Put in the blender, pour into a bowl and leave to cool. When cold, stir in the buttermilk. There should be 2–3 parts soup to 1 of buttermilk. Add lemon juice to taste – about ½ lemon. Serve very cold. Serves 6–8. This is a delicious and unusual summer soup; the combination of flavours is excellent, and it makes a quite substantial start to a light meal.

Lentil Soup I

1 lb brown (continental) lentils
1 onion
2 Tbs olive oil
2½ pt chicken, game or vegetable stock
1 stalk celery
1 carrot
2 cloves garlic
1 bay leaf
2 sprigs parsley
salt and black pepper

Pick over the lentils, wash them well in a colander and drain. Chop the onion and brown in the oil in a heavy pan. Add the lentils and stir around in the oil. Heat the stock and pour on. Bring to a boil, lower the heat and add the sliced vegetables, herbs and seasonings. Simmer gently for 45–50 minutes, or until the lentils are soft but unbroken. Adjust seasoning and serve as it is, or sieved if you prefer, or put half in the blender and mix the two halves together. Serves 6–8.

Lentil Soup II

1 onion
1 carrot
1 leek
2 stalks celery
3 Tbs olive oil
$\frac{1}{2}$ lb brown (continental) lentils
$2\frac{1}{2}$–3 pt game stock
salt and black pepper

Chop the vegetables but keep them in separate piles. Heat the oil in a heavy pan, and cook the onion in it for 2–3 minutes. Add the chopped celery, carrot and leek. After another 5 minutes add the washed and drained lentils. Stir around for a minute or two, then pour on the heated stock. Simmer until the lentils and the vegetables are soft, 45–50 minutes. Season carefully with salt and freshly ground black pepper. Thin with more stock if necessary. When made with a well-flavoured game stock, this soup is really delicious. Serves 8–10.

Lettuce and Hazelnut Soup

3 lettuces
1 bunch spring onions *or* one medium onion
2 oz butter
$1\frac{1}{2}$ pt light stock: chicken, veal *or* vegetable
4 Tbs thin cream
2 oz chopped hazelnuts

Wash and drain the lettuces. Blanch for 5 minutes in lightly salted boiling water. (If you have no stock, reserve the water, and add $\frac{1}{2}$ a stock cube to it.) Drain the lettuces well, pressing out as much moisture as possible, and chop them. Chop the spring onions or onion finely. Melt the butter in a heavy pan and cook the chopped onions in it until they are transparent. Add the chopped lettuce and stir well until all is coated in butter. Cook for another 3 or 4 minutes, then pour on the heated stock. Simmer for 20 minutes, then put through the fine mesh of a vegetable mill or the blender and return to the cleaned pan. Stir in the cream, taste for

27

seasoning, re-heat and serve with the chopped nuts sprinkled on top of the tureen or each individual bowl. Serves 4–5.

Minestrone

¼ lb dried haricot beans
1 large onion
1 large leek
½ lb tomatoes
2 stalks celery
1–2 carrots, depending on size
1 clove garlic
4 Tbs olive oil
2½ pt stock *or* water
2 oz short macaroni
salt and black pepper
1–2 Tbs extra olive oil (optional)
¼ lb grated Parmesan
6 Tbs chopped parsley (optional)

Put the beans to cook very slowly in a small pan. When they reach the boil, turn off the heat and leave covered by the side of the fire for 1 hour. Chop the vegetables. Heat the oil in a large pan, add the chopped vegetables and let them stew gently in the oil for 8–10 minutes. Heat the stock and pour onto the vegetables. Add the beans with their cooking liquid. Bring to the boil and simmer gently until the beans are tender, about 1 hour. Add the macaroni and cook for another ¼ hour. Taste and adjust seasoning, adding plenty of ground black pepper. If you like the taste of olive oil, you can add an extra spoonful now, at the very end of the cooking. Most people mix the grated cheese into the soup, but I prefer to serve it separately in a bowl, with another bowl of freshly chopped parsley so that each person can help themselves. Serves 8–10.

Pumpkin Soup

2 lb pumpkin
½ lb potatoes
½ lb tomatoes
1½ pt chicken *or* vegetable stock
1 large onion
1½ oz butter
salt and black pepper
½ Tbs chopped fresh basil, when available *or*
    4 Tbs chopped parsley
¼ gill cream (optional)

Peel the pumpkin and cut in 1-inch cubes. Peel the potatoes
and cut in similar sized pieces. Skin the tomatoes and chop
coarsely. Put all three vegetables in a large pan with the
stock. Bring to the boil and simmer, covered, for 15–20
minutes, till all are soft. Meanwhile chop the onion finely
and stew gently in the butter till soft. When the mixed
vegetables are cooked, push through the medium mesh of
the vegetable mill (or the blender if you prefer), reserving
about ½ pt of the liquid, or the soup may be too thin. Return
the sieved soup to the clean pan and adjust the consistency
by adding as much of the reserved liquid as is needed to
make a soup like thin cream. Stir in the onion and its juices
and add salt and black pepper to taste. Add the basil if
available; I would not substitute dried basil in this case as it
destroys the fresh taste of the soup. Stir in the cream if used;
this is purely a matter of taste: the cream makes it slightly
richer and smoother, but it is also good without. Serve in
bowls sprinkled with chopped parsley if no basil is available.
Serves 8. A delicious and unusual soup, a warm orange in
colour.

A Soup of Mixed Root Vegetables

½ lb parsnips
½ lb carrots
½ lb turnips *or* swedes
2 oz beef dripping *or* butter
2½ pt beef stock
salt and black pepper
chopped parsley

Cut all the vegetables in slices (half or quarter them first if they are very large). Melt the fat in a pan and cook them all together gently for 5 minutes, stirring now and then. Heat the stock in a large deep pan. When it is very hot, lift the sliced vegetables from the fat with a slotted spoon, and drop them into the stock. Simmer for 10 minutes, or until the vegetables are just tender but not mushy. Put through the coarse mesh of a vegetable mill, re-heat in the cleaned pan and season with salt and black pepper. Add plenty of chopped parsley or have a bowl of it on the table. Serves 8. This is one of my favourite winter soups; it seems equally good with swedes or turnips, carrots or parsnips, or a mixture of them all. It can also be put in the blender, although I prefer a coarser texture.

Soupe au Pistou

1 onion
2 small leeks
2 small carrots
2 small courgettes
½ lb string beans
2 medium potatoes
¼ pt olive oil
½ lb fresh white haricot beans (1½ lb in pod) *or*
    ¼ lb dried white haricots
salt
2 oz shell pasta *or* short macaroni

Pistou
4 cloves garlic
2 tomatoes
12 sprigs basil *or* 4 Tbs chopped leaves
2 oz grated Parmesan

Dice the onion, leeks, carrots, courgettes (unpeeled), string beans and potatoes, keeping them in separate piles. Heat a layer of olive oil (about 4 Tbs) in a large heavy saucepan and cook the onion and leeks gently until they are pale golden. Pour in 2 pt boiling water and add the carrots and the haricot beans. (If using dried ones, they must be pre-cooked until half tender.) Bring back to the boil, add salt, cover and simmer for 45 minutes. Then add the potatoes, courgettes and string beans. Simmer for another 30 minutes. Add the pasta, and cook uncovered for another 10 minutes, or until it is just tender. Meanwhile prepare the *pistou*. Pound the garlic in a mortar. Halve the tomatoes, squeeze out the seeds and juice, and grill until browned. Chop the basil and add to the garlic in the mortar, then add the chopped grilled tomatoes, discarding the skins. Pound again until you have a fairly smooth paste, then add 4 Tbs olive oil drop by drop. When it is amalgamated, pour the sauce into the heated tureen, and add a ladleful of the boiling hot soup. Mix well, then add the rest gradually. Leave for 5 minutes before serving. Serve the grated cheese separately. Serves 10.

Iced Beetroot Soup

2 raw beetroot
1 cucumber
1 pt beef *or* duck stock
2–4 Tbs lemon juice
2 Tbs white wine vinegar
½ pt thin cream

Peel the beetroot and chop into small pieces. Cook in 2 pt lightly salted water until tender – about 1½ hours. Peel the cucumber and cut in slices. Add it to the beetroot and cook for another 5 minutes. Put through the fine mesh of a vegetable mill or in the blender, adding a pint of good beef or duck stock. Season with 2–4 Tbs lemon juice, or 2 Tbs lemon juice and 2 Tbs white wine vinegar. Chill in the refrigerator for several hours or overnight, pour into a chilled tureen and swirl in the cream – don't mix it in too thoroughly, as it looks prettier with a marbled effect. This makes 4 pt, and will serve 10–12 people.

Solferino Soup

$\frac{1}{4}$ lb butter
1 onion
4 leeks
1$\frac{1}{2}$ lb tomatoes
1$\frac{1}{2}$ lb potatoes
1 clove garlic
2 qt chicken, veal *or* vegetable stock
$\frac{1}{4}$ lb tiny carrots
2 Tbs chopped parsley

Melt half the butter in a heavy pan and cook the sliced onion in it for 2–3 minutes while you slice the white part of the leeks. Add them to the onion and cook gently until well softened, about 8 minutes. Add the peeled and roughly chopped tomatoes, the peeled potatoes cut in slices and the chopped garlic. Pour on the heated stock and simmer for 30 minutes. Slice the little carrots thinly and cook separately in a few spoonfuls of the stock kept back from the rest of the soup. When they are just tender but still slightly crisp, drain the liquid back into the soup and keep the carrots warm in the covered pan for a garnish. When the soup is cooked, put through the fine mesh of a vegetable mill or the blender and return to the cleaned pan. Re-heat, season carefully, add the remaining butter, the carrots and the chopped parsley, and serve. Serves 10–12.

Tomato and Cucumber Soup

1 cucumber
1 bunch spring onions *or* 1 medium onion
1$\frac{1}{2}$ oz butter
salt and black pepper
$\frac{3}{4}$ lb tomatoes
lemon juice
cayenne
sugar
1 Tbs sour cream

Slice the peeled cucumber and the spring onions. Melt the butter in a heavy pan and stew the sliced vegetables in it gently for about 5 minutes. (If you have to use an ordinary onion instead of the spring onions cook it alone for a few minutes in the butter before adding the cucumber.) Pour on 1½ pt boiling water and simmer uncovered for 30 minutes. Season with salt and black pepper. Put the tomatoes (unpeeled) in a pan half full of boiling water. Cover and cook over medium heat for 10 minutes. Lift out the tomatoes and press them through the medium mesh of a vegetable mill. Discard the skins and pour the cucumber soup through the vegetable mill on top of the tomatoes. Mix well, season to taste with lemon juice, a little cayenne and a pinch of sugar, and more salt and black pepper if necessary. Stir in the sour cream. Serve hot or chilled. The freshness of the almost raw tomatoes makes a delicious contrast to the bland cucumber base. Serves 4. This soup freezes well.

Turnip Soup

1½ lb young turnips
2 oz butter
¾ pt light stock : chicken, veal *or* vegetable
¾ pt creamy milk *or* milk and cream mixed
2 Tbs chopped fresh chervil *or* parsley
salt and black pepper

Peel the turnips very thinly and slice them. Melt the butter and cook the sliced turnips in it slowly for 5 minutes. (If the turnips are not as young as they should be, blanch them first by putting them, sliced, in a pan of cold water and bringing to the boil. Boil for 2 minutes, then drain and throw away the water.) After the turnips have cooked for 5 minutes in the butter pour on the heated stock. Simmer gently until the turnips are soft, about 20 minutes. Put the soup through the fine mesh of a vegetable mill together with the heated milk, or put all together in the blender. Return to the cleaned pan and re-heat, season with salt and black pepper, and serve sprinkled with chopped chervil or parsley. Serves 4–6. This soup freezes well.

Watercress and Cucumber Soup

1 bunch watercress
1 cucumber
1 large potato
2 oz butter
$\frac{3}{4}$ pt chicken stock
$\frac{3}{4}$ pt milk
salt and black pepper
4 Tbs cream

Chop the watercress, stalks and all. Peel the cucumber and chop it. Peel the potato and slice it thinly. Melt the butter in a heavy pan and cook the watercress and cucumber gently for 4 minutes, stirring now and then. Add the sliced potato and stir until coated with fat and well mixed. Heat the stock and milk together and pour on. Season lightly with salt and simmer gently for 25 minutes. Cool slightly, push through the medium mesh of a vegetable mill and return to the cleaned pan. Re-heat, adjust seasoning, and stir in the cream. Alternatively, for a more elegant soup, reserve a few of the best leaves of the watercress. Put the soup in the blender instead of the vegetable mill, and scatter the fresh leaves (chopped if they are very large) on top before serving. Serves 4–6. This soup freezes well.

Cold Avocado Soup

1 large avocado *or* 2 small ones
1$\frac{1}{2}$ pt chicken stock
$\frac{1}{4}$ pt yoghurt
lemon juice
salt

Peel the avocado and remove the stone. Chop the flesh and put it in the blender with the cold stock. Blend till smooth, then add the yoghurt and blend again. Add lemon juice to taste and a pinch of salt. Chill for 2 hours. Serve in white cups. Serves 4–5. This soup is a beautiful pale green but it must not be made far in advance or both the colour and the flavour will be lost.

Barley Broth

3 pt mutton stock
2 oz pearl barley
salt and black pepper
½ lb carrots
1 lb leeks
½ lb turnips
¼ lb onions
¼ lb celery
½ cup chopped parsley

Heat the stock in a deep pot, and skim if necessary. Wash the barley well and put it into the stock when it is boiling. Add some salt. Dice the vegetables in equal sized pieces and add them to the stock. Simmer for 1 hour. Season with plenty of salt and freshly ground black pepper. Serve with a good handful of freshly chopped parsley in each bowl. Serves 8–10.

Raw Carrot and Tomato Soup

¼ pt carrot juice
¼ pt tomato juice
¼ pt yoghurt

If making your own juices, allow 1 lb carrots and ¾ lb raw tomatoes. Put the vegetable juices and the yoghurt in the blender, or mix with an electric mixer. Pour into glasses and serve immediately. Serves 2–3.

Carrot and Tomato Soup

¾ lb carrots
¾ lb tomatoes
2 oz butter
1½ pt chicken stock
½ pt milk and cream mixed
salt and black pepper
a bowl of chopped parsley

Slice the carrots; skin and chop the tomatoes. Melt the butter in a saucepan, put in the carrots and tomatoes and stew gently for 5 minutes. Heat the stock and pour it on. Bring to the boil and simmer until the carrots are very soft, about 35 minutes. Put through the medium mesh of the vegetable mill and return to the pan. Heat the milk and cream and stir into the soup. Add salt and black pepper to taste, and serve with a bowl of chopped parsley on the table, or put some in each bowl. Serves 6. A smoother version can be made by putting in the blender with the milk and cream.

Cauliflower Soup

1 medium cauliflower
2 oz butter
1½ pt light chicken stock
4 Tbs thin cream
salt and black pepper

Divide the cauliflower into sprigs and wash them well. Reserve one and chop the rest. Melt the butter in a saucepan and put in the chopped cauliflower. Cook gently in the butter for 5 minutes, stirring it about. Heat the stock and pour it into the pan. Bring to the boil, cover and simmer for 20 minutes. Let the soup cool slightly, then pour it into the blender. Return to the cleaned pan and re-heat. Taste for seasoning and stir in the cream. Serve in cups, either hot or chilled, with a little finely chopped raw cauliflower on top of each cup. Serves 4–5. This freezes well, except the garnish, which must be omitted until ready to serve.

Celery Consommé

1 head celery
2 pt beef stock
salt and black pepper

Scrub the celery well, and chop it coarsely – leaves, root and all. Put in a pan with the cold stock and bring slowly to the boil. Simmer gently for 15–20 minutes, or until the stock is well flavoured. Strain, return to the cleaned pan. Re-heat and season with salt and black pepper. Serve hot with cheese straws. Serves 4–6. This delicate soup makes an ideal start to a rich meal.

(Hot or Cold) Green Pea Soup

1 lb shelled peas *or* 2 $\frac{1}{2}$ lb packets frozen peas
$\frac{1}{2}$ pt milk
$\frac{1}{2}$ pt thin cream
salt and black pepper
1 oz butter (for a hot soup only)
a few fresh mint leaves (for a cold soup only)

Cook the peas in the minimum of lightly salted water, then put in the blender, reserving 1 Tbs whole peas for garnishing. Add the milk and cream and blend again. Return to the cleaned pan and re-heat, seasoning carefully with salt and black pepper. For a hot soup, add the butter and garnish with a few whole cooked peas in each cup. For a cold soup, omit the butter, chill for several hours or overnight, and garnish with chopped fresh mint. Serves 6.

Split Pea Soup

$\frac{1}{2}$ lb split peas
1 ham bone *or* bacon end
2 medium onions
1 clove garlic (optional)
4 Tbs olive oil *or* 2 oz butter
salt and black pepper

Cook the peas with the ham bone in 2 pt water until tender. Put aside. Chop the onions and cook in the oil (or butter) until soft and golden, adding the garlic half-way through. Throw away the ham bone or bacon and mix the onions into the soup. Re-heat, seasoning with salt and black pepper. Serves 6.

Potato and Onion Soup

2 large onions
3 oz butter
2 large potatoes
1 pt chicken stock
1 pt creamy milk *or* milk and cream mixed
salt and black pepper

Chop the onions and cook in the butter until transparent. Peel the potatoes, halve them, and slice each half thinly. Add them to the onions and stir around for a minute or two until coated with fat and well mixed. Heat the stock and pour on. Season with salt and pepper and simmer until the potatoes are soft, about 20–30 minutes. Heat the milk and stir it in. Mix well, taste and adjust seasoning. Serve as it is, or put through the medium mesh of a vegetable mill, or in the blender, according to your taste. If made into a smooth soup, sprinkle with a garnish of chopped parsley. Serves 6.

Provençal Soup

1 lb potatoes
1 lb tomatoes
½ lb onions
1 clove garlic
2 pt stock
2 lb green peas (in pod) *or* ½ lb frozen *petits pois*
1½ oz butter
salt and black pepper

Peel the potatoes and cut them in quarters. Skin the tomatoes and cut in quarters. Slice the onions and crush the garlic. Shell the peas. Put the potatoes, tomatoes, onions and garlic in a pan with the stock. Bring to a boil and simmer slowly for 1½ hours. Put through the medium mesh of a vegetable mill and return to the cleaned pan. Cook the peas separately and add to the re-heated soup. Adjust seasoning. Serves 6.

(Hot) Sorrel Soup

½ lb sorrel *or* mixed sorrel, spinach and lettuce
2 oz butter
1¼ pt chicken stock
salt and black pepper
2 egg yolks
¼ pt cream

Wash and dry the green leaves. Heat the butter in a heavy pan, put in the leaves and cook gently for 6 minutes. Heat the stock and pour on. Bring to simmering point, add a little salt and cover the pan. Simmer for 25 minutes. Put through the medium mesh of the vegetable mill. Return to the cleaned pan and re-heat. Add salt and black pepper to taste. Beat the egg yolks with the cream, stir in a ladleful of the hot soup, then return the mixture to the pan. Re-heat without allowing to boil. Serves 4.

(Cold) Sorrel Soup

½ lb sorrel *or* mixed sorrel, spinach and lettuce
2 oz butter
2 medium potatoes
1¼ pt chicken stock
salt and black pepper
½ pt buttermilk
lemon juice

Wash and dry the green leaves. Peel the potatoes, cut in half, and slice thinly. Heat the butter in a saucepan, put in the leaves and cook gently for 4 minutes. Add the potatoes and cook another 2 minutes. Heat the stock and pour on. Bring to simmering point, add a little salt and cover the pan. Simmer for about 25 minutes. Cool slightly and purée in the blender, adding the buttermilk. Season with salt and black pepper, and a little lemon juice. Chill in the refrigerator. Serves 5.

Mushroom Soup

½ lb mushrooms
1½ pt chicken stock
¼ pt yoghurt *or* sour cream
lemon juice
2 Tbs chopped parsley

Chop the mushrooms. Heat the stock and add the mushrooms when it is almost boiling. Bring to the boil and simmer for 15 minutes. Cool slightly, then put in the blender. Add the yoghurt or sour cream, then blend again. Add lemon juice to taste, and salt and black pepper if needed. Serve hot in white cups, with a little finely chopped parsley on top of each. Serves 4–5.

Cold Spinach Soup

½ lb frozen chopped spinach
½ pt sour cream
¼ pt tinned *vichysoisse*
approximately ¼ pt buttermilk
the juice of 1 lemon
1 Tbs tomato ketchup
a few drops Tabasco

Cook the frozen spinach and squeeze out as much moisture as possible. Mix the sour cream with the *vichysoisse*, beat in the spinach, and thin to the desired consistency with buttermilk, remembering it becomes thicker when chilled. Flavour with lemon juice to taste, and add the tomato ketchup and Tabasco. Chill for several hours, and serve in white cups. Serves 4–5. This makes a pretty green soup, quite thick, and of a creamy consistency though not in fact rich

Tomato Consommé

6 tomatoes
1 head celery
2 leeks
1 carrot
2 egg whites
2 pt beef stock
¾ lb minced beef
2 Tbs lemon juice
salt and black pepper and sugar

Chop the vegetables and beat the egg whites until stiff. Put them all in a large pan with the stock and the minced beef. Bring slowly to the boil and simmer for 1 hour. Strain through a muslin cloth. Re-heat in the cleaned pan and add lemon juice, sugar, salt and black pepper to taste. Serve in individual cups, either quite plain or with a spoon of whipped or sour cream, or a few croûtons in each cup. Serves 6.

Terry's Tomato Soup

1 medium onion
2 oz butter
1½ lb tomatoes
1 pt light stock: chicken, veal *or* vegetable
salt and black pepper
sugar
2 Tbs chopped chervil, basil *or* chives

Chop the onion finely and cook it gently in the butter until soft. Add the peeled and roughly chopped tomatoes. After a few minutes softening in the butter, stirring now and then, pour on the heated stock. Season with salt, black pepper and a pinch of sugar. Simmer for 20 minutes. Pass through the medium mesh of a vegetable mill. Serve in individual cups, and sprinkle each one with finely chopped fresh basil, chervil, chives or parsley, as available. Serves 4.

Spring Vegetable Soup

½ lb young carrots
½ lb young turnips
2 small leeks
1 stalk celery
3 oz butter *or* 6 Tbs olive oil
3 pt light stock: chicken, veal *or* vegetable
½ lb shelled peas (about 2 lb in the pod)
salt and black pepper

Chop the carrots, turnips, leeks and celery and stew them very gently in the butter or oil in a covered pot for 10–15 minutes. Heat 2½ pt of the stock and pour on. Simmer gently for 30 minutes. Meanwhile cook the peas in the remaining ½ pt of stock until soft, and put in the blender. When the mixed vegetables are cooked, stir in the purée of green peas, re-heat, season lightly, and serve. Serves 6–8.

A Vegetable Consommé

½ lb carrots
1 lb leeks
1 red pepper (or green)
½ celeriac *or* ½ head celery
½ lb tomatoes
3–4 sprigs parsley, with root if possible
salt and black pepper
lemon juice

Clean the carrots and leeks and slice finely. Chop the pepper removing the seeds. Peel the celeriac, or scrub the celery, root, leaves and all, and chop. Chop the unpeeled tomatoes coarsely. Put all the vegetables with the parsley in a deep pot with 2 pt cold water. Bring slowly to the boil and simmer for 2–3 hours. Pour through a strainer, return to the cleaned pan, re-heat and season with salt, black pepper and a little lemon juice. Serves 4–6. Serve hot or chilled.

Watercress and Bean Sprout Soup

2 pt duck *or* chicken stock
1 bunch watercress, chopped
½ lb bean sprouts
lemon juice
soy sauce
salt and black pepper

Heat the stock until almost boiling, then put in the watercress. Simmer for 2 minutes, then add the bean sprouts. Simmer for 3 more minutes, add lemon juice, a dash of soy sauce, salt and black pepper to taste, and serve. Serves 6.

Vichysoisse

4 good-sized leeks
1 onion
2 medium potatoes
1½ oz butter
2 pt chicken stock
2 sprigs parsley
1 celery stalk
salt and black pepper
¼ pt thick cream
2 Tbs chopped chives

Chop the leeks and the onion, and slice the potatoes thinly. Melt the butter in a heavy pan, put in the leeks and the onion, and cook gently until golden and soft. Add the potatoes and stir around until coated with butter. Pour in the heated stock, add the parsley and celery, season with salt and black pepper, and simmer until the potatoes are soft, about 20–30 minutes. Discard the parsley and celery and put the soup in the blender after it has cooled slightly, adding the cream. Chill for at least twelve hours before serving. Serve in chilled cups sprinkled with chopped chives. Serves 8.

Soufflés and Timbales

Cheese Soufflés in Artichokes

6 globe artichokes

Cheese soufflé mixture
1 oz butter
2 Tbs flour
⅓ pt milk
3 oz grated Gruyère
3 egg yolks, 4 egg whites
salt and black pepper

Cook the artichokes as usual. Drain and cool. When cool enough to handle, pull out the centre bunch of leaves, leaving a hollow space well enclosed with leaves. Scrape out the choke with a small sharp spoon. Make the soufflé mixture: melt the butter, stir in the flour, and cook 2–3 minutes. Heat the milk and pour on. Blend, and simmer gently for 4–5 minutes, stirring often. Stir in the grated cheese and season well with salt and pepper. Beat the egg yolks and stir in off the fire. Beat the whites until stiff, and fold into the mixture. Spoon the mixture quickly into the artichokes. Place the artichokes on a greased baking sheet and cook for 15 minutes at 400°. It should be less set than the usual soufflé, resembling a thick foamy sauce. The remaining leaves of the artichoke are pulled off and dipped in the soufflé, then the heart is eaten with a knife and fork. Serves 6. This makes an unusual start to a meal and is very filling.

Serve alone.

Steamed Broccoli Ring

½ lb broccoli
1 oz butter
1½ Tbs flour
¼ pt thin cream
salt and black pepper
3 oz grated Gruyère, Emmenthal *or* Parmesan
4 eggs

Cook the broccoli until just tender in lightly salted water. Drain well, reserving the liquid, and chop finely. Melt the butter, stir in the flour and cook for 3 minutes. Heat $\frac{1}{4}$ pt of the reserved cooking water with the cream, and pour into the roux when it is almost boiling. Stir until smooth and cook gently for 4 minutes. Season quite highly with salt and black pepper, then stir in the grated cheese. When smooth, add the chopped broccoli and mix well. Remove from the fire and stir in the beaten egg yolks. Then beat the whites until stiff and fold in. Pour into a buttered ring mould set in a baking tin half full of water and steam for 40 minutes at 325°. When set and lightly browned, turn onto a flat dish and fill the centre with a thick tomato sauce. Alternatively, cook in a soufflé dish for 20 minutes at 400°, and serve with a garlic and yoghurt sauce or a spicy tomato sauce. Serves 4.

Tomato and cucumber salad or a green salad (if serving a tomato sauce).

Courgette Soufflé

6 oz cooked puréed courgettes ($\frac{3}{4}$ lb uncooked)
2 oz butter
3 Tbs flour
a scant $\frac{1}{4}$ pt cooking water
a scant $\frac{1}{4}$ pt creamy milk *or* milk with a little
    cream added
2 Tbs grated Parmesan
salt and black pepper
4 eggs

To make the purée, slice the unpeeled courgettes in $\frac{1}{2}$-inch slices and cook in just enough boiling water to cover, for 12 minutes. Drain, reserving the water, and mash with a fork or push through the coarse mesh of a vegetable mill. Dry out the purée for a few minutes in the cleaned pan, stirring over gentle heat. To make the soufflé mixture: melt the butter, stir in the flour and cook for 2 minutes. Blend with the stock and milk, heated together, and simmer for 4 minutes. Stir in the cheese, and season with salt and pepper. Stir in the courgette purée, and mix well. Remove from heat and add the beaten egg yolks. Whip the whites and fold in. Pour into a

buttered soufflé dish and bake for 20 minutes at 400°.
Serves 4–5.

Lettuce and watercress salad.

Carrot Soufflé

1 lb carrots
1 pt chicken stock
1 tsp butter and 1 tsp flour
salt and black pepper
2 eggs

Slice the carrots and cook until tender in the stock. Drain,
reserving the liquid. Put in the blender with 6 Tbs of the
liquid. Return to a clean pan and stir in a paste made by
mixing the butter and flour. Add by degrees, and stir until
slightly thickened. Season, and stir in the beaten yolks off
the fire. Whip the whites stiffly and fold into the soufflé. Pour
into a buttered dish and bake for 20 minutes at 350°, or until
risen slightly and set. Serve immediately. Serves 3.

French beans or broccoli; grilled mushrooms.

Timbale of Green Peas

1 lb shelled *or* frozen green peas
4 Tbs soft breadcrumbs
2 Tbs milk
salt and black pepper
2 oz softened butter
3 eggs

Cook the peas and make into a purée by putting them
through the medium mesh of a vegetable mill. Stir in the
breadcrumbs, soaked in the milk and squeezed dry. Season.
Beat in the softened butter in small pieces. Beat the egg yolks
and stir in. Whip the whites until stiff and fold in. Pour into
a buttered pudding basin and place in a saucepan with
boiling water half-way up the basin. Cover. Bring the water
back to the boil and steam for 1 hour. Turn out on a hot
dish and serve with a tomato sauce. Serves 3–4.

Serve alone.

Soufflé aux fonds d'artichauts

Soufflé mixture
2 oz butter
3 Tbs flour
a scant ½ pt milk
4 oz grated cheese, preferably Gruyère and
    Parmesan mixed
salt and black pepper
4 eggs, separated

4 artichoke bottoms, cooked

Make the soufflé: melt the butter, stir in the flour, and cook
for 3 minutes, stirring constantly. Pour on the heated milk
all at once, and stir until smooth. Cook over gentle heat for
5 minutes, then stir in the grated cheese. Stir until melted
and season well with salt and black pepper. Remove from
the heat and stir in the beaten egg yolks. Beat the whites
until stiff and fold into the mixture. Have the artichoke
bottoms cut in small cubes. Pour half the soufflé mixture
into a buttered soufflé dish, then make a layer of the chopped artichoke bottoms, then pour on the remaining soufflé
mixture. Bake for 20 minutes at 400°. Serves 5–6. An alternative method of serving this dish is to have 6 cooked artichoke bottoms and place each one in a small soufflé dish.
Divide the soufflé mixture among them and make 6 individual soufflés. Cook for 12–15 minutes at 400°. Serves 6.

Spinach Soufflé

1 lb spinach
2 oz butter
3 Tbs flour
½ pt milk *or* buttermilk
¼ lb cream cheese (Philadelphia *or* similar)
salt and black pepper
4 eggs

Cook the spinach as usual until just tender. Turn into a
colander to drain. When cool enough to handle, squeeze it
in your hands until as much moisture as possible has been
expressed. Chop it quite finely on a board. (If planning to

serve a spinach sauce with the soufflé, cook an extra $\frac{1}{2}$ lb spinach and reserve $\frac{1}{3}$ of the chopped drained spinach for the sauce.) Melt the butter, blend with the flour and pour on the heated milk or buttermilk. Stir until a thick smooth sauce is obtained, then beat in the cream cheese, chopped in small pieces. Beat until smooth and well amalgamated. Stir in the chopped spinach and season well. Cool slightly, then mix in the beaten egg yolks. When ready to cook, whip the egg whites until stiff, then fold into the mixture. Pour into a buttered soufflé dish and bake for 25 minutes at 350°. Serve with a spinach sauce, a mushroom and tomato sauce or both. Serves 4–5.

Serve alone.

Timbale Vert

> 1 cos lettuce *or* outer leaves of 2 cos lettuces
> $\frac{1}{2}$ lb spinach
> $\frac{1}{2}$ lb sorrel, when available, *or* $\frac{1}{2}$ lb extra
>   spinach
> 1 large endive *or* $\frac{1}{2}$ lb chicory
> 1 lb potatoes
> 2 oz butter
> 4 eggs
> salt and black pepper

Wash the greens and throw them into a large pan of boiling salted water. Cook for 5 minutes, drain, squeezing out as much moisture as possible with your hands. Chop them roughly. Make a dry purée with the potatoes. In a warmed bowl, beat the butter into the hot purée, and when it is melted stir in the chopped greens. Mix well, season with salt and black pepper. Add the beaten egg yolks. Beat the whites until stiff and fold in. Pour into a buttered soufflé dish or ring mould (in which case level the surface with a palette knife), and cook standing in a baking tin of water for about 40 minutes at 325°. It will not rise as much as a soufflé, but should be just firm to the touch and lightly browned on top. It can be served in the soufflé dish, or turned out of the mould. This can be served as an accompaniment to a main dish, or as a main course on its own, accompanied by a tomato or cream cheese sauce. It is quite substantial, and will serve 6 as an extra dish, or 4 as a main course.

Peperonata, baked corn.

Turnip Soufflé

6 oz cooked puréed turnip (allow about
   ¾ lb raw turnips)
2 oz butter
3 Tbs flour
a scant ¼ pt cooking water
a scant ¼ pt milk
2 Tbs finely chopped parsley
salt and black pepper
4 eggs

Have a well-dried purée of turnips and reserve ¼ pt of the cooking water. Melt the butter and add the flour. Cook gently for 3 minutes, stirring constantly. Heat the milk and the turnip water together and pour on to the butter and flour mixture. Stir till smooth, bring to the boil, and simmer 5 minutes. Stir in the puréed turnips and chopped parsley and season well with salt and black pepper. Remove from the fire and beat in the beaten egg yolks. Whip the whites until stiff and fold in. Pour into a buttered soufflé dish and cook for 20 minutes at 400°. Serves 4–5. This soufflé can also be made with parsnips or Jerusalem artichokes instead of turnips.

Serve alone.

Pastry, Breads and Dumplings

Short Pastry (for Quiches, etc.)

8 oz plain flour
a pinch of salt
6 oz very cold butter
1 egg yolk (optional)
iced water

Sift the flour into a large bowl with salt and grate in the butter. Mix well, stir in the yolk, and add enough iced water to make the mixture hold together. Make into a ball and leave in a cool place for 30 minutes, or longer, before using. This makes enough pastry to line a 10-inch flan ring. The egg yolk is optional; it gives a richer pastry.

Cheese Pastry

8 oz plain flour
a pinch of salt
3 oz grated Cheddar cheese
3 oz very cold butter
approximately 3 fl oz iced water

Sift the flour into a large bowl with the salt. Mix in the grated cheese with the blade of a knife. Grate the butter into the bowl. Rub in very quickly with the finger tips. Add just enough iced water to hold together. Make into a ball and chill for 30 minutes. Roll out and line a 9–10-inch flan ring. This makes an unusual and excellent pastry for vegetable cuiches. It can be used for any vegetable or mixture of vegetables, only remember to omit any other cheese that occurs in the recipe.

Onion and Bacon Quiche

¾ lb short pastry
1½ lb onions
2 oz streaky bacon rashers
3 oz butter
2 eggs and 1 egg yolk
¼ pt cream
salt and black pepper

Line a 10-inch flan ring with pastry, brush with beaten egg yolk and pre-bake for 10 minutes at 400°. Slice the onions and cook in the butter until soft. Chop the bacon and add it to the onions. When all is golden, remove from the fire. Beat two eggs with the cream and add salt and black pepper. Mix with the onions and bacon and taste for seasoning. Pour into the pastry case and bake for 30 minutes at 400°. Serves 6. This can also be made with 2 lb leeks instead of onions.

Grilled mushrooms; tomato and cucumber salad.

Courgette Quiche

¾ lb short pastry
1 lb courgettes
2 eggs and 1 yolk
¼ pt thick cream
salt, black pepper and nutmeg

Line a 9–10-inch flan tin with the pastry, brush with beaten egg yolk and pre-bake for 10 minutes at 400°. Cut the courgettes in ½-inch slices and cook in boiling salted water for 12 minutes. Drain, pressing out excess moisture with the back of a wooden spoon. Beat two eggs with the cream and season well with salt, black pepper and nutmeg. Pour over the courgettes, mix lightly, and pour into the pre-baked pastry case. Bake for 30 minutes at 350°. Serves 5–6.

Grilled tomatoes; boiled leeks.

Chicory Quiche

¾ lb short pastry
1 lb chicory
2 oz butter
1 tsp lemon juice
2 eggs and 1 yolk
¼ pt thick cream
salt, black pepper and nutmeg
1 oz grated Gruyère

Line a 9-inch flan ring with the pastry, brush with beaten egg yolk and pre-bake for 10 minutes at 400°. Cut the chicory in ¾-inch slices. Melt the butter with the lemon juice in a covered sauté pan. Cook the chicory in it for 10 minutes, stirring once or twice. Drain. Beat two eggs with the cream. Add salt, black pepper and nutmeg to taste. Mix with the chicory and stir in the grated cheese. Pour the mixture into the pastry case. Cook for 20 minutes at 375° until risen slightly and golden brown. Serves 4–5.

Tomato and cucumber salad.

Quiche of Herbs and Cheese

¾ lb short pastry
1 egg yolk
1 small cos lettuce
1 bunch watercress
¼ lb spinach
¼ lb sorrel, when available
1 bunch parsley
½ lb Brie
½ pt thin cream
2 eggs
black pepper

Line a 10-inch flan ring with the pastry and pre-bake for 10 minutes at 400°, having first brushed it with beaten egg yolk to prevent it rising up. (Alternatively weigh it down with a greased paper full of dry beans for 10 minutes, then remove them and return it to the oven for a further 5 minutes.)

Throw all the green stuff into a large pan of boiling water for 5 minutes, then drain it. Press in a colander to extract as much moisture as possible. Turn it onto a board and chop roughly, in pieces about ½-inch square. Cut the rind off the cheese and chop the firm parts. Put it in a bowl in a very low oven (200°) with half the cream until melted, 10–15 minutes. Put in the blender or through a sieve to make it smooth. Beat the eggs with the remaining cream and combine with the cheese mixture. Scatter the chopped green stuff in the pastry case and pour the cheese mixture over. Sprinkle with pepper and bake at 350° for 30 minutes. Serves 6. An unusually good dish. Do not attempt to substitute any other cheese for Brie. If unavailable make the quiche with cheese pastry, filled with herbs, cream and eggs.

Tomato and onion salad.

Spinach and Tomato Quiche

¾ lb cheese pastry
1 lb spinach, spinach beet *or* chard
½ lb onions
¾ lb tomatoes
approximately 3 oz butter
1 clove garlic
salt and black pepper
2 eggs and 1 yolk
¼ pt thin cream

Line a 10-inch flan ring with the pastry (ordinary short pastry can be substituted for the cheese pastry if easier), brush with beaten egg yolk and pre-bake for 10 minutes at 400°. Chop the spinach or spinach beet, stalks and all, and cook in half the butter until softened. Chop the onions and cook in half the remaining butter until soft and golden. Peel and chop the tomatoes; cook them in the remaining butter until softened, 4–6 minutes. Mix the tomatoes and the onions together, add the crushed garlic and season with salt and black pepper. Spread half the mixture over the bottom of the pastry case, put the spinach over it, and cover with the remaining tomato and onion. Beat two eggs and the cream and pour over the top. Bake for 30 minutes at 375°. Serves 6.

An excellent dish which can be kept and eaten when still warm, or the next day when cold. A perfect dish to take on a picnic.

Lettuce, mushroom and bacon salad.

Tomato and Mustard Quiche

$\frac{3}{4}$ lb short pastry
1–2 Tbs *Moutarde de Dijon* (*Grey Poupon*, for
    preference)
1 lb tomatoes
4 eggs and 1 yolk
$\frac{1}{2}$ pt thick cream
salt and black pepper
2 oz grated Gruyère

Line a 10-inch flan ring with the pastry, brush with the beaten egg yolk, prick the bottom with a fork and pre-bake for 10 minutes at 400°. When it has cooled, spread a thin layer of *Moutarde de Dijon* over the bottom. Skin the tomatoes and chop coarsely, discarding seeds and juice. Beat four eggs, add the cream and season carefully with salt and black pepper. Stir in the tomatoes and cheese, keeping back a handful. Pour into the pastry case and scatter the reserved cheese over the top. Bake at 325° until golden and puffed up, 35–40 minutes. Serve immediately. Serves 6.

Cucumber and watercress salad.

Onion Bread

1 lb strong white flour
$\frac{1}{2}$ oz yeast
1 tsp salt
just over $\frac{1}{2}$ pt tepid water
1 lb onions
2 oz butter

Sift the flour into a large warm bowl. Put the yeast in a cup with 2 tablespoons of the water. Stand in a warm place – the linen cupboard, plate warmer, the back of the stove or on a radiator – for 10 minutes. Dissolve the salt in a little hot water in a measuring jug. When the yeast is ready, cream it with a teaspoon. Make the salty water in the jug up to half a pint with cooler water. Make a well in the centre of the flour and pour in the yeast mixture. Cover quickly with the flour round the edges, and pour on the salty water, mixing with a wooden spoon. Do not pour quite all on in case it is too much; it is hard to give exact quantities as flours vary. When just moist enough to pick up all the bits around the edge of the bowl – slightly more moist than pastry would be at this stage – turn out on a floured board and knead with the hands for 5 minutes, sprinkling with the flour as needed. After a few minutes it should become smooth and elastic, and no longer stick to the board. Sprinkle the bowl with flour, put the dough in it, and cover with a towel also sprinkled with flour. Put in the same warm place for 2 hours, by which time it should have doubled in size. Punch down with your fist and turn out onto the floured board. Knead again for 5 minutes then lay on a greased and floured baking sheet in the shape of a round flat loaf. Return to the warm place for another 45 minutes to rise again. Meanwhile slice the onions evenly into rings. Melt the butter in a sauté pan or large saucepan, and cook the onions in it gently with the lid on. Stir them now and then, and cook until they are soft but do not allow them to brown. When the bread is ready to bake, pile the onions on top of it and spread them in an even layer with a palette knife. Bake for 15 minutes at 450°, then turn down the oven to 425° and cook another 30 minutes. If the onions start to get burnt, cover with a sheet of foil. Makes a large loaf, enough for 8 people. Excellent with paté.

Cold dishes of vegetables dressed in oil and vinegar or lemon; vegetable stews.

Onion Shortcake

4 oz flour
1 tsp baking powder
¼ tsp salt
3½ oz butter
about 3 fl oz milk
1 lb onions
1 egg
¼ pt cream
salt and black pepper

Sift the flour with the salt and baking powder. Cut 1 oz butter in small pieces and rub into the flour, or cut in with two knives. Mix with enough milk to make the right consistency dough. Turn onto a floured board and knead once or twice. Put aside while you make the onion mixture. Slice the onions thinly and evenly. Melt the remaining butter in a heavy frying pan and cook them gently until they are soft. Stir now and then so that they do not stick. Beat the egg with the cream; season with salt and black pepper. When the onions are soft, lift them out of the pan with a slotted spoon, leaving behind the juice. Put them into a bowl and beat in the egg and cream mixture. Taste for seasoning and adjust. Roll out the shortcake till ¼ inch thick; alternatively it can be patted out with the floured heel of the hand. Place in a shallow round dish or a flan ring. Pour the onion mixture in and cook for 25 minutes at 425°. Serve hot or warm. Serves 4.

Tomato and cucumber salad; lettuce and watercress salad.

Green Gnocchi

½ lb cooked spinach
1 oz butter
salt and black pepper
nutmeg
6 oz Ricotta
1 oz grated Fontina *or* Parmesan
2 eggs   2½ Tbs flour

Chop the spinach finely and put through the medium mesh of a vegetable mill. Return the purée to the cleaned pan and

57

stir over gentle heat until well dried. Stir in the butter, salt and black pepper and a grating of nutmeg. When all is smooth and hot, stir in the mashed Ricotta cheese. Stir again until smooth, then shake in the Fontina or Parmesan. Stir again until smooth and melted, then remove from the fire and stir in the beaten eggs and the flour. Pour the mixture into a shallow dish and leave to cool. When cold, place in the refrigerator overnight, or even longer – this can be left in the refrigerator for 2–3 days without harm. Do not cover the dish. When ready to serve, take large teaspoons of the mixture with two floured spoons, and roll on a floured board into oval shapes. Bring a large pan of very lightly salted water to the boil, reduce to a gentle simmer, and drop in a batch of the gnocchi. Simmer gently all the time, watching them carefully. After 5 minutes lift them out with a flat skimmer and drain. Place them in a heated shallow dish in a warm place while you cook the rest of the gnocchi. Some people sprinkle them with grated cheese and melted butter and gratiné them under the grill, but I prefer them quite plain, served with a bowl of grated Parmesan handed separately. A jug of melted butter can be handed also. Serves 3–4. Having once unwisely made potato gnocchi for eight, I resolved never to do them in large quantities again. But if you like, these quantities can be increased by half as much again, to serve 5–6. More than this is impractical if you are doing the cooking yourself, as the poaching of many batches takes too long.

Serve alone.

Herb Dumplings

4 oz plain flour
2 tsp baking powder
a pinch of salt
1 oz butter
1 egg
approximately $\frac{1}{2}$ gill milk
3 Tbs finely chopped fresh herbs: chervil,
    dill, parsley

Sift the flour with a pinch of salt and baking powder. Cut

the butter in small pieces and rub into the flour. Beat the egg and add enough milk to make up to 3 fl oz. Add the chopped herbs to the egg and milk and pour onto the flour mixture gradually, mixing with the blade of a knife. Stop as soon as the mixture becomes clinging and soft. Add a drop more milk if still too dry. Using two large teaspoons, take small scoops of the mixture and drop onto the surface of the casserole, about 15 minutes before serving. Makes about 12 dumplings. Serves 6.

Mixed vegetable casserole.

Leek Pudding

½ lb self-raising flour
¼ lb shredded suet
6 leeks
salt and black pepper

Sift the flour, add the suet, and make into a stiff paste with water. Roll out and line a pudding basin, reserving ⅓ for the lid. Cut the leeks in thick slices and put them in the suet-lined basin. Add salt and black pepper, and about 3 Tbs water. Cover with a suet lid and seal. Steam in a large pan of boiling water coming half-way up the sides of the bowl for 2½ hours. Serves 4–6. Excellent with a dish of stewed beef.

A simple tomato salad.

Potato and Herb Pie

1½ lb short pastry
1 lb new *or* waxy potatoes
2 oz butter
salt, black pepper and nutmeg
¼ pt thick cream
4 Tbs chopped fresh herbs: chervil, chives, parsley, dill
1 egg yolk

Roll out half the pastry and line a 9-inch flan ring. Slice the peeled potatoes thinly and evenly. Arrange in layers in the pastry, dotting each layer with butter, seasoning with salt, black pepper and grated nutmeg. Cover with a pastry lid and brush with beaten egg yolk. Bake for 1 hour at 350°. Heat the cream, season with salt and black pepper and stir in the herbs. Lift off the lid and pour the cream over the potatoes. Replace the lid and put back into the oven for 5 minutes. Serves 6.

A mixed salad.

Pissaladière

Dough
$\frac{1}{4}$ lb strong white flour
$\frac{1}{2}$ tsp salt
$\frac{1}{4}$ oz yeast
1 tsp oil

Filling
1$\frac{1}{2}$ lb onions
$\frac{1}{2}$ gill olive oil
2 cloves garlic (optional)
salt and black pepper
8 anchovy fillets
5 black olives

Sieve the flour and the salt. Mix the yeast with 2 tablespoons warm water. Put in a warm place for 10 minutes. Make a well in the flour, pour in the yeast, and stir in approximately $\frac{1}{2}$ gill tepid water and the oil. Turn onto a floured board and knead for about 4 minutes, until smooth and slightly elastic. Put in a bowl with a floured cloth over it and leave in a warm place for about 2 hours, until doubled in size. Turn out and knead again for about 4 minutes, then roll out, or press with the heel of the hand, into a large circle between $\frac{1}{4}$ and $\frac{1}{8}$ inch thick with a slightly raised edge. Lay on an oiled baking sheet. To make the filling: slice the onions and cook very gently in the oil in a covered pan. Allow 45 minutes, stirring often, for them to become really soft without colouring. (Add the garlic after 30 minutes if used.) When done, turn them into a strainer to drain off the remaining oil. Season well with salt and black pepper, and pour over the dough. Arrange the anchovy fillets in a lattice pattern over the top, with a stoned olive in each square. Have the oven heated to 400°, put in the pissaladière, turn down the heat to 350°, and cook for about 25–30 minutes, until the edges are golden and the filling slightly coloured also. Serves 6.

A tomato salad.

Pirog

Yeast dough
1 lb strong white flour
salt
¾ oz fresh yeast
a pinch of sugar
¼ pt tepid water
3 egg yolks
¼ pt tepid milk
8 oz butter

Filling I
the heart of a green cabbage
2 hard-boiled eggs
1 oz butter
salt and black pepper

Filling II
½ lb young carrots
2 hard-boiled eggs
1 oz butter
salt and black pepper

Filling III
½ lb mushrooms
2 hard-boiled eggs
2 oz butter
salt and black pepper

Sift the flour with a pinch of salt into a large warmed bowl. Put the yeast and the sugar into a cup with the tepid water. Leave in a warm place for 10 minutes, till it starts to bubble. Beat the eggs with the milk. Cream the butter. Make a well in the centre of the flour, pour in the yeast mixture and cover it with the rest of the flour. Pour on the egg and milk mixture and stir with a wooden spoon till blended. Beat in the creamed butter and turn onto a floured board and knead briefly. Return to the bowl and cover with a floured cloth. Leave in a warm place – the linen cupboard, plate warmer, the back of the stove, or on top of a radiator – for 2 hours, by which time it should have doubled in size. Punch down with your fist, turn out and knead again briefly. Roll out on a floured baking sheet till a large oval shape. Put the filling (see below) on one half of the oval and cover with the other half. Pinch the edges together, sealing with a little beaten egg. Leave to rise in the same warm place for 15–20 minutes. Bake in the oven for 20 minutes at 400°. To serve, lay on a board and cut in thick slices. It is like a delicious loaf with a vegetable filling.

Filling I: Cut the heart of the green cabbage in half and cook until just tender in boiling salted water, drain very well and chop. Melt the butter in a saucepan, toss the cabbage in it, add the chopped eggs, and season quite highly with salt and freshly ground black pepper.

Filling II: Cook the carrots, whole or in halves according to size, in boiling salted water until tender. Drain well and chop them. Melt the butter in a saucepan, toss the carrots in it, add the chopped eggs and season well with salt and black pepper.

Filling III: Slice the mushrooms and cook gently in a covered sauté pan in the butter. When soft, add the chopped eggs and mix. Season with salt and black pepper.

Vegetable hors-d'oeuvres : ratatouille, peperonata or piperade.

Pizza

Dough
½ lb strong white flour
½ tsp salt
½ oz yeast
2 tsp olive oil

Filling
1 lb onions
4–6 Tbs olive oil
1½ lb tomatoes (fresh *or* tinned)
1 Italian Mozzarella cheese *or* 6 oz Danish
    Mozzarella
1 clove garlic
1 Tbs chopped fresh basil *or* marjoram *or*
    ½ tsp dried basil *or* marjoram
salt and black pepper
8 anchovy fillets *or* 8 black olives *or* 12 thin
    slices small hot sausage

Make the dough and leave to rise while you make the filling.
Sieve the flour. Put the yeast in a cup with 2 tablespoons
warm water and leave in a warm place for 10 minutes. Stir
into a well in the flour, then mix in about ¼ pt tepid water
and the oil. Turn out and knead until smooth – about 4
minutes. Put on a plate and cover with a floured cloth in a
warm place for 2 hours, until doubled in size. Meanwhile
make the filling. Chop the onions and stew them gently in
oil in a covered pan for 30 minutes. Drain off all the oil and
season with salt and black pepper. Skin the tomatoes and
chop coarsely. Cook briskly in a little oil until softened and
most of the juice has evaporated – about 12–15 minutes.
Slice the cheese thinly. Roll or press out the dough into a
large circle between ¼ and ⅛ inch thick – I use a mixture of
both methods, rolling to start with, then finishing by pulling
and pressing. Leave a thicker rim round the edge to enclose
the filling. Place on a greased baking sheet. Cover the dough
with the onions, then the sliced cheese, then the tomatoes.
Mince or crush the garlic and scatter over the tomatoes with
the basil, salt and black pepper. Lay the anchovy fillets, or
the stoned olives, or the sliced sausage, over the top. (I find

pizza much improved by some hot or sharp flavour, but as children rarely like anchovies or olives I have found tiny slices of a hot salami-type sausage – the Italian *peperoni*, the Polish *cabanos*, or the rather coarse Spanish *chorizo* – make a good substitute.) Put the pizza in the oven heated to 400°, turn down immediately to 350°, and cook for about 30 minutes, until golden. Serves 8–10. There are endless variations of fillings for pizza; one alternative is to omit the onions, increase the tomatoes to 2 lb, and lay the sliced cheese over the tomatoes, leaving out anchovies, etc.

A green salad.

Egg Dishes

Eggs with Watercress Sauce

8 eggs
2 large slices stale bread
approximately 1 oz butter
1 clove garlic

Watercress sauce
1 bunch watercress
$\frac{1}{2}$ pt chicken stock
$\frac{1}{2}$ oz butter and 1 Tbs flour
$\frac{1}{8}$ pt cream, or more according to taste
salt and black pepper

Cook the eggs for exactly 5 minutes in boiling salted water, then put them in a bowl of cold water and shell as soon as they are cool enough to handle. (Alternatively they can be poached.) Keep them hot. Remove the crusts from the bread and cut each slice in 4 triangles. Heat the butter and when it is very hot fry the croûtons until golden on each side. Cut the clove of garlic in half, score each cut surface with a knife, and rub the fried bread on each side with it. Keep warm while you make the sauce. Chop the watercress and simmer in the stock for 5 minutes. Pour the contents of the pan into the blender, or push through the fine mesh of the vegetable mill. Melt the butter, stir in the flour and cook for 2–3 minutes, stirring constantly. Pour in the blended watercress and stock and stir until smooth. Simmer gently for a few minutes, then add the cream. Season with salt and black pepper. Lay the eggs in a shallow dish and pour the sauce over them. Surround with the croûtons. Serves 4–6.

Serve alone.

Lentils with Hard-boiled Eggs

2 oz beef dripping *or* duck fat
1 onion
2 carrots
1 stalk celery
1 lb brown lentils
1 clove garlic
stock: beef, duck *or* game
½ lb piece bacon *or* a ham bone
black pepper
6 hard-boiled eggs

Melt the dripping in a heavy pan. Chop the onion and cook in the fat until golden. Add the sliced carrots and the diced celery. Stir around for a few minutes, then add the lentils, washed but not soaked. When they are well coated with fat, add the minced garlic and pour on enough stock to almost cover them. Put in the bacon (any odd corner or end will do, even a piece of rind failing all else) and season with black pepper. Simmer gently for 45 minutes. When the lentils are soft, the liquid should have almost boiled away. Pour into a serving dish and lay the halved hard-boiled eggs on top. Throw away the bacon, unless it is a nice piece, in which case cut it in slices and lay on top with the eggs. Serves 4–6.

Serve alone, or with a cucumber and watercress salad and a raw mushroom salad.

Stuffed Eggs Guacamole

6 eggs
4–6 large lettuce leaves

Guacamole
1 large avocado
2 tomatoes
4 spring onions *or* ½ small onion
1 small green pepper
1 green chillie
salt and black pepper
1 Tbs lemon juice
1 Tbs olive oil

Cook the eggs for 12 minutes in boiling water, and cool in a bowl of cold water. Make the guacamole: peel the avocado and remove the stone. Cut the flesh into small dice. Skin the tomatoes and chop them also, discarding the seeds and juice. Chop the spring onions and the pepper, discarding all the seeds. Pour boiling water over the chillie and leave for 2 minutes, then drain and chop finely, avoiding all the seeds. Mix all together, seasoning with salt and black pepper. Stir in the lemon juice and olive oil. Cut the shelled eggs in half and remove the yolks. Chop 2 or 3 of them and stir into the guacamole. Spoon the mixture into the egg whites and arrange on a bed of lettuce leaves. Serves 4.

Spinach and yoghurt, sweet corn mayonnaise.

Stuffed Eggs Rémoulade

6 eggs
1 head celery

Sauce rémoulade
1 egg yolk
salt and black pepper
1 heaped tsp *Moutarde de Dijon (Grey Poupon)*
1 Tbs white wine vinegar
1 Tbs tarragon vinegar
¼ pt olive oil
2 Tbs sour cream

Boil the eggs for 12 minutes, then cool in a bowl of cold water. When cold, remove the shells and cut them in half. Take out the yolks and reserve them. Scrub the celery and chop finely, reserving the best leaves for a garnish. Make the sauce: mash one of the reserved egg yolks in a bowl, and beat in the raw yolk until a smooth paste. Add a pinch of salt and black pepper. Beat in the mustard and add the vinegar very gradually. Then add the oil drop by drop, as for a mayonnaise. When finished, taste for seasoning and add the sour cream. Mix the chopped celery with the sauce and spoon into the egg whites. (Two or three of the hard-boiled egg yolks can be chopped and added to the mixture, or they can be used for another dish.) Garnish the stuffed eggs with the celery leaves. Serves 4.

Mixed bean salad; mixed chicory salad.

Eggs Sardou

6 artichoke bottoms
1½ lb fresh spinach *or* 2 lb frozen chopped
    spinach
1 oz butter
1 Tbs flour
salt and black pepper
nutmeg
2 Tbs cream
6 poached eggs
Sauce hollandaise (see p. 178)

Cook the artichoke bottoms (see p. 200) and keep hot. (I find it easier to cook whole artichokes and discard the leaves after cooking.) Make a well-seasoned spinach purée by cooking the fresh spinach, chopping and putting through the fine mesh of a vegetable mill. Return to the cleaned pan and dry out as much as possible over gentle heat. (If using frozen chopped spinach, simply cook as usual, then dry out as above.) Melt the butter, stir in the flour and cook for 1 minute. Stir in the spinach purée and simmer for 3 minutes. Season well with salt, black pepper and grated nutmeg. Add the cream. Have the poached eggs well drained and still hot. Make the sauce hollandaise. Place the artichoke bottoms on a flat dish, divide the spinach purée among them, and lay an egg on each. Cover with sauce hollandaise and serve immediately. Serves 6. This dish takes a lot of work, so do not try and do anything else at the same time.

Serve alone.

Eggs St Germain

1 lb shelled peas (about 3½ lb oldish peas in
  the pod)
½ pt chicken stock
1 oz butter
2 Tbs cream
salt and black pepper
4 eggs
Cream sauce (see p. 183)

Cook the peas in the stock until soft. Drain and reserve the
stock. Put the peas in the blender with ¼ pt of the stock.
Return the purée to the cleaned pan and stir in the butter,
cut in small bits, over a gentle heat. Add the cream, salt and
black pepper to taste. Cook the eggs for 5 minutes exactly in
boiling salted water, cool and shell. Make the cream sauce
using the remaining stock. Put the eggs in a shallow dish and
pour on the pea purée. Spoon a little of the sauce over each
egg, and hand the rest separately. Serves 4.

Serve alone.

Piperade

1 Spanish onion
1 green pepper
1 red pepper
4 large tomatoes
4 Tbs olive oil
2 cloves garlic
salt and black pepper
5 eggs

Chop the onion; cut the peppers in strips, discarding seeds
and inner white part; skin and chop the tomatoes; mince the
garlic. Heat the oil in a sauté pan and cook the onion until it
starts to soften and colour. Add the peppers and cook for 10
minutes over a low flame. Add the tomatoes and the garlic
and cook another 10 minutes. Season with salt and black
pepper. Beat the eggs lightly and pour into the piperade.
Cook for 2–3 minutes, stirring now and then, until the eggs

have thickened like lightly scrambled eggs. Serve immediately. Serves 3–4.

A green salad.

Poached Eggs on Spinach Purée

1½ lb fresh spinach *or* 2 lb frozen chopped
   spinach
1 oz butter
2 tsp flour
salt, black pepper and nutmeg
4 eggs
Cream sauce (see p. 183)

Cook the spinach and drain well. Chop and push through the fine mesh of a vegetable mill. (If using frozen chopped spinach, cook according to directions on the packet, and dry out as much moisture as possible.) Melt the butter, stir in the flour, and add the spinach purée. Cook until smooth, and simmer for 4 minutes, stirring often. Season with salt, black pepper and a little grated nutmeg. Poach the eggs and lay on a cloth to drain. (Alternatively you can use eggs boiled for exactly 5 minutes, cooled and shelled.) Keep the eggs warm while you make the sauce (see p. 183). Put the eggs in a shallow dish, pour over the spinach purée, and spoon a little sauce over each egg. Hand the rest of the sauce separately. Serves 4.

Serve alone.

Aubergine Omelette

1 medium aubergine
about 1 Tbs olive oil
4 eggs
salt and black pepper
about ½ oz butter

Peel the aubergine, cut in ¼-inch slices, then cut each slice in thin strips. Salt the strips and leave to sweat. After 30 minutes squeeze them dry in a cloth. Heat enough oil to cover the bottom of the frying pan, and cook the strips until soft and golden. Drain on soft paper. Keep warm. Beat the eggs, season with salt and black pepper, and make an omelette. When almost set, sprinkle the aubergines in an even layer across one half of the omelette, fold it over and turn onto a heated platter. Serve immediately. Serves 2.

A green salad.

Sweet Pepper Omelette

1 small red pepper
1 small green pepper
1 Tbs olive oil *or* ½ oz butter
4 eggs
salt and black pepper
½ oz butter

Skin the peppers by placing them under a hot grill and turning until blackened on all sides. When cool, remove all the skin and cut the flesh in thin strips after removing all the seeds. Soften for 2 minutes in a little butter or oil before adding to the omelette. Beat the eggs, season with salt and black pepper, and make an omelette with the butter. When almost set, sprinkle the strips of pepper in an even layer across one half of the omelette, and fold it over onto a hot dish. Serve immediately. Serves 2.

A green salad.

Potato Purée with Poached Eggs

2 lb floury potatoes
¼ pt creamy milk
3 oz butter
salt and black pepper
6 poached eggs *or oeufs mollets*
4 Tbs grated Gruyère *or* Emmenthal

Make a purée with the potatoes. Heat the milk and butter in a small pan with salt and plenty of black pepper. Beat

71

into the potato purée over a very gentle heat. When really smooth – the purée should be quite thin – pour it into a shallow gratin dish. Lay the poached eggs or *oeufs mollets* in the purée, sprinkle over the grated cheese, and brown quickly under a hot grill. Serves 3–6, depending on the rest of the meal. An excellent dish for a light supper.

A green salad.

Poached Eggs on Hop Shoots

1 bunch hop shoots
4–6 eggs (1 per person)
Sauce hollandaise (see p. 178)

Wash the hop shoots well – make sure they have not yet been sprayed – and tie them in a bundle. Lower them into boiling salted water and cook until just tender, about 10 minutes. Drain well. Meanwhile make the sauce hollandaise and keep it warm in a bowl over hot water. Poach the eggs and lay on a cloth to drain. Arrange the hops on a flat dish, lay the eggs on top, and pour the sauce over them. Serves 4–6. When hop shoots are unobtainable, this dish can be made with sprue, the thin stalks of asparagus.

Serve alone.

Scrambled Eggs with Sweet Corn

4 ears corn-on-the-cob *or* 1 packet frozen corn
   or 1 14-oz tin kernel corn
4 rashers streaky bacon
1 oz butter
6 eggs
salt and black pepper

If using fresh corn, cut the kernels off the cobs with a sharp knife, and scrape off all the juice as well. Simmer in a very little lightly salted water until tender, about 5 minutes. Drain. Chop the bacon. Fry the bacon in the butter until golden. Add the cooked (or tinned) corn and stir over a moderate heat. Season with salt and black pepper. Beat the eggs and pour onto the corn. Stir constantly with a wooden spoon until just cooked, and well mixed. Serve with crusty French bread and butter. Serves 3–4.

Grilled tomatoes ; leaf spinach.

Scrambled Eggs with Mushrooms

6 oz mushrooms
2 oz butter
8 eggs
salt and black pepper
croûtons

Slice the mushrooms and cook in half the butter until soft. Drain them and keep hot. Scramble the eggs in the remaining butter, season well with salt and black pepper. When they are almost set, stir in the mushrooms and cook a few moments longer. Garnish with croûtons of bread fried in butter. Serves 4.

Fried cucumber, baked tomatoes.

Scrambled Eggs with Tomatoes

$\frac{1}{2}$ lb tomatoes
2 oz butter
8 eggs
salt and black pepper
sugar
a few leaves of basil, when available
croûtons

Peel the tomatoes and chop them, discarding seeds and juice. Cook gently in half the butter for a few moments, until softened. Season with a little salt and black pepper and a pinch of sugar, adding a few chopped leaves of fresh basil when available. Scramble the eggs as usual in the remaining butter, adding the tomatoes when they are three-quarters cooked. Serve garnished with croûtons of bread fried in butter. Serves 4.

Courgettes stewed with herbs ; succotash.

Scrambled Eggs with Red Peppers

1 large red pepper
2 oz butter
1 Tbs oil
8 eggs
salt and black pepper

Skin the pepper by placing it under a hot grill and turning until the skin is blackened. Remove with a knife. Cut the pepper in strips, discarding the pith and seeds. Heat $\frac{1}{2}$ oz butter and the oil in a frying pan. Cook the pepper for about 3 minutes, until softened. Beat the eggs with salt and black pepper and scramble in the remaining butter. Half-way through the cooking add the pepper, and mix well with the eggs as they finish cooking. Serves 4.

Steamed broccoli; grilled mushrooms.

Fritters and Pancakes

Fritter Batters

Batter I (French batter)

¼ lb flour
salt
2 Tbs arachide oil
¼ pt tepid water
1 egg white

Sift the flour with a pinch of salt. Stir in the oil, then mix in the tepid water until you have the consistency of thickish cream. (You may need slightly more than ¼ pt.) Leave for about 2 hours in a cool place. Just before using, beat again and fold in the stiffly beaten egg white. This makes an excellent light batter, suitable for all types of fritters.

Batter II (Japanese batter or tempura)

1 egg
¼ pt iced water
¼ lb flour

Beat the egg, stir in the iced water and the sifted flour. Use immediately. This mixture gives a golden coating to the food, familiar to all those who eat in Oriental restaurants.

Batter III (American batter)

3 oz flour
salt
1 egg
¼ pt flat ale

Sift the flour with a pinch of salt. Make a well in the middle and break in the egg. Mix the egg and the flour with a whisk, stirring in the ale gradually at the same time, until all are amalgamated into a smooth batter. Stand for about 2 hours if possible, before using. If preferred, the egg can be separated, and the white folded in at the last moment. A good all-purpose batter.

Batter IV (Soda water batter)

Make as for Batter I, substituting soda water for water. Do not stand, but use as soon as prepared. Another light batter particularly suited to vegetables.

Batter V (English)
3 oz flour
salt
1 egg
¼ pt water

Sift the flour with a pinch of salt into a large bowl. Make a well in the centre and break in the egg. Using a wire whisk, beat the egg, gradually incorporating the flour around the edges. At the same time, slowly pour in the water, beating continually and timing the process so that by the time all the water is poured in, all the flour has been amalgamated. If it seems too thick, add a little more water. Leave to stand for 2 hours if possible. Alternatively, the egg can be separated, and the stiffly beaten white folded in at the last moment. This makes a lighter batter, but has the disadvantage of having to be used immediately. If you want to keep some for the next day, it is better to use the whole egg unbeaten. Store the remaining batter in a covered container in the refrigerator.

Brussels Sprouts in Batter

½ lb tiny brussels sprouts
fritter batter

Throw the sprouts into boiling salted water and cook briskly until almost tender, about 5 minutes. Drain well, and pat dry in a cloth. Dip each one in fritter batter and drop into deep fat or oil heated to about 360°. Cook until they rise to the surface, and are golden brown and soft in the centre. Drain on soft paper and serve with a tomato sauce. Serves 4.

Potato pancakes; baked corn.

Fritto Misto of Vegetables

fritter batter
2 lemons (optional)

2 tomatoes
2 courgettes
2 small onions
or
2 small beetroot, already cooked
½ cucumber
1 small aubergine
or
1 small aubergine
2 courgettes
2 tomatoes

Choose a selection of vegetables that make a colour contrast, and prepare them as follows: cut the unpeeled tomatoes and courgettes in thin slices, the tomatoes vertically, the courgettes diagonally. Peel the onions and slice thinly, being careful not to divide up the slices into rings. Peel the cooked beetroot and slice equally thinly; slice the unpeeled cucumber and aubergine in similar fashion. Keep the vegetables separate, and dip each batch in batter, using tongs to lift them out and scraping off excess batter on the edge of the bowl. (If using beetroot, do it last of all as it colours the batter.) Have a pan of deep oil heated to about 360° and drop in the slices in small batches. Turn them over halfway, and as soon as they are golden and puffed up on both sides, lift out and drain on soft paper. When all are cooked, arrange them on a hot platter, or make a mixture of each vegetable on individual dishes. Serve with quartered lemons, or skordalia (see p. 179). Serves 4.

Serve alone.

Aubergine Fritters

½ lb aubergines
fritter batter
2 lemons (optional)

Cut the unpeeled aubergines in thin slices. Sprinkle with salt and leave to drain for 30 minutes. Dry the slices and dip them in the batter. Lift them out with tongs, scraping off excess batter. Drop them into oil, heated to about 360°, a few at a time, and cook for about 3–4 minutes. Turn them over halfway through with a slotted spoon. Drain on soft paper and keep warm while you fry the next batch. Serve with skordalia, or simply lemons cut in quarters. Courgette or cucumber fritters can be made in the same way, substituting ½ lb courgettes or 1 large unpeeled cucumber. Serves 4.

Serve alone.

Corn Fritters

½ lb corn kernels cut off the cob (about 2–3 ears)
4 Tbs thick cream
2 Tbs flour
½ tsp baking powder
salt and black pepper
½ tsp sugar

Cut the corn off the cobs with a sharp knife, scraping the juice into the mixing bowl. Stir the cream into the corn, add the flour, baking powder and seasonings and mix. Heat a griddle, grease it with a small piece of butter, and drop spoonfuls of the corn mixture onto it. Flatten them with a palette knife, and try to allow a few holes to develop in the little flat cakes. Cook until golden brown, approximately 4 minutes each side. Serves 4–5.

Boiled leeks; beetroot with dill.

Pancake Batters

Batter I (plain)
8 oz plain flour
¼ tsp salt
2 eggs
a scant ½ pt milk
a scant ½ pt water

Sift the flour with the salt into a large bowl. Make a well in the centre. Beat the eggs and pour them into the well. Mix the milk and water in a jug. Using a wire whisk, start to beat the eggs, incorporating the flour little by little round the edges, and pouring in the milk and water with the other hand. Do it carefully so that by the time the jug is empty all the flour has been drawn into the mixture. Continue to beat for two minutes, until all is perfectly smooth. Leave in a cool place for 1–2 hours, if possible, before using. The mixture should resemble fairly thick but unwhipped cream. If it is too thick, add a little more liquid before using. In any case, beat well for 1–2 minutes before cooking. Have a very hot pan lightly greased with butter. I have a heavy pancake pan and a griddle, but prefer to use an omelette pan as it is lighter and easier to handle. Pour on a large spoonful of the batter and tilt the pan till a round even pancake has formed. Cook over a moderate heat until the surface has solidified, then turn (or toss) and cook the other side for about 1 minute. Lay the pancakes in a warm place, separated by the folds of a clean cloth, until you are ready to use them. Serves 6–8. This makes a fairly large amount of batter. It can be made in half quantities or half can be stored in the refrigerator until the following day. These pancakes make a good first course or a main dish, filled with any of the suggested fillings.

Batter II (wholemeal)

4 oz wholewheat flour (obtainable from
   health food shops)
4 oz plain white flour
¼ tsp salt
2 eggs
½ pt milk
½ pt water

Make as for Batter I (plain). (The wholewheat flour absorbs more liquid, hence the extra milk and water.) Serves 6–8. This makes a more substantial pancake than the plain batter, suitable for a main course. Fill with spinach filling (see p. 81), ratatouille (see p. 110) *or* tomatoes in sour cream (see p. 82).

79

Batter III (buckwheat)

4 oz buckwheat flour (obtainable from health
   food shops)
4 oz plain white flour
½ tsp salt
2 eggs
½ pt milk
½ pt water

Make as for Batter I (plain). (The buckwheat flour absorbs
more liquid, hence the extra milk and water.) Serves 6–8.
This makes a filling pancake, suitable for a main course.
Fill with tomato and onion filling (see p. 81) *or* mushrooms
in sour cream (see below).

Batter IV (spinach)

½ lb raw spinach *or* ½ lb frozen chopped
   spinach
Batter I (plain)

Cook the spinach and drain as well as possible. Make the
batter as before, and stir in 4 fl oz spinach purée. Stand fo
2 hours before using. For a very smooth batter run through
the blender. Serves 6–8. This can be made in half quantities. It makes an unusual green pancake, excellent with
tomato sauce, with a mushroom stuffing and served with a
sauce mornay or filled with either mushrooms or tomatoes
in sour cream (see below and p. 82).

Pancake Fillings

Here are some suggested fillings. Other vegetable dishes
which make suitable fillings are COURGETTES, CARROTS and
TOMATOES (see p. 122) and RATATOUILLE (see p. 110).

Mushrooms in sour cream

6 oz mushrooms, flat if possible
1–1½ oz butter
¼ pt sour cream *or* fresh cream and a little
   lemon juice
salt and black pepper

Slice the mushrooms and cook in the butter until soft. Add the cream, mix and season to taste.

Spinach filling

1 lb raw spinach *or* 1 lb frozen leaf spinach
½ onion
1 oz butter
1 tsp flour
¼ pt sour cream
approximately 4 Tbs buttermilk (or milk)
salt and black pepper

Cook the spinach in the usual way, drain it well, and chop it. Chop the onion finely. Brown it in the butter; when soft, add the flour and blend. Stir in the cream and cook gently till smooth, thinning with a little buttermilk. Stir in the chopped spinach, re-heat, and season with salt and black pepper. This makes an excellent filling for buckwheat or wholemeal pancakes.

Tomato and onion filling

1 medium onion
¾ lb fresh tomatoes *or* a 14-oz tin
1 oz butter
1 Tbs olive oil
1 clove garlic
1 heaped tsp flour
salt and black pepper
sugar
ground celery seed *or* substitute celery salt for
    plain salt
2 Tbs chopped basil *or* marjoram when
    available

Chop the onion coarsely. If using fresh tomatoes, skin them and chop coarsely. Heat the butter and oil and cook the onion with the lid on until quite soft, stirring now and then, about 10 minutes. Add the crushed garlic and cook another minute, then stir in the flour and cook for another minute before adding the tomatoes. Simmer until thick and soft, about 8 minutes. Season carefully. This makes 1 cup.

Tomatoes in sour cream
1 lb tomatoes
1 oz butter
1 tsp flour
salt and black pepper
a pinch of sugar
2 Tbs chopped fresh basil, when available
$\frac{1}{4}$ pt sour cream

Skin the tomatoes and chop them coarsely. Melt the butter and cook the tomatoes until softened, about 5 minutes. Add the flour, salt and black pepper, sugar, and fresh basil when available. Stir in the sour cream and cook gently until well mixed and blended, another 3–4 minutes. Excellent with spinach pancakes.

Spinach Pancakes

Pancake batter IV (spinach) (see p. 80)
Mushrooms in sour cream (see p. 80)

Tomato sauce
1 lb tomatoes
2 oz butter
1 clove garlic
2 Tbs chopped fresh basil, if available
salt and black pepper
sugar

Make the batter, and while it is standing make the mushroom filling. Then make the tomato sauce: skin and chop the tomatoes coarsely. Melt the butter and cook the tomatoes with the crushed garlic and basil for about 8 minutes, adding salt, black pepper and a pinch of sugar. Keep both fillings hot while you make the pancakes. Heat a griddle or large crêpe pan. When very hot, grease lightly with a small piece of butter. Pour half a ladle full of batter onto the centre of the pan, and tilt to form a large thin crêpe. Make six in all, keeping them hot and assemble on a flat dish like a layer cake, in the following order: pancake, $\frac{1}{3}$ of the mushroom filling, second pancake, $\frac{1}{3}$ of the tomato sauce, third pancake, and so on, finishing with a layer of tomato sauce.

Cut in quarters to serve. Serves 4. An excellent dish, very pretty and well worth the trouble.

A lettuce salad.

Celeriac Croquettes

1 celeriac weighing approximately ¾ lb
¾ lb potatoes
2 egg yolks and 1 whole egg
1 oz butter
salt and black pepper
dry breadcrumbs

Cut the celeriac into pieces and cook in boiling salted water until tender. Peel the potatoes and cook separately. Dry out both celeriac and potatoes as much as possible, then push through the medium mesh of the vegetable mill. Mix the two purées and return to the cleaned pan. Dry out again as much as possible stirring over a low flame. Beat in the butter, and season with salt and black pepper. If the purée still seems slightly moist, stir in ½ Tbs flour. Stir in 2 egg yolks off the flame, and mix well. Pour into a shallow dish, cover with a greased piece of saran-wrap, and put in the refrigerator for several hours, or overnight. (This makes the purée drier, and easier to handle.) The next day, divide into equal sized pieces, form into rolls like corks, and dip in beaten egg and white breadcrumbs. Fry in a mixture of butter and oil, or deep fry if preferred. Serve immediately. Fried parsley makes a nice garnish if the croquettes are to be eaten on their own, in which case hand a tomato sauce separately. Makes 16–18 croquettes. Serves 6.

Ratatouille ; green rice.

Individual Vegetable Dishes

Fried Aubergines

2 medium aubergines
flour
salt and black pepper
1–2 lemons

Leave the aubergines unpeeled and cut across in very thin slices. Sprinkle them with salt and leave to drain for about 30 minutes, then pat dry in a cloth or soft paper. Coat the slices in seasoned flour by shaking them in a bag, then drop them one by one into a pan of oil heated to about 360°, shaking off the excess flour. Do not try to cook too many at one time as they must have room to float freely. Turn them over once with a slotted spoon so that they brown on both sides. In about 3–4 minutes they should be golden brown. Lift them out and drain on soft paper. Keep them hot while you fry the next batch, but wait until the oil has reached the correct temperature before putting the second lot in. Serve with lemon quarters, a garlic sauce such as skordalia, a yoghurt sauce or a spicy tomato sauce. Serves 4. Do not try to do much more than this quantity, as if the slices are really thin it will take some time to get them all cooked and they should be eaten soon after cooking. FRIED COURGETTES are made as above, substituting $\frac{1}{2}$ lb courgettes cut in very thin diagonal slices. For FRIED CUCUMBER use a large cucumber, unpeeled and thinly sliced.

Serve alone.

Middle Eastern Aubergines

4 medium aubergines
4 onions
6 large tomatoes
olive oil
4 cloves garlic
salt and black pepper

Peel the aubergines and cut them in ½-inch slices. Sprinkle with salt, leave for 30 minutes and pat dry. Slice the onions thinly. Peel and slice the tomatoes. Heat some oil in a large frying pan and fry the aubergine slices until golden on both sides. Drain. Fry the onions in the same pan, adding more oil if necessary. When they are golden, put them in a thick layer at the bottom of a fireproof casserole. Fry the sliced tomatoes briefly, allowing 2–3 minutes only to soften them. Make alternate layers of aubergines and tomatoes on top of the onions, sprinkling each layer with finely minced garlic, salt and black pepper. Pour over ½ pt water. Cover and cook very gently over a low flame, or in a low (325°) oven, for about 30 minutes, until the vegetables are very soft. Leave to cool. When cold, turn out on to a flat dish. Serves 4.

Leek vinaigrette; potato salad.

Terry's Aubergines

2 large aubergines
1 Spanish onion
1 lb tomatoes
olive oil
salt and black pepper
sugar
¼ lb Mozzarella, thinly sliced

Cut the aubergines in ½-inch slices, salt them, and leave to drain in a colander. Cut the onion in half, then cut each half in ¼-inch slices. Divide the slices into rings. Peel the tomatoes, discard the seeds and juice and cut the flesh in strips like the onion. Heat some olive oil in a broad heavy frying pan and fry the aubergine slices until brown on both sides. Place the slices on a flat dish and keep warm. Add more oil to the pan and cook the onion until it is soft, then add the tomatoes and cook the mixture a few minutes more. Season with salt, black pepper and a little sugar. Spoon the tomato and onion mixture over the aubergine slices and top with the sliced cheese. Bake in a moderate oven (350°) for 30 minutes. Serves 4.

A green salad.

French Beans Provençale

½ lb tomatoes
¼ lb tiny onions
1 lb very small French beans
1 clove garlic
1 oz butter
2 Tbs olive oil
salt and black pepper

Skin the tomatoes, cut them in half horizontally and remove the seeds with the point of a knife. Peel the onions; if they are really small, leave them whole, otherwise cut them in half. Cut off the ends of the beans, leaving them whole. Mince or crush the garlic. Heat the butter and oil in a sauté pan with a lid. Put in the onions and cook gently until they are lightly coloured, turning them around in the oil. Add the tomatoes, cut side downwards, and cook another 2–3 minutes. Add the beans, garlic, salt and black pepper, cover the pan and cook gently for 40 minutes, stirring now and then. Test the beans to make sure they are just tender before serving. Also good cold. Serves 6.

If hot, fried or sautéed potatoes, and grilled mushrooms; if cold, cauliflower vinaigrette, and raw mushroom salad.

Red Cabbage Cooked in the Viennese Fashion

1 large red cabbage
1 Spanish onion
3 oz beef dripping *or* other fat
2 Tbs sugar
1 large cooking apple
3 Tbs red wine vinegar *or* cider vinegar
salt and black pepper
$\frac{1}{2}$ pt beef stock
1 Tbs flour
$\frac{1}{2}$ gill cream, sour cream *or* yoghurt

Cut the cabbage in quarters, discard the outer leaves and the central core, then shred each quarter finely. Chop the onion. Melt the fat in a deep heavy casserole and cook the onion until it starts to soften and colour. Add the sugar and stir around until all is golden. Put in the cabbage and mix well. Chop the unpeeled apple and add to the cabbage. Add the vinegar and some salt and black pepper. Stir well, cover and cook for 15 minutes over a low flame. Heat the stock and pour into the casserole. Cook for 2 hours on top of the stove or in a low oven (310°). When the time is up, mix the flour and cream to a paste in a cup and add to the cabbage by degrees, stirring all the time, on top of the stove. Cook over a low flame for 3–4 minutes to cook the flour and thicken the sauce. Taste, and add more sugar or vinegar if necessary – the sweet and sour elements should be nicely balanced – or more salt and black pepper. Serves 8. This dish is improved by being made a day in advance and re-heated in a covered casserole in a moderate oven (350°) for one hour. Excellent with all game, boiled ham or bacon, and sausages of all sorts.

Potato cakes or potato scones; braised fennel.

Courgettes in Cheese Soufflé Sauce

2 large courgettes *or* 4 smaller ones

Cheese soufflé sauce
2 oz butter
3 Tbs flour
½ pt milk
3 oz grated Gruyère
2 eggs, separated

Poach the whole courgettes in boiling salted water for 10 minutes, then drain. Cut a thin sliver off each side of the courgettes, then cut lengthwise into slices about ⅓-inch thick. (If using small courgettes, cut in half, after removing a very thin sliver to flatten the base.) Lay each slice on a greased baking sheet. Make the sauce: melt the butter, stir in the flour, and cook for 3 minutes, stirring continuously. Add the heated milk, and stir until smooth. Simmer for 5 minutes, stirring now and then, then beat in the grated cheese. Stir over gentle heat until melted and smooth. Season well with salt and black pepper. Remove from the heat and beat in the beaten egg yolks. Whip the whites until stiff, then fold into the sauce. Using two teaspoons, cover each of the courgette slices with the sauce, heaping it up thickly. Place the baking sheet in the oven pre-heated to 400°, and cook for 15 minutes, when the sauce should be puffed up and golden brown. Serve immediately. Serves 4. TOMATOES IN CHEESE SOUFFLÉ SAUCE can be made as above, substituting 3 large tomatoes for the courgettes. Cut the raw tomatoes horizontally in ½-inch slices, and bake covered with the sauce.

Serve alone.

Braised Celery

3 heads celery
2 oz butter
⅓ pt stock: beef, chicken, game, veal *or* vegetable
about 1 Tbs lemon juice
salt and black pepper

Bring a large pan of water to the boil. Remove the outside stalks of the celery, trim the stumps, and cut the inner stalks down to make a neat 'heart'. Cut each heart in half and throw into the boiling water. Cook for 5 minutes, then drain. Rub a heavy pan with some of the butter and lay the celery hearts in it in one layer. Dot with the remaining butter. Pour over the stock and add salt, black pepper and the lemon juice. Cover with the lid and cook very gently on top of the stove for 1½–2 hours, depending on the size and age of the celery. Turn them over every half hour, and add a little more stock if necessary. After 1½ hours test with a skewer to see when they are soft. Remove them to a clean dish and pour the juice over them, or thicken it slightly by stirring in 1 tsp flour rubbed into 1 tsp butter. Stir until smooth and slightly thickened, taste for seasoning, and pour over the celery. Serves 6. When made with a good flavoured beef or game stock this is really delicious. It can be cooked in the oven, but like braised chicory, I prefer to cook it on top of the stove as it is easier to watch the celery hearts while they cook. If they go in the oven, however, put them in a shallow buttered dish and cover with foil. Allow 1½–2 hours at 350°.

Cabbage cooked in milk; baked tomatoes.

Celery Mornay

3 heads celery
2 oz butter
⅓ pt stock: beef, chicken, veal, game *or*
    vegetable
about 1 Tbs lemon juice
salt and black pepper

Sauce mornay
¾ pt milk
½ bay leaf, ½ small onion, 2 cloves
6 black peppercorns and ½ tsp salt
1 oz butter and 2 Tbs flour
¼ pt thin cream
grated nutmeg
4 oz grated Gruyère

Braise the celery with the butter, stock, lemon juice, and seasonings. (See page 90.) While it is cooking, make the sauce: put the milk in a small pan with the bay leaf, onion, cloves, peppercorns and salt and bring slowly to boiling point. Remove from the heat, cover the pan, and leave to infuse for 15–20 minutes. Melt the butter, stir in the flour and cook for 2 minutes. Pour in the strained milk and blend. Simmer for 4 minutes, then add a little grated nutmeg and extra salt and pepper if needed. Stir in the cream and the cheese, reserving one ounce. When the celery is tender, lift it out of its juices and lay it in a gratin dish. Beat the juice into the sauce and pour it over the celery. Scatter the remaining cheese over the top and brown under a hot grill until golden. (Alternatively, it can be made in advance and browned in the oven while it is re-heating – approximately 25 minutes at 400°.) Serves 6.

Braised Chicory

1½ lb chicory
1½ oz butter
lemon juice
salt and black pepper

Bring a large pan of water to the boil, throw in the chicory, cook for 5 minutes and drain. Rub a shallow sauté pan with some of the butter, put in the chicory in one layer, and dot with the remaining butter. Squeeze over about 2 Tbs lemon juice, and sprinkle with salt and black pepper. Add 1 Tbs water and cook over a gentle heat for 45 minutes, turning the chicory over from time to time. If the liquid shows signs of boiling away, add another Tbs water. To cook in the oven, lay in a shallow buttered dish, again in one layer if possible, and dot with butter and lemon juice as above. No water is necessary. Cover with a buttered piece of aluminium foil and cook for 1 hour at 350°. In both cases, it is best to transfer the chicory to a clean dish to serve. Sprinkle with more lemon juice. Serves 4.

Brussels sprouts fried in batter; grilled tomatoes.

Chicory Mornay

1½ lb chicory
1½ oz butter
lemon juice
salt and black pepper

Sauce mornay
¾ pt milk
½ bay leaf, 1 slice onion, 2 cloves
salt and 6 black peppercorns
nutmeg *or* mace
1 oz butter and 1 Tbs flour
¼ pt thin cream
4 oz grated Gruyère

Braise the chicory with the butter, lemon juice, salt and pepper. (See page 91.) While it is cooking, make the sauce: put the milk in a small pan with the bay leaf, onion, cloves, peppercorns, a pinch of grated nutmeg or mace, and the salt. Bring slowly to the boil and leave, covered, by the side of the fire for 20 minutes to absorb the flavours. Melt the butter, stir in the flour and cook for 1 minute over gentle heat. Pour in the strained milk and blend. Simmer gently for 4–5 minutes, stirring often. Adjust the seasoning, and add the cream and the cheese, reserving one quarter. Stir until smooth. When the chicory is cooked, transfer it to a clean dish, draining the juice away carefully. Pour the sauce over the chicory (do not add the juice as it will be bitter) and scatter the remaining cheese over the top. Brown under a hot grill. (Or make in advance and re-heat for about 25 minutes in a hot oven – 400°.) Serves 4–6.

Steamed broccoli, grilled tomatoes, lettuce salad.

Braised Fennel

3 heads fennel
2 oz butter
⅓ pt stock: beef, chicken, game *or* vegetable
1 Tbs lemon juice
salt and black pepper
1 tsp butter
1 tsp flour

Trim the fennel, cutting off any discoloured leaves and scrubbing well under running water. Cut each root in half and lay them in one layer in a sauté pan. Cut the butter in small pieces and scatter over them. Pour over the stock and add the lemon juice, salt and black pepper. Cover with the lid and cook very gently on top of the stove for 1½–2 hours, turning them over from time to time, and adding more stock if necessary. When they are soft (test by piercing with a fine skewer), transfer them to a shallow dish and thicken the juice slightly by stirring in the butter and flour which you have mixed to a paste. Stir until smooth and pour over the fennel. Serves 4–6.

Green rice ; courgettes, carrots and tomatoes.

Fennel Mornay

3 heads fennel

Sauce mornay
¾ pt milk
½ bay leaf, 1 slice onion, 2 cloves
salt and 6 black peppercorns
nutmeg *or* mace
1 oz butter and 1 Tbs flour
¼ pt thin cream
4 oz grated Gruyère

Trim the fennel, cutting off any discoloured leaves. Drop into a large pan of boiling salted water, and simmer for 30 minutes, or until tender. While they are cooking, make the sauce: put the milk in a small pan with the bay leaf, onion, cloves, peppercorns, a pinch of grated nutmeg or mace, and the salt. Bring to boiling point, remove from the heat and leave covered for 20 minutes to infuse. Melt the butter, stir in the flour and cook for 1–2 minutes, stirring often. Pour in the strained milk and blend. Simmer for 4 minutes, stirring often. Stir in the cream and the grated cheese, reserving a quarter of it. Stir until smooth. When the fennel are soft, drain them well and cut each one in half. Lay them in a shallow dish and pour the sauce over them. Scatter the remaining cheese over the top and brown under the grill. Alternatively, make in advance and re-heat for 25 minutes in a hot oven – 400°. Serves 4.

Boiled rice; French beans Provençale.

Creamed Leeks

2 lb leeks
1½ oz butter
½ Tbs flour
¼ pt cream
salt and black pepper
a pinch grated nutmeg

Wash and trim the leeks, and cut in 1-inch slices. Bring ½ inch lightly salted water to the boil in a broad heavy pan and put in the leeks. Cover the pan and cook for 10 minutes, shaking the pan from side to side occasionally. Drain the leeks, reserving the water. Shake them about over gentle heat for a few minutes to dry them out, then turn onto a flat surface and chop with a long knife. You should have about 2½ cups of chopped leeks. Melt the butter in the cleaned pan, put in the leeks and re-heat. Add the flour, stir to blend for 1 minute, then pour on ¼ pt of the reserved cooking water (if there is less than ¼ pt, make up with water), re-heated in a small pan with the cream. Stir until well mixed and blended. Season well with salt and black pepper, and a little freshly grated nutmeg. Simmer for a few minutes, then pour into a serving dish and surround with croûtons (small triangular pieces of toast, or bread fried in butter). Serves 6.

Beetroot fritters; broccoli.

Spinach Purée

2 lb raw spinach
1½ oz butter
1 small onion
1 clove garlic (optional)
1 tsp flour
½ pt thin cream
salt and black pepper

Cook the washed spinach very gently in the water clinging
to its leaves, stirring now and then. When it releases its moisture turn up the heat slightly and add salt. When tender,
drain very well and chop roughly with a knife. Melt the
butter in the cleaned pan, chop the onion very finely and
stew gently in the butter until soft. Add the minced or
crushed garlic half-way through; do not allow to burn. Stir
in the flour, blend with the heated cream and season well
with salt and black pepper. When smooth and blended,
stir in the chopped spinach. Stir well, pour into the blender
to make a purée. Return briefly to the pan to re-heat and
adjust seasoning. Serves 4–6. This dish can be made in
advance and reheated. If serving alone, surround with garlic
croûtons (triangles of bread, fried until golden in butter and
rubbed on each side with a cut clove of garlic).

Hot potato salad; beetroot fritters.

Jerusalem Artichokes Hollandaise

1½ lb Jerusalem artichokes

Sauce hollandaise
4 oz best butter
3 egg yolks
1 Tbs white wine vinegar
¼ bay leaf
4 black peppercorns.

Scrub the artichokes and cook until tender in boiling salted
water. Drain them in a colander and remove the skins as
soon as they are cool enough to handle. Cut them in thick
slices and put them in a hot dish. Make the sauce hollan-

daise (see p. 178) and pour over them. Serves 4. An excellent first course which is quite filling.

Serve alone.

Home Baked Beans

¾ lb haricot beans
1 medium onion
1 Tbs olive oil
2 oz bacon rashers
2 cloves garlic
salt and black pepper
2–3 Tbs chopped parsley

Soak the beans for about 3 hours, then drain. Chop the onion and cook in the oil until it starts to soften. Chop the bacon and add to the onion. Mince the garlic finely and add to the bacon. Pour in the drained beans, barely cover with cold water, and add salt and black pepper. Cover the casserole and bake in a low oven (275°) until the beans are tender, about 2 hours. Stir once or twice adding water if necessary. Drain off any excess liquid and stir in 2–3 Tbs chopped parsley before serving. Serves 4–6.

Courgettes stewed with herbs; grilled tomatoes.

French Beans with Bacon

1 lb very small French beans
4 oz streaky bacon rashers
¼ oz butter
salt and black pepper
1 small onion

Cut the ends off the beans but leave them whole. Bring a pan of lightly salted water to the boil, throw in the beans, and cook until just tender. Drain. Chop the bacon, melt a tiny bit of butter in a frying pan and fry the bacon slowly until crisp. Add the beans to the pan and stir around until well mixed and hot. Add salt and black pepper to taste. Pile on a flat serving dish and scatter the very finely chopped raw onion over the top. Serves 6.

Hashed potatoes or rösti; baked tomatoes.

Dried Beans Provençale

½ lb haricot beans
2 Tbs olive oil
½ lb tomatoes
1 clove garlic
salt and black pepper
3 Tbs finely chopped parsley

Soak the beans for 2–3 hours, then cover with fresh water and bring to the boil. Simmer gently until soft, adding salt towards the end. (Alternatively, use ½ lb beans already cooked, or tinned beans well rinsed under the cold tap.) Heat the oil and cook the skinned and chopped tomatoes with the minced garlic for about 5 minutes, until softened. Add the beans and cook another 5 minutes, until well mixed and heated. Stir in the parsley and add salt and black pepper to taste. Serves 4. An excellent dish to serve with boiled bacon.

Braised celery; turnips with mustard.

Beetroot with Dill

1¼ lb small cooked beetroot
1 oz butter
¼ pt cream
salt and black pepper
2 Tbs chopped fresh dill

Cut the beetroot in quarters if small, or in chunks or thick slices if larger. Melt the butter in a sauté pan and turn the beetroot about in it until coated all over with the butter, and quite hot. Pour in the cream and add plenty of salt and black pepper. Stir around until all is well mixed and hot. Sprinkle on the chopped dill and serve. Serves 4–6.

Corn fritters; steamed broccoli.

Beetroot in Sour Cream

1½ lb small cooked beetroot
1 oz butter
¼ pt sour cream
salt and black pepper

Have the beetroot freshly cooked if possible, or buy them from a reliable greengrocer. Cut them in thick slices and toss in butter in a sauté pan until coated all over. Pour over the sour cream and season well with salt and black pepper. Put on the lid and leave over a very gentle heat for about 8 minutes to heat through thoroughly. Stir occasionally. Serves 4–6.

Stewed mushrooms ; green rice.

Carrot Purée

1 lb carrots
1 oz butter
salt and black pepper

Slice the carrots and cover with cold water. Add salt, bring to the boil, and simmer until soft. Drain and return to the pan to dry out, stirring for 2 minutes over a gentle heat. Push the carrots through the medium mesh of a vegetable mill and return the purée to the pan. Stir over low heat to dry out as much moisture as possible, then beat in the butter. Season with salt and black pepper and serve.

Boiled leeks or leek pudding ; steamed broccoli.

Carrot Purée with Stock

1 lb carrots
¾ pt chicken stock
salt and black pepper
½ oz butter

Slice the carrots and cook in the stock until soft. Drain, reserving about 6 Tbs of the liquid. Put in the blender with

98

the liquid. Return to the cleaned pan and re-heat, but do not try to dry out as this is meant to be a moist purée. Season with salt and black pepper and add the butter. Serves 3. A very nourishing dish which is easily digested, ideal for babies and invalids.

Green peas with cucumber; potato pancakes.

Cauliflower Cooked in Stock

1 cauliflower
1½ oz butter
about ½ pt light stock: chicken, veal *or*
    vegetable
salt and black pepper

Divide the cauliflower into sprigs and chop. Melt 1 oz butter in a heavy pan, put in the cauliflower and stir over a gentle heat for 4–5 minutes. Pour on a little boiling stock, enough to half cover the cauliflower, add salt and cover the pan. Simmer until just tender, and the liquid is almost evaporated. If there is still much left, remove the cauliflower with a slotted spoon and keep warm while you boil up the stock to reduce to a few spoonfuls. Add the remaining butter and a little black pepper and pour over the cauliflower. Serves 4–5.

Carrot risotto; French beans Provençale.

Cauliflower Polonaise

1 medium cauliflower
1 oz butter
4 Tbs dry breadcrumbs
1 hard-boiled egg
2 Tbs chopped parsley
lemon juice
salt and black pepper

Cook the cauliflower until just tender in boiling salted water. Drain upside down in a colander. Place on a round serving dish and keep hot. Melt the butter, and when it is very hot put in the breadcrumbs and stir around until all are well browned, being careful not to let them burn. Add the chopped hard-boiled egg and the parsley, stir over a gentle heat until all are well mixed and hot, adding a little lemon juice and salt and black pepper to taste. Pour over the whole cauliflower and serve. Serves 4.

Tomato and courgette casserole; French beans and bacon.

Gratin of Chicory

1½ lb chicory
1½ oz butter
1 tsp lemon juice
2 eggs
¼ pt thick cream
salt, black pepper and nutmeg
1 oz grated Gruyère

Cut the chicory in 1-inch slices. Cook gently in the butter and lemon juice in a covered sauté pan for 10 minutes, stirring once or twice. Drain the chicory in a colander while you beat the eggs with the cream, adding salt and black pepper to taste, some freshly grated nutmeg and the cheese. (This amount of cheese will give only a very slight flavour; if you want a stronger cheesey taste double the quantity.) Mix the drained chicory with the egg and cream mixture and pour into a buttered gratin dish. Cook for 15 minutes at 400°. Serves 4.

Boiled French beans; grilled tomatoes.

Chinese Cabbage

1 Chinese cabbage
about ½ pt chicken stock
salt and black pepper
lemon juice

Cut the cabbage in slices. Put ½-inch chicken stock in a heavy saucepan, bring to the boil and then pile in the cabbage. Cook until tender, about 8–10 minutes, stirring often. There should be very little stock left. Serve in its own juice, adding salt, black pepper and a squeeze of lemon juice. Serves 4. A useful dish for those on a diet as it contains no fat.

Baked corn; potato croquettes.

Gratin of Courgettes

1½ lb courgettes
2 eggs
¼ pt thick cream
salt and black pepper
nutmeg
2 oz grated Gruyère

Cut the courgettes in ½-inch slices and cook them for 12 minutes in boiling salted water. Press them in a colander to get rid of as much moisture as possible. Turn them into a shallow fireproof dish, which has been rubbed with butter, and chop them roughly with the edge of a palette knife. Beat the eggs with the cream, season with salt and pepper, add some grated nutmeg and the cheese. Pour over the courgettes and put in a hot oven (400°) for 15 minutes, until slightly risen and browned. Serves 4–5.

Seakale or salsify; fennel and tomato salad.

Poached Courgettes with Herbs

1 lb courgettes
1½ oz butter
2 Tbs chopped dill *or* chervil

Cut the unpeeled courgettes in ¾-inch slices, throw them in a pan of boiling salted water and cook for 10 minutes. Drain in a colander. Melt the butter in a covered sauté pan and toss the courgettes in it. Add the chopped herbs, cover and stew gently for 4 minutes. Serves 4.

Corn fritters; grilled tomatoes.

Corn Pudding

4 ears corn-on-the-cob *or* 12 oz frozen *or*
    tinned corn
2 eggs
½ pt very creamy milk or milk and cream
    mixed
1 oz butter
½ tsp salt
1 tsp sugar
black pepper

Scrape the corn off the cobs, being careful not to waste any
of the juice (see BAKED CORN, below). Put the corn in a
bowl and add the beaten eggs, the milk, the melted butter,
and the salt, sugar and black pepper. Have a buttered
soufflé dish ready and pour the corn into it. Bake in a
moderate oven (350°) for 45 minutes. Serves 6.

Beetroot with dill ; a green salad.

Baked Corn

6 ears corn-on-the-cob
2 oz butter
salt and black pepper

Cut the corn kernels off the cobs, using a sharp knife and
cutting downwards onto a flat surface. Then scrape the cobs
well with the edge of the knife to get as much as possible of
the milk (this is best done into a bowl). Put the corn and the
juice into a buttered baking dish, add the butter cut in small
pieces, and plenty of salt and black pepper. Cook in a
moderate oven (350°) for 45 minutes. Serves 3–4.

Potato pancakes ; fried cucumber ; grilled tomatoes.

Celeriac Purée

1 celeriac, weighing about 1 lb
½ lb potatoes
2 oz butter
4 Tbs cream
salt and black pepper
1 Tbs finely chopped parsley

Peel the celeriac and cut in chunks. Cover with cold water, add a little salt, and boil until tender when pierced with a skewer, 25–30 minutes. Peel the potatoes and boil until tender. Drain both vegetables and dry out slightly over gentle heat. Force through the medium mesh of a vegetable mill. Return to the cleaned pan and beat the purée over a low flame. Add the butter and the cream, beating all the time. Season well with salt and black pepper. Pour into a serving dish and sprinkle with finely chopped parsley. Serves 4.

Boiled carrots; turnips with mustard.

Cucumbers Stewed in Cream

2 cucumbers
2 oz butter
4 Tbs cream
salt and black pepper

Peel the cucumbers and cut them in 1-inch chunks. Slice each piece downwards into 9 rectangular sticks, sprinkle them with salt, and leave to drain for 30 minutes. Pat dry in a cloth. Melt the butter in a sauté pan, put in the cucumber, and cover the pan. Cook gently for 10 minutes, shaking the pan occasionally. Add the cream, re-heat, season and serve. Serves 4–6. A light moist dish that goes well with other vegetable dishes, or with veal or chicken.

Grilled mushrooms; a simple tomato salad.

Stewed Mushrooms

1 lb mushrooms
6–8 Tbs sunflower-seed oil *or* nut oil
2 large cloves garlic
salt and black pepper
2 Tbs chopped parsley
lemon juice

Slice the mushrooms. Heat the oil in a broad pan and cook the sliced mushrooms with the minced garlic, turning them over now and then, until all are softened. Season with salt and black pepper, squeeze over lemon juice to taste, and sprinkle with chopped parsley. Serves 3–4.

French beans Provençale ; celeriac purée.

Mushrooms in Sour Cream

1 lb mushrooms
2 oz butter
½ pt sour cream
salt and black pepper
lemon juice

Wipe the mushrooms, trim the stalks and slice. Heat the butter in a sauté pan and put in the mushrooms. Stir around until coated with butter and leave to stew gently until they have softened, about 8 minutes, stirring occasionally. Pour in the cream and stir around to mix well. Simmer gently for 3–4 minutes, season with salt and black pepper, and add a little lemon juice to taste. Serve immediately. Serves 4.

Rice salad ; grilled tomatoes.

Braised Onions

1 lb Spanish onions
2 oz beef dripping *or* duck fat
½ pt stock: beef, chicken, etc.
¼ oz butter
1 dessertspoon flour
2 Tbs cream
salt and black pepper

Slice the onions and cook them gently in the melted fat (if you have no dripping or duck fat, butter or margarine will do), for about 8 minutes. Heat the stock and add to the onions. Simmer uncovered for 30 minutes, stirring occasionally. Work the butter and flour into a paste in a cup and add by degrees to thicken the sauce. Simmer until smooth, stirring constantly. Add the cream, season well and serve. Good with hard-boiled eggs. Serves 4.

Potato pancakes; French beans with bacon.

Fried Parsley

Take very fresh parsley and divide into sprigs. If it is necessary to wash it, dry it very well in a soft cloth. Have a pan of deep oil (I use a mixture of nut oil and sunflower-seed oil) heated to approximately 325°. It must not be too hot or the parsley will shrivel up and burn. Drop in the sprigs, a few at a time, and cook for 2–3 minutes, turning over with a slotted spoon. Drain well before serving. They should be bright emerald green and very crisp, slightly like the fried seaweed one gets in Chinese restaurants. This was a very popular garnish for fried fillets of sole in England in the 1920s; nowadays it is rarely seen which is sad as it is both elegant, delicious, and highly nutritious. It is good served with all dishes of fried vegetables, fritters, etc., but nothing with a sauce.

Seakale with Cream Sauce

1 lb seakale
¼ pt thin cream
lemon juice
salt and black pepper
1 Tbs very finely chopped parsley

Wash the seakale and trim the roots. If you have an asparagus pan (not the upright steamer type) or a small fish kettle, leave the stalks whole, otherwise you may have to cut them in half. Bring a pan of lightly salted water to the boil and drop in the seakale. Simmer until tender, about 20 minutes. Drain well, and lay in a shallow dish. Heat the cream until almost boiling, flavour with a little lemon juice and add salt and black pepper to taste. Pour over the seakale and scatter the very finely chopped parsley over the dish. Serves 3–4.

Rösti ; broccoli.

Baked Tomatoes

1½ lb tomatoes
1 oz butter
salt and black pepper
¼ pt sour cream

Take 1 lb tomatoes and cut them in half horizontally. Butter a shallow fireproof dish and arrange the tomatoes in it. Dot with the butter and sprinkle with salt and black pepper. Cook in a moderate oven (350°) for 20 minutes. Meanwhile skin the remaining tomatoes and put in the blender with the sour cream. Season with salt and black pepper and heat until boiling in a small pan. When the tomatoes are cooked, pour over the sauce and serve. Serves 4–6.

Rice salad with herbs ; broccoli salad.

Tomatoes with Mozzarella

4 large tomatoes *or* 6 medium ones
salt and black pepper
1 Mozzarella cheese (6–8 oz)

Cut the unpeeled tomatoes in ½-inch slices. Arrange them on a large flat ovenproof dish, or divide them between as many individual dishes as you have guests. (The white porcelain dishes with two handles meant for *oeufs au plat* are ideal.) Sprinkle the tomato slices with salt and black pepper. Cut the cheese in ¼-inch slices and lay over the tomatoes. Cook in a hot oven (400°) until the cheese has melted and gone a golden brown, about 15 minutes. Serves 4–6 as a first course.

Boiled broccoli; stewed mushrooms.

Turnips with Mustard

1½ lb small French turnips, long or round
1 oz butter
1 Tbs *Moutarde de Dijon (Grey Poupon)*
salt and black pepper
2 Tbs freshly chopped parsley

If the long French turnip is not available, use ordinary round ones, but they must be young and tender. Cut them in ¾-inch slices, cover with cold water, add a little salt and bring to the boil. Cook until tender, about 12–15 minutes if they are really young, and drain well. Melt the butter in the cleaned and dried pan and turn the slices around in it until they are coated all over, but do not fry. Stir in the mustard, season with salt and black pepper and serve in a shallow dish sprinkled with parsley. Serves 4–6.

Green rice; cauliflower polonaise.

Mixed and Stuffed Vegetable Dishes

Courgette and Tomato Casserole

$\frac{3}{4}$ lb courgettes
1 lb tomatoes
4 large slices stale white bread, crusts removed
2 oz melted butter
$\frac{1}{4}$ lb cheese: Mozzarella, Gruyère or Cheddar
1 heaped Tbs chopped fresh basil, when available
salt and black pepper

Slice the unpeeled courgettes very thinly indeed, and scatter them with salt. Leave for about 30 minutes to sweat, then pat dry in a cloth or soft paper. Skin the tomatoes and slice thinly. Cut the bread in cubes and pour the melted butter over them. Butter a broad soufflé dish and put half the courgette slices in one layer in the bottom. Season lightly with salt and black pepper, then lay half the tomatoes over them. Scatter half the basil (if available) over the tomatoes and a sprinkling of sugar. Slice the cheese very thinly and lay half the slices over the tomatoes, then cover with half the buttered bread cubes. Repeat the layers, sprinkling with salt and black pepper, finishing with the remaining bread. Bake for about 1 hour at 375°. Serves 4. This is one of the few vegetable dishes that is not a lot of trouble to make, yet provides a perfect dish to serve as a main course without needing any accompaniment, although a lettuce salad goes well with it.

Lettuce salad.

Ratatouille

1 Spanish onion
2 large red peppers
2 large green peppers
1 lb courgettes
1 lb tomatoes
3–4 cloves garlic
approximately ¼ pt sunflower-seed oil
salt and black pepper

Chop the onions, cut the peppers in strips, slice the cour-gettes (or chop if they are large) and skin and chop the tomatoes. Mince the garlic. Heat some oil in a broad heavy pan, put in the chopped onions and cook until slightly softened, about 10 minutes. Add the peppers and cook for a further 10 minutes, then mix in the tomatoes and minced garlic, adding more oil as required to prevent sticking. Cook until the mixture is softened and well-mixed, a further 10–15 minutes. Season well with salt and black pepper, and serve hot, warm or cold. Serves 4–6. Like many dishes this is best made a day in advance to allow the flavours to develop, and re-heated. This is my version of ratatouille; made this way, omitting the aubergines (which absorb such a quan-tity of oil) and using sunflower-seed oil, it is a lighter dish, a cross between peperonata and ratatouille.

If hot, chicory quiche; if cold, French bean vinaigrette and raw mushroom salad.

Mixed Vegetable Casserole

6 small onions
6 new potatoes
4 small leeks
4 small courgettes
4 stalks celery
6 small carrots
½ lb tomatoes
1 small cauliflower
2¼ oz butter
1 pt chicken *or* vegetable stock
1 dessertspoon potato flour *or* plain flour
2 Tbs chopped parsley

Leave the onions and potatoes whole. Cut the leeks, courgettes and celery in 1-inch slices. Cut the carrots in half. Peel and quarter the tomatoes. Divide the cauliflower into sprigs. Melt 2 oz butter, stew the onions gently, adding the leeks, courgettes, celery and tomatoes after a few minutes. Heat the stock and add it. Put in the potatoes and cauliflower, bring to the boil and simmer until all the vegetables are tender, about 1 hour. Mix the remaining butter and flour to a paste in a cup, and add by degrees to thicken the sauce. Simmer for 3 minutes to cook the flour, stir in the parsley and serve. Serves 6.

Herb dumplings or pirog with cabbage filling.

Mixed Vegetable Mould

¾ lb young parsnips
¾ lb young carrots
¾ lb young turnips, swedes *or* kohlrabi
salt, black pepper and lemon juice
6 oz butter
4 Tbs chopped mixed herbs: parsley, chervil,
    tarragon, dill

Grate each vegetable coarsely, keeping them in separate piles. Butter a charlotte mould or soufflé dish thickly. Make a layer of the grated parsnips in the bottom of the dish, and

111

sprinkle with salt and black pepper. Cover with a layer of carrots, more salt and pepper, then turnips, swedes or kohlrabi. Melt 2 oz of the butter, pour evenly over all and cover with a sheet of foil. Bake for 1 hour at 350°, then turn out onto a hot flat dish. Heat the remaining butter with the chopped herbs and add lemon juice to taste. Pour over the mould after turning out, or hand separately. Serves 6. I would not recommend making this dish without an electric grater.

Baked tomatoes ; boiled leeks.

A Dish of Mixed Spring Vegetables

1 bunch spring onions
1 bunch (*or* ½ lb) new carrots
1 lb green peas in the pod
1 lb broad beans in the pod
2 oz butter
½ pt chicken stock
1 heaped tsp potato flour
4 Tbs cream
salt and black pepper, sugar

Trim the onions, using the bulbs only. Cut the carrots into ½-inch slices. Shell the peas and beans. Melt the butter in a sauté pan with a lid. Cook the onions gently for 3–4 minutes, then add the carrots. Stir until well coated with fat, then pour on the heated stock. Add salt, black pepper and a little sugar. Cover and simmer gently for 15 minutes, then add the broad beans. Simmer again for 5 minutes, then add the peas. In about 10 minutes all the vegetables should be tender. Mix the flour with the cream and add, cook 2–3 minutes and adjust the seasoning. Serves 2–3 as a main dish with rice, or 4 as an accompaniment.

Boiled rice ; a green salad.

A Simple Vegetable Stew

1 aubergine (about $\frac{1}{2}$ lb)
$\frac{1}{2}$ lb courgettes and $\frac{1}{2}$ lb string beans
1 lb tomatoes and 1 onion
2 potatoes and 1 green pepper
$\frac{1}{3}$ pt olive oil
$\frac{1}{3}$ pt hot water
salt and black pepper
2 Tbs parsley

Cut the unpeeled aubergine in quarters and slice thinly.
Cut the courgettes in diagonal slices. Chop the beans in
1-inch pieces. Peel the tomatoes and cut in slices. Slice the
onion and the peeled potatoes. Cut the pepper in strips. Put
all the vegetables into a casserole and pour over the oil and
water. Throw in the chopped parsley, salt and black pepper.
Bring to boiling point, then cover the dish and cook either in
the oven at 350°, or on top of the stove over a low heat for
$1\frac{1}{2}$ hours, stirring occasionally. Serves 4–6. This simply-
made dish is good either hot or cold, or it can be made in
double quantities and eaten hot the first day, then cold on
the following day.

Onion bread or pirog.

Vegetables in Curry Sauce

1 cauliflower
$\frac{1}{2}$ lb tiny carrots
$\frac{1}{2}$ lb small courgettes
$\frac{1}{2}$ lb Jerusalem artichokes, when available
$\frac{1}{2}$ lb French beans
$\frac{1}{2}$ lb shelled broad beans *or* peas

Curry sauce
$1\frac{1}{2}$ oz butter and $2\frac{1}{2}$ Tbs flour
$1\frac{1}{2}$ Tbs light curry powder *(Spice Islands or
    Sea Isle)*
$\frac{1}{2}$ pt thin cream
approximately 2 Tbs fruit juice *or* juice from
    sweet pickle
2 Tbs sliced blanched almonds

Divide the cauliflower into sprigs, leave the carrots whole, slice the unpeeled courgettes in ¾-inch slices, slice the Jerusalem artichokes likewise, cut the French beans in 1-inch chunks. Cook each separately in the minimum of lightly salted water, reserving it afterwards, while you keep the vegetables hot. To make the sauce: melt the butter, stir in the flour and cook for 3 minutes, adding the curry powder halfway through. Measure 1 pt of the vegetable stock, heat it, and blend with the roux. Stir until smooth and simmer for 3 minutes. Add the cream and blend again, then the fruit juice. When all is smooth and well mixed, pour over the vegetables in a serving bowl and mix. Scatter the sliced almonds over the top. Serves 6. Alternatively omit the nuts and add 4 hard-boiled eggs, cut in chunks. Best made a day in advance and re-heated; this curry is also good cold.

Serve alone, or with boiled rice for a more substantial dish.

Cold Stuffed Tomatoes

6 large tomatoes, preferably the French ridged
type

Cucumber and cheese filling
½ lb curd *or* cream cheese
2 Tbs lemon juice
2 Tbs olive *or* sunflower-seed oil
salt and black pepper
½ cucumber, diced
4 Tbs chopped chives

Make the filling (see p. 159). Skin the tomatoes by covering with boiling water for exactly 1 minute, then plunging into cold water. Do not leave a moment longer as they must stay firm. Cut a slice off the tops and remove the insides carefully with a small sharp-edged teaspoon. Sprinkle the insides with salt and leave to drain upside down for 20 minutes. Shake dry, sprinkle a pinch of caster sugar into each tomato, and divide the filling among them. Chill again, or serve immediately. Serves 6 as a first course.

Lentil vinaigrette; broccoli salad.

Stuffed Aubergines

3 aubergines
about 3 Tbs olive oil
about 2 oz butter
1½ lb tomatoes
1 Spanish onion
2 cloves garlic
salt and black pepper
2 Tbs dry breadcrumbs
2 Tbs finely chopped parsley

Cut the unpeeled aubergines in half lengthwise. Run a small knife around the edge between the skin and the flesh, without puncturing the skin. Sprinkle the cut surface with salt and turn upside down to drain for 30 minutes. Heat 2 Tbs each of oil and butter in a broad frying pan. Dry the aubergines and cook them in the oil and butter, allowing about 6–8 minutes on each side. Drain again. When cool enough to handle remove the flesh from the skins, taking care to leave the skins intact, and chop it. Peel the tomatoes, discard the juice and seeds and chop the flesh. Chop the onion and mince or crush 1 clove garlic. Heat about 1 Tbs each of oil and butter in the same pan and cook the chopped onion in it gently until soft. Add the aubergine, tomatoes and garlic. Cook all together for 15 minutes, stirring often and seasoning well with salt and black pepper. Fill the skins with the mixture. Toss the breadcrumbs in more hot butter with a peeled clove of garlic; when lightly browned, discard the garlic and mix in the parsley. Stir around together until nicely mixed, scatter over the top of the aubergines, and cook in a moderate oven (350°) for 30 minutes. Serves 6 as an accompaniment to a main course, or 3 as a separate course.

French beans; grilled mushrooms or mushrooms in sour cream.

Stuffed Cabbage

1 green cabbage

Stuffing
1 lb mixed greens: lettuce, spinach,
  watercress, dandelion, corn salad, endive,
  sorrel, nettle tops, herbs, etc.
¼ lb uncooked rice
1 bunch spring onions *or* 1 onion
¼ lb sliced ham
¼ lb mushrooms
salt and black pepper
chicken stock

Have as varied and tasty a mixture of greens as you can.
After washing, throw them into a large pan of boiling water
and cook for 4 minutes. Drain, reserving the water in the
pan, and cool. When cool enough to handle, squeeze between the hands to press out as much moisture as possible. Turn
onto a board and chop. Choose 5 or 6 large perfect cabbage
leaves and blanch in the same water for 4 minutes. Drain.
Make the stuffing: wash the rice, drain and put it in a large
bowl. Slice or chop the spring onions, or slice the ordinary
onion, and mix with the rice. Chop the ham and the mushrooms, and add to the stuffing. Stir in the chopped greens
and add salt and plenty of black pepper. Lay a clean piece
of muslin in a pudding basin and arrange 4 or 5 of the cabbage leaves in it to form a casing. Spoon the stuffing in
carefully and cover with another leaf. Tie the muslin around
it loosely, remembering the rice will swell. Bring a large pan
of chicken stock (enough to cover the cabbage) to the boil
and lower in the cloth. Cover with the lid and simmer for
1 hour. Lift out and drain for a minute, then untie the
muslin and turn the cabbage out carefully onto a flat dish.
Serve with a tomato sauce. Serves 4.

Serve alone.

116

Stuffed Cabbage Leaves

2 oz rice
1 small onion
1 oz fat (beef dripping, butter *or* margarine)
salt and black pepper
1 lb raw minced pork
1 green cabbage
1¼ pt beef *or* chicken stock
1 oz butter
1 Tbs flour
1 egg yolk
½ gill sour cream

Boil the rice until barely tender. Drain. Chop the onion finely and brown it in the fat in a frying pan. Add the pork and cook lightly, stirring often, until browned. Add the drained rice and mix well. Season with salt and black pepper and leave to cool. Separate the cabbage leaves, discarding the outermost ones. Cut out the thickest part of the stalk in a V-shape, and throw them, a few at a time, into a large pan of boiling water. Let them cook for 4 minutes, then lift them out and drain, while you cook the others. When cool, wrap each one around a mound of the stuffing, making a little enclosed roll. Cut up the unused leaves in strips and lay at the bottom of a casserole. Lay the stuffed leaves on top of this bed. Heat the stock. Pour enough to almost cover them. Bring to the boil, cover and cook in the oven at 350° for 45 minutes. Drain off the stock, reserving ½ pt for the sauce. Melt the butter, stir in the flour and add stock to make a thin sauce. Stir until smooth, adding salt and black pepper to taste. Beat the egg yolk with the sour cream, stir in a little of the boiling stock, and return all to the pan. Stir until smooth, without allowing it to boil. Arrange the cabbage leaves in a dish, and hand the sauce separately. Serves 6. Alternatively serve with a garlic and yoghurt sauce, or egg and lemon sauce.

Serve alone.

Cold Stuffed Leaves of Chinese Cabbage

1 Chinese cabbage
$\frac{1}{4}$ lb uncooked rice
2 oz chopped almonds *or* whole pine kernels
$\frac{1}{2}$ lb tomatoes
1 bunch spring onions *or* 1 medium onion
$\frac{1}{2}$ cup chopped parsley
salt
black pepper
approximately $\frac{3}{4}$ pt chicken stock
lemon juice

Choose about 12 perfect leaves of the Chinese cabbage and blanch them by throwing for 1 minute into a pan of boiling water. Drain. To make the stuffing: wash and drain the rice and put it in a large bowl. Add the chopped almonds, the sliced spring onions or chopped onion, the skinned and chopped tomatoes and the chopped parsley. Add salt and plenty of black pepper and mix well. Spread each cabbage leaf carefully on a board, being careful not to tear them as they are very fragile, and lay about 1$\frac{1}{2}$ Tbs stuffing on each one. Roll them up. Slice the remaining cabbage and put in the bottom of a broad saucepan to make a bed for the stuffed leaves. Lay the wrapped leaves on top and pour over enough stock to half cover them. Bring to the boil and simmer for 30 minutes. Lift out the stuffed leaves and lay them on a flat dish. Sprinkle generously with lemon juice and leave to cool. Serve cold, with more lemon. Serves 3–4. When Chinese cabbage is not available, substitute leaves of spinach beet or cos lettuce.

Fennel salad; radish and cucumber salad.

Stuffed Green Peppers

6 green peppers
1 medium onion
3 Tbs sunflower-seed oil
1 clove garlic
2 Tbs pine kernels
¼ lb rice
1 pt chicken stock
2 Tbs raisins
salt and black pepper
a pinch of mace *or* grated nutmeg
a pinch of *quatre-épices or* cinnamon
1 oz butter

To make the filling, chop the onion and cook in oil in a fry-ing pan until slightly coloured. Add the minced or crushed garlic and the pine kernels, and cook another 2–3 minutes. Add the washed rice and stir around until coated with oil. Pour on ½ pt heated stock, and the raisins, salt, pepper and spices and simmer until the rice is almost tender, about 15 minutes, stirring now and then. Leave to cool. To pre-pare the peppers, cut a thin slice off the top and remove the interior membrane and all the seeds with a small sharp knife. Rinse with water to remove any remaining seeds. Spoon in the stuffing when it has cooled, and stand the peppers up-right in a deep dish with a lid. Heat the remaining stock with the butter and pour on. Cover with the lid or a double layer of foil and cook in a moderate oven (350°) for 45 minutes. Serve hot or cold with a bowl of yoghurt or garlic sauce with yoghurt. Serves 6. This filling can be used in the same way for stuffing other vegetables, or made in larger quantities and served as a *pilaff*, in which case increase the quantity of stock in proportion to the rice by half, and cook the rice for an extra 10 minutes.

Ratatouille (hot or cold); a lettuce salad.

Stuffed Leaves of Spinach Beet

10 large leaves spinach beet
2 medium onions
1½ oz butter
6 oz mushrooms
½ lb breadcrumbs
1 egg
salt and black pepper
nutmeg
1 clove garlic
½ pt chicken stock
1 egg yolk
1 Tbs lemon juice

Remove the stalks from the spinach beet leaves. Throw the leaves into a pan of boiling water, cook 1 minute and drain. To make the stuffing, slice onions and cook in the butter until they soften. Slice the mushrooms and add to the onions. Stir both together until almost cooked. Remove from the fire and stir in the breadcrumbs, add the beaten egg and season with salt, black pepper, a pinch of grated nutmeg and the crushed garlic if used. Mix well and leave to cool. Put 1 Tbs of the cooled stuffing on each leaf and roll up carefully. Slice the stalks and lay in the bottom of a saucepan. Place the stuffed rolls on top. Heat the stock and pour over. Simmer 30 minutes, then lift out the rolls and lay on a flat dish, reserving the cooking stock. Beat the egg yolk and lemon juice in a cup. Strain the cooking liquid into a small pan and bring back to the boil. Pour a little into the egg and lemon, stir and return to the pan. Stir over a gentle heat until slightly thickened but do not boil. Hand separately. Serves 4.

Baked (or grilled) tomatoes; cucumber and watercress salad.

Stuffed Vegetable Marrow

1 vegetable marrow
3 oz brown rice
1 large onion
2 oz streaky bacon rashers
1 oz butter
1 Tbs oil
2 small courgettes
½ aubergine
2 small carrots
2 cloves garlic (optional)
salt and black pepper
Thick tomato sauce (see p. 196)
2 Tbs chopped fresh basil *or* marjoram, when
    available

Peel the marrow in strips, giving a striped effect. Cut it in half horizontally, and scoop out the flesh with a spoon leaving a wall about ¾-inch thick. Sprinkle the interior with salt and leave upside down to drain while you make the stuffing and the sauce. Cook the rice in a covered pan in 12 fl oz lightly salted water with ½ oz butter for 30 minutes, when it should be almost tender. Drain well. Chop the onion finely and cook in the butter and oil until golden. Add the chopped bacon and fry until coloured. Add the unpeeled, chopped courgettes, and the unpeeled, chopped aubergine and 2 cloves of garlic. Slice the carrots, boil in a small pan until almost tender, then chop and add to the stuffing. When all is slightly softened and cooked, stir in the rice and season well with salt and black pepper. Cook another 3–4 minutes, then leave to cool. Make the sauce (see p. 196), adding the herbs (if available) with the seasoning. Pat the inside of the marrow dry with a cloth and fill with the stuffing. Lay the hollowed out top half on top of the mounded stuffing. Lay in an oiled piece of aluminium foil in a baking tin. Pour the sauce over and around the marrow. Wrap the foil tightly round it and cook in a moderate oven (350°) for 45 minutes. Slide out of the foil with its sauce onto a heated dish. Serves 4. Like all stuffed vegetable dishes, this has the advantage of cooking equally well in a pre-set oven. It can be left, cold and already wrapped, in the oven pre-set to cook at 350° for 1 hour (the extra time allows for the heating of the oven), and will keep hot in its foil casing until you are ready to eat it.

Serve alone, or with a lettuce salad.

Stuffed Mushrooms (Cold)

6 very large flat mushrooms
olive oil

Aubergine filling
2 medium-sized aubergines
½ Spanish onion
½ lb tomatoes
salt and black pepper
3 Tbs olive oil
1 Tbs lemon juice *or* wine vinegar
2 Tbs finely chopped parsley

Lay the mushrooms on a baking sheet gills uppermost, and brush them lightly with olive oil. Cook in the oven at 350° until soft, about 20 minutes. Remove from the oven and leave to cool. Make the aubergine filling (see AUBERGINE SALAD p. 156). When the mushrooms are cool, spoon the salad onto them, and sprinkle with finely chopped parsley. Serves 6 as a first course.

Cucumber and watercress salad; spinach and yoghurt salad.

Courgettes, Carrots and Tomatoes

¼ lb new carrots
1 lb courgettes
½ lb tomatoes
olive oil
salt and black pepper

Slice the carrots and par-boil for 5 minutes. Drain. Cut the unpeeled courgettes in ½-inch slices. Skin and slice the tomatoes. Cover the bottom of a sauté pan with olive oil. Put in the courgettes and cook gently for 10 minutes with the lid on, stirring frequently. Add the drained carrots and cook another 10 minutes. Add the tomatoes and cook for another 15 minutes, until all is soft and slightly mushy. Season with salt and black pepper. Serves 4–6. This makes a delicious vegetable dish on its own, faintly like a ratatouille, and is excellent used as a filling for pancakes.

Potato pancakes ; steamed broccoli.

Stewed Courgettes with Tomatoes

1 lb courgettes
1½ oz butter
½ lb tomatoes
salt and black pepper
1–2 Tbs chopped basil, chervil *or* parsley

Cut the unpeeled courgettes in ½-inch slices, throw into boiling salted water and cook for 8 minutes. Drain in a colander. Melt the butter, add the peeled and roughly chopped tomatoes and simmer for 4–5 minutes. Add the courgettes and simmer for another 4–5 minutes. Add salt and black pepper to taste, sprinkle with chopped herbs and serve. Serves 4–6.

Boiled leeks ; boxty.

Leeks and Carrots

2 lb leeks
1 lb carrots
1½ oz butter
salt and black pepper
2 Tbs chopped parsley

Cut the leeks in 1-inch slices, cook for 10 minutes in a covered pan in ½-inch lightly salted water. Drain well. Cut the carrots in ½-inch slices, cook until tender in boiling salted water and drain. Melt the butter in a heavy pan, put in the carrots and leeks and mix well. Add plenty of salt and black pepper; stew gently until all are well heated and softened, sprinkle with chopped parsley. Serves 4–6. For a more substantial dish, add ¾ lb freshly boiled potatoes, peeled and cut in quarters just before serving.

Potato soufflé; purée of Brussels sprouts.

Green Peas with Cucumber

1 cucumber
3 lb fresh peas in the pod *or* ½ lb frozen *petits pois*
2 oz butter
a sprig of mint
1 tsp sugar
salt and black pepper

Cut the peeled cucumber in 1-inch slices, and cut each slice downwards into 9 sections. Bring ½ inch lightly salted water to the boil in a heavy pan and throw in the cucumber and the shelled peas. Add the butter, mint, sugar, salt and black pepper. Cook gently in the covered pan, shaking from time to time, until the peas are tender. Do not drain but serve in their cooking liquor. (If using frozen peas, cook the cucumber alone in the butter for 5–8 minutes, then add the peas and 2 Tbs only water. Cook another 4–5 minutes, until the peas and cucumber are cooked.) Serves 4. Excellent with salmon trout, or with veal.

Grilled mushrooms; potato pancakes.

Vegetable Marrow with Tomatoes

1 small vegetable marrow
2 oz butter
½ lb tomatoes
chopped parsley

Peel the marrow, remove the seeds, and cut in chunks about 1 by 1½ inches. Sprinkle with salt and drain for 30 minutes. Pat dry in a cloth. Melt the butter in a sauté pan and put in the marrow. Cover and cook gently, stirring now and then, for about 8 minutes. Peel the tomatoes and chop coarsely.

Add them to the marrow after 8 minutes, re-cover, and cook for another 8–10 minutes. When both vegetables are soft and mixed into a delicious stew, season carefully with salt and black pepper, sprinkle with chopped parsley. Serves 4.

Bubble and squeak; cauliflower polonaise.

Peperonata

2 lb peppers, mixed red, green and yellow
1 Spanish onion
1 lb tomatoes
approximately $\frac{1}{4}$ pt olive oil *or* sunflower-seed oil
2 cloves garlic (optional)
salt and black pepper

Remove the stalks and seeds from the peppers. Cut the flesh in strips. Chop the onion; skin and chop the tomatoes. Heat the oil in a sauté pan and add the onion. Cook gently for 5 minutes, then add the peppers. Cover and stew slowly for 15 minutes, then add the tomatoes and the minced garlic, stir well, and cook for another 10–15 minutes. Season well with salt and black pepper. Serve hot, warm or cold. Serves 4–6.

Serve hot with onion bread or pirog or cold with French beans vinaigrette and broccoli salad.

Braised Root Vegetables

$\frac{1}{2}$ lb carrots
$\frac{1}{2}$ lb parsnips
$\frac{1}{4}$ lb turnips *or* swedes
$1\frac{1}{2}$ oz beef dripping *or* butter
$\frac{1}{2}$ pt good beef stock
salt and black pepper
2 Tbs chopped parsley

Cut the vegetables in thin even slices. Melt the fat in a heavy sauté pan with a lid, and put in the vegetables. Stir around until coated with fat, and cook gently for 5 minutes, stirring now and then. Heat the stock and pour on, cover the pan and simmer for 20–30 minutes, until all are soft. Stir occasionally. Season well with salt and black pepper and serve sprinkled with chopped parsley. Serves 4–5.

Champ or colcannon; French beans with bacon.

Succotash

approximately $\frac{1}{2}$ pt fresh corn, cut off the cob
approximately $\frac{1}{2}$ pt broad beans
$1\frac{1}{2}$ oz butter
salt and black pepper

It is difficult to give exact quantities for this dish, as much depends on the size and age of the vegetables, but the quantities should be roughly equal. Cook the corn in very little boiling salted water until just tender and drain. Cook the beans in the same way; unless very young the outer skins should be removed before or after cooking. When both vegetables are well drained, mix and stir over a gentle heat with the butter and plenty of salt and black pepper. Serves 4. I do not consider this dish worth making with tinned or frozen vegetables, as it can be very starchy unless both vegetables are fresh.

Courgettes stewed with herbs; beetroot fritters.

Potato, Rice and Cous-cous

Boxty

$\frac{1}{2}$ lb mashed potatoes
$\frac{1}{2}$ lb raw potatoes
1 small onion, put through the garlic press
1 large egg
2 Tbs flour
2 oz butter
$\frac{3}{4}$ tsp salt
$\frac{1}{2}$ tsp black pepper

Peel and grate the raw potatoes. Put in a bowl of cold water, then squeeze dry in a clean cloth. Mix with the freshly mashed potatoes in a large bowl. Add the crushed onion, beaten egg, flour, melted butter and seasonings. Have a very hot griddle or frying pan and cook the mixture immediately, or it will discolour. Drop spoonfuls on to the lightly greased griddle, three or four at a time, and cook until golden brown on both sides (3–4 minutes on each). Serve immediately. Makes 12–14 small pancakes, serves 4–5. Boxty, like champ and colcannon, is a traditional Irish dish. As the Irish have made potatoes their staple diet for hundreds of years, it is not surprising that they have learned to make these dishes so delicious. The actual potatoes have a flavour unlike any others I have ever tasted, with a delicious floury consistency. Boxty is like a potato pancake, the mixture of cooked and raw potato making it better than any other. But like all potato pancakes it is only good eaten within minutes of being cooked, otherwise it quickly loses its excellence. Eat with ham and eggs, grilled bacon or other vegetable dishes.

Beetroot fritters; stewed leeks; corn fritters.

Colcannon

1 lb kale, cabbage, spring greens *or* Brussels
   sprouts
1 bunch spring onions *or* 1 leek *or* 1 onion
¼ pt milk
1 lb potatoes
2 oz butter
salt and black pepper

Cook the greens in a little rapidly boiling water. Drain well
and chop. Chop the spring onions, leek or onion and cook in
the milk in a small covered pan until tender. Put aside. Cook
the potatoes, drain and dry over gentle heat. Make a purée
and beat in the milk and onion mixture. Stir in the chopped
greens. Mix in the butter and plenty of salt and black
pepper. Beat well until very hot and well mixed. Serves 4.
Excellent with sausages or boiled bacon. This is also good
made in a frying pan. Leave out the milk and cook the
spring onions in water. Drain off the water. Make a dry
purée of potatoes and mix with the onions and greens.
Season well. Heat the butter in a frying pan and spread in
the mixture, flattening with a palette knife. Cook gently
until well browned underneath, about 30 minutes. Turn
out on a flat dish and cut in wedges like a cake. Serve with
fried ham and eggs or grilled bacon rashers.

Courgettes or vegetable marrow with tomatoes; boiled leeks.

Potato Soufflé

1 lb potatoes
⅔ pt milk
½ small onion
1 clove
6 peppercorns
nutmeg, ¼ bay leaf, celery salt
1 oz butter
4 eggs
2 Tbs grated cheese (optional)

Boil the potatoes, drain, and put them through the medium

mesh of a vegetable mill. You should have $\frac{3}{4}$ lb dry purée. While they are cooking, put the milk in a small pan with the seasonings and flavourings. Bring to simmering point, then leave covered at the side of the heat to infuse for 15–20 minutes. Strain the milk and beat it into the purée. Separate the eggs and beat in the yolks. Beat the egg whites until stiff and fold in. Pour the mixture into a buttered soufflé dish and sprinkle the grated cheese over the top, if liked. Bake at 400° for 20 minutes or at 350° for 25 minutes. Serve alone or with a tomato sauce.

A green salad.

Souffléd Potatoes

1½ lb floury potatoes
3 eggs
approximately 2 Tbs thin cream *or* top of the milk
2 oz grated Parmesan *or* Gruyère
salt and black pepper

Make a dry purée with the potatoes and beat in the yolks of the eggs. Add enough thin cream or milk to make a smooth thick cream. Beat in the cheese, and season highly with salt and black pepper, bearing in mind the bland mass of egg whites still to be incorporated. At the last moment, beat the egg whites until stiff and fold in. Have a pan of deep oil heated to a temperature of about 360°. Drop spoonfuls of the potato mixture in, about a dessertspoon at a time, but do not put in more than will float freely without crowding. Cook until golden brown on the underneath, about 3–4 minutes, then turn them over with a slotted spoon and brown on the other side. Drain on soft paper while you cook another batch; move them quickly to a hot dish and serve as soon as possible. Serves 4. If you like, the cheese can be omitted, in which case add some nutmeg, otherwise the mixture is a bit too bland.

French beans; beetroot in sour cream.

Potato Pancakes

1 lb potatoes
1 medium onion
2 eggs
2 Tbs flour
salt and black pepper
arachide oil

Grate the potatoes and onion finely. Put them in a bowl and add the beaten eggs. Sprinkle in the flour, stir well and add salt and black pepper to taste. Mix very well. Do not prepare in advance or the mixture will discolour and separate. Heat a thin layer of oil in a large pan or griddle; when it is hot, drop in spoonfuls of the mixture, flattening them into round cakes with a palette knife. Cook over moderate heat until nicely browned on the underneath, about 5 minutes, then turn over and brown the other side. Serves 4–6. It is sometimes easier to make one huge pancake. This takes longer to cook but does not need constant attention. When the oil is hot, pour the contents of the bowl into the pan and flatten with a palette knife. After about 15–20 minutes over a moderate heat, loosen the edges with a palette knife and see if the underneath is nicely browned without being burnt. Invert a flat dish over the pan and turn the cake out, heat a little more oil in the pan, and slide the pancake back for another 10–15 minutes to brown the other side. When ready to serve, turn out again onto a flat round platter and cut in wedges like a cake. Serves 4–6. Excellent with cold meat, fried eggs and bacon or ham and eggs.

Steamed broccoli; courgette and tomato casserole.

Risi e Bisi

1 onion
3 oz butter
2 oz *prosciutto or* streaky bacon rashers
½ lb rice
1½ pt chicken stock
1 pt shelled peas *or* 1 lb frozen *petits pois*
salt and black pepper
1 oz freshly grated Parmesan

Chop the onion finely and cook in 2 oz butter until it starts to soften. Chop the *prosciutto* or bacon and add to the onion. Stir until all is lightly coloured. Add the washed and drained rice, stir well. Heat the stock until almost boiling and pour on half of it. Add the peas and simmer gently until the rice is cooked, adding more stock by degrees. (If using frozen peas, add only towards the end.) When the rice is tender all the stock should have been absorbed. Season with salt and black pepper. Pour into a serving dish, sprinkle with grated Parmesan and dot with the remaining butter. Serves 4.

Leeks mornay; baked or grilled tomatoes.

Cauliflower with Rice

1 cauliflower
6 oz rice
½ lb sliced ham
¼ lb grated Cheddar
1½ oz butter
2 Tbs flour
¼ pt milk
½ gill cream
salt and black pepper

Cut the cauliflower in sprigs and cook in boiling salted water until tender. Drain, reserving the liquid, and keep warm. Cook the rice and drain. Chop the ham and grate the cheese. Make a sauce with ¼ pt of the reserved cooking water mixed with the milk, blended in the usual way with a roux of butter and flour. Stir in the grated cheese until smooth. Season well,

131

and add the cream. Arrange the rice around the edges of a round shallow dish, or use a ring mould. Lay the sprigs of cauliflower in the centre with the chopped ham filling up the crevices, and pour half the sauce over the centre of the dish. Serve the rest separately. Place in a low oven for 10 minutes to heat through. Serves 4 as a main course.

Serve alone, or with a simple salad.

Green Rice

½ lb rice
1 clove garlic *or* 1 small onion
2 oz butter
½ lb frozen chopped spinach
salt and black pepper
grated nutmeg
1½ oz grated Parmesan

Boil the rice and drain. Leave in a low oven or plate warmer for 15 minutes to dry. Mince the garlic and cook gently in the butter without allowing it to brown. Cook the spinach and drain; dry out the purée as much as possible by stirring over very gentle heat. Stir the garlic and butter into the spinach purée, and season well with salt and black pepper, and a little grated nutmeg. Mix with the rice and pour into a shallow serving dish. Sprinkle with some of the grated cheese and brown under the grill. Serve the remaining cheese separately. Alternatively, put the rice in a buttered ring mould, and leave in a cool oven, or plate warmer, for 20 minutes, then turn out onto a flat dish. Sprinkle with some of the cheese, and serve the rest in a small bowl. Serves 4.

Baked tomatoes; poached courgettes with herbs.

Peas with Cous-cous

½ lb *cous-cous*
light stock: chicken, veal *or* vegetable
1 lb shelled *or* frozen peas
4 oz butter
salt and black pepper

Put the *cous-cous* in a bowl and pour over it ½ pt cold water. Leave for 10 minutes to absorb the water, then put in a muslin-lined strainer and steam for 40 minutes over the boiling stock. Turn out into a bowl and break up any lumps with a fork. Cook the peas in boiling salted water until tender and drain. Mix the peas with the *cous-cous* and add the butter, cut into small pieces. Stir in the bowl, set in a saucepan of very hot water, until the butter has melted and all is hot and well mixed. Season with salt and black pepper. Serves 6.

Baked tomatoes; cucumbers stewed in cream.

A Vegetable Cous-cous

¾ lb *cous-cous*
2½ pt chicken stock
6 small onions
4 leeks
4 carrots
2 stalks celery
4 courgettes
6 tomatoes
1 packet (¼ tsp) saffron
salt and black pepper
½lb chick peas, pre-soaked and cooked
Hot sauce (see p. 188)

Put the *cous-cous* in a bowl and pour over it ¾ pt cold water. Leave for 10 minutes to absorb. Put the chicken stock in a pot, add the whole onions and bring slowly to the boil. When the stock reaches the boil, add the leeks, carrots and celery, all cut in thick slices. Put the *cous-cous* in a muslin-lined strainer over the pot and cover with a lid. Keep boiling gently for 30 minutes, then remove the strainer and add the unpeeled courgettes cut in thick slices to the stock. Stir the *cous-cous* and break up any lumps with a fork. Replace it and cover with the lid. After 10 minutes, add the whole peeled tomatoes to the stock. Cook another 5 minutes after it returns to the boil and remove from the heat. Turn the *cous-cous* into a heated dish and break up with a fork. Add the cooked chick peas and saffron to the vegetables and pour into a large tureen. Make the hot sauce, using stock from the vegetables. Hand separately. A jointed chicken can be cooked with the vegetables. Serve with soup plates, knife, fork and spoon. Serves 8.

Serve alone.

Bubble and Squeak

½ lb mashed potatoes
½ lb cooked spring greens, spring cabbage *or* kale
2 oz butter
salt and black pepper

Mix the mashed potatoes and the chopped greens in a bowl. Melt half the butter and stir into the mixture. Season well with plenty of salt and black pepper. Melt the remaining butter in a heavy frying pan and when it is hot, pile in the potato and cabbage mixture. Flatten with a palette knife, and cook over a low heat until very hot and browned on the underneath, about 25 minutes. Turn out on a flat dish and serve. Serves 3–4.

Brussels sprouts fried in batter; leeks and carrots.

Champ

1½ lb hot mashed potatoes
1 bunch spring onions
¼ pt milk
2 oz butter
salt and black pepper

Cook the chopped onions in the milk in a small pan until soft. Drain them, keeping back the milk. Mix the chopped onions into the hot potato and beat in the butter in small pieces. Add enough of the milk to make a creamy purée and season well with salt and black pepper. Beat over gentle heat until smooth. Serves 4. This is a traditional Irish dish. The butter should really be melted and poured into a well in the middle of the potato, but I prefer to mix it in as above.

Grilled tomatoes ; cauliflower polonaise.

Gratin Dauphinois

1½ lb waxy potatoes
1 large egg
¾ pt creamy milk
1 clove garlic
3 oz grated Gruyère *or* Fontina
salt and black pepper
nutmeg

Peel the potatoes and slice them very thinly and evenly. Mix with the beaten egg, milk, crushed garlic, and cheese, and season with salt, black pepper and grated nutmeg. Pour into a very shallow buttered gratin dish and bake for 1 hour at 350°. Serves 4–6. GRATIN SAVOYARD is made as above omitting the cheese and substituting chicken stock for the milk.

Boiled leeks and carrots ; French beans Provençale or grilled mushrooms.

Hashed Potatoes

2 lb potatoes
1 Spanish onion
salt and black pepper
1 oz butter
2 Tbs olive oil

Bake the potatoes in a hot oven (400°) until soft, about 1 hour. Peel them and grate coarsely. Grate the onion finely and mix lightly with the potatoes, seasoning with salt and

135

black pepper. Heat the butter and oil in a frying pan. When it is really hot but not yet smoking, put in the potato. Flatten with a palette knife and cook over a low flame for 30–40 minutes, lifting the edges now and then to make sure it is not burning. Tip out on a flat dish to serve. It should be brown and crusty on top. Serves 4. Serve with fried eggs and bacon, or grilled steaks or chops.

Grilled or fried tomatoes; steamed or boiled broccoli.

Potato Paste

8 fl oz water
2½ oz butter
6 oz flour
3 eggs
10 oz mashed potato
salt and black pepper
nutmeg

Boil the butter and water in a largish pan. When the butter has melted, take off the heat and add the flour. Stir hard until it makes a thick smooth paste. Break in the eggs one at a time, and beat each one in until it is a smooth mixture and comes away from the sides of the pan. Beat in the hot mashed potatoes (they should be freshly cooked and well dried), until all is well mixed and smooth. Season with salt and black pepper and a little grated nutmeg. Leave to cool. Chill in the refrigerator until next day if possible, or at least for a few hours. Use for gnocchi, potato cakes or potato scones.

Gnocchi

potato paste

Make the paste and form into ovals like pigeon's eggs, on a floured board. Bring a large pan of water to the boil and drop them in in batches. Simmer gently for 5 minutes, then lift out with a slotted spoon and drain on a cloth while cooking another batch. Serve with a thick tomato sauce (see p. 196) poured over all in a shallow dish. Serves 4–6.

A green salad.

Potato Cakes

potato paste

Make the paste and form into small round flat cakes on a floured board. Either fry them in butter or bacon fat until browned on both sides, or cook in a fairly hot oven (375°–400°) on a buttered baking sheet until lightly risen and browned, about 10–15 minutes. Makes about 16 cakes. Serves 6–8. Good with bacon and eggs, or eaten hot with butter.

Stewed leeks; beetroot with dill.

Potato Scones

potato paste
3 Tbs chopped fresh herbs *or* 1½ oz grated
  cheese

Make up the paste and add the herbs or cheese. Form into flat round cakes, about ¾ inch thick, and cook on a very hot lightly greased griddle or frying pan until golden on both sides. Makes about 16; serves 6–8.

Baked tomatoes; baked corn.

Potato Croquettes

1½ lb potatoes
1 egg and 2 egg yolks
salt and black pepper
nutmeg
fine dry breadcrumbs
nut oil

Boil the potatoes and make a dry purée. Beat in the 2 egg

yolks, one at a time. Season with salt, black pepper and a little grated nutmeg. Spread out on a floured board and when cool divide into equal parts (about 15), and form into rolls. Coat in the whole beaten egg and the breadcrumbs. Heat some nut oil, or a mixture of butter and oil, and fry until golden, turning on all sides. Drain on soft paper. Serve as soon as possible. Serves 4–5.

Celery mornay; leeks and carrots.

Rösti

1½ lb waxy potatoes
4 oz butter
salt and black pepper

Boil the potatoes in their skins. When cool enough to handle, peel them and slice them thinly, or grate coarsely. Heat the butter in a heavy frying pan and put in the potatoes, adding salt and black pepper. Stir them around in the hot butter, then press into a flat cake and leave for 25–30 minutes. Turn out on a flat dish to serve. Serves 4–5.

Braised onions; beetroot in sour cream.

Potato Cake with Leeks

2 leeks
1½ lb freshly mashed potatoes
2 oz butter
salt and black pepper

Slice the leeks and cook in 1½ oz butter until soft. Mix with the mashed potatoes, adding salt and black pepper to taste. Melt the remaining butter in a frying pan and when it is hot, pile in the potato and leek mixture. Spread into a flat cake with a palette knife and cook gently until browned underneath, about 25–30 minutes. Turn out onto a flat dish and cut in wedges like a cake. Serves 4–6. This can also be made by substituting 2 sliced medium onions for the leeks. Good with fried eggs and bacon.

Baked tomatoes; steamed broccoli.

Deep Fried Potatoes

Use waxy potatoes. Peel them and slice them thinly and evenly, using an electric grater with a slicing attachment, or a mandoline. Throw the slices into a bowl of cold water for a few minutes, then drain them and pat dry in a cloth. Cook in batches in hot deep oil (310°) for 5–8 minutes. They should be floating on the top when cooked, crisp and golden brown on the outside and soft in the middle. Stir them round occasionally to prevent them sticking. Drain on soft paper and serve immediately, sprinkled with salt.

Succotash; onions in white sauce.

Fried Potatoes

This is particularly good when made with the fat from roasting a duck or goose, or good beef dripping. Peel the raw potatoes and cut them in half, then slice each half thinly and evenly. Heat some fat in a heavy frying pan, enough to cover the bottom to the thickness of about ½ an inch, and when it is very hot put in the sliced potatoes. Cook them over a moderate heat for about 30 minutes – the exact timing will depend on the thickness of the slices – turning them over now and then with a palette knife so that the top ones go to the bottom to brown, and so on. When all are more or less browned and tender throughout, sprinkle them with salt and a little finely chopped parsley, and serve.

Purée of turnips; salsify or seakale.

Sautéed Potatoes

1½ lb waxy potatoes
approximately 1 oz butter
approximately 2 Tbs olive oil
salt
2 Tbs chopped parsley

Peel the potatoes and cut them in cubes about ½-inch square. Put enough butter and oil in a frying pan to cover the bottom by about $\frac{1}{4}$ inch and heat. When it is very hot put in the potatoes. Fry them until they are golden brown on all sides and soft in the centre, turning them often. They will take about 20 minutes to cook. There should be almost no fat left at all by the end of the cooking; if there is, drain it off carefully. Add salt and chopped parsley to the potatoes in the pan, stir around and serve immediately. Serves 4.

Braised endives; carrot purée.

A Purée of Potatoes, Parsnips and Cabbage

1 lb potatoes
1 lb parsnips
the heart of a green cabbage weighing about
    1 lb
2 oz butter
salt and black pepper

Boil the potatoes and drain. Push through the medium mesh of a vegetable mill. Peel the parsnips and cut in pieces. Boil until tender and push through the same mesh as the potatoes. Cut the cabbage heart in quarters, remove the inner core and slice the rest. Cook until just tender in boiling salted water. Drain it well and chop finely. Mix the potato and parsnip purée in a heavy pan over a gentle heat and stir in the chopped cabbage. Put in the butter, cut in small pieces, and season well with plenty of salt and black pepper. Serve very hot. Serves 6. Excellent with boiled ham or bacon.

Courgettes, carrots and tomatoes; French beans with bacon.

Sweet Potato Purée

$1\frac{1}{2}$ lb sweet potatoes
salt and black pepper
2 oz butter
$\frac{1}{4}$ pt cream
chopped parsley

Peel the potatoes and cut in pieces. Cover with lightly salted water and cook until tender. Drain very well and dry out by

140

stirring for a few minutes over gentle heat. Push through the medium mesh of the vegetable mill and return to the cleaned pan. Stir in the butter and cream, and add salt and black pepper to taste. Pour into a serving dish and sprinkle with chopped parsley. Serves 4–5. Do not attempt to make this purée with yams, as they are too moist.

Grilled mushrooms; beetroot fritters.

Baked Sweet Potatoes

1 medium-sized sweet potato per person
butter
salt and black pepper

Scrub under a running tap and leave to dry. Heat the oven to 400°, and put the potatoes on the middle rack. Allow 45–60 minutes, testing to see if they are done by squeezing them gently with a cloth. Serve exactly like ordinary baked potatoes, with butter, salt and black pepper. Sweet potatoes are more suitable than yams for this as their flesh is of a fluffier consistency.

Carrot Risotto

1 onion
2½ oz butter
4 rashers bacon
½ lb rice
1½ pt chicken stock
6 oz young carrots
black pepper
1 oz freshly grated Parmesan

Chop the onion and cook gently in 2 oz butter until soft. Add the chopped bacon and cook until golden. Stir in the rice and half the boiling stock. Add the carrots, thinly sliced. Cook gently until the liquid has been absorbed, then add half the remaining boiling stock. Cook until the rice is tender, adding boiling stock by degrees. Only use as much as is required; by the time the rice is cooked the liquid should be almost totally absorbed. Season with black pepper and dot with the remaining butter. Scatter the grated cheese over the top. Serves 4 as a main course.

Gratin of courgettes ; grilled mushrooms ; spinach.

Salads, Aspics and Mousses

Arabic Salad

1 Arab *or* Greek loaf *(pitta)*
1 large cucumber
4 tomatoes
1 onion
2 cloves garlic
2 Tbs chopped parsley
2 Tbs chopped mint
1 large lemon *or* 2 small ones
olive oil
1 heart of cos lettuce

Split the bread open and leave overnight to dry, or place in the sun for a few hours. Chop the peeled cucumber and tomatoes into similar sized squares. Break up the bread into small pieces. Put the bread in the bottom of a large bowl and cover with the tomatoes, the cucumber, the sliced onion, the crushed garlic and the chopped herbs. Squeeze the lemon and measure the juice. Pour it over the vegetables and add twice as much olive oil. Chill in the refrigerator for 3–4 hours. Before serving, chop the lettuce and mix all together. Serves 6. This is similar to the Spanish salad on page 151, but the mint and the sharper dressing make it unmistakeably Arabic.

Serve alone.

Arabic Parsley Salad

$\frac{1}{2}$ pt crushed wheat *(burghul)*
$\frac{3}{4}$ pt finely chopped parsley
$\frac{1}{4}$ pt finely chopped mint
1 bunch spring onions
2 large tomatoes
$\frac{1}{4}$ pt olive oil
$\frac{1}{4}$ pt lemon juice
salt and black pepper

Soak the crushed wheat (obtainable from health food shops) for 1 hour in cold water; drain and squeeze in the hands to press out as much water as possible. Put in a large bowl and mix with the chopped parsley and mint. Chop the spring onions and the peeled tomatoes and mix with the crushed wheat. Add the lemon juice and oil gradually, beating in with a wooden spoon. Add salt and freshly ground black pepper to taste, and more oil or lemon as required. Serve on a large platter with a border of sliced tomato, and a bowl of small crisp lettuce leaves with which to eat it. Serves 6. An unusual salad, except in Lebanon where it is almost a national dish, this is refreshing and very nutritious.

Cucumber with yoghurt; fennel and radish salad.

Aubergine Meza

2 large aubergines
$\frac{1}{4}$ pt *tahini* (sesame seed paste)
$\frac{1}{4}$–$\frac{1}{2}$ pt lemon juice
salt and black pepper
2 cloves garlic
olive oil
1 Tbs finely chopped parsley

Bake the aubergines in a moderate oven for 45 minutes or grill until soft. Cut in half and scoop out the flesh. Pound in a mortar (or push through the medium mesh of a vegetable mill) until reduced to a smooth purée. Beat in *tahini* and lemon juice alternately. Stir in crushed garlic, salt and black pepper to taste. Pour onto a flat dish and make swirls on the top. Pour a dribble of olive oil over the top and scatter with the parsley or a dusting of red pepper. Serves 6. A very good dish, similar to homus but with an individual smoky flavour from the baked or grilled aubergines. Eat with hot Arab (or Greek) bread, the flat oval loaves sold in Greek and Cypriot shops under the name of *pitta*. *Tahini* can be bought in the same shops, or in health food stores.

Serve alone.

Celery (or Celeriac) Rémoulade

2 heads celery *or* 1 celeriac

Sauce rémoulade
2 hard-boiled egg yolks and 2 raw egg yolks
a pinch of salt and pepper
1 Tbs *Moutarde de Dijon* (*Grey Poupon* for
   preference)
2 Tbs white wine vinegar
2 Tbs tarragon vinegar
$\frac{1}{2}$ pt sunflower-seed oil
$\frac{1}{4}$ pt sour cream

Scrub the celery well under a running tap, and cut it across in thin strips. Reserve any good leaves for the garnish. Make the sauce: put the hard-boiled egg yolks into a mortar or heavy bowl, and mash to a paste. Beat in the raw egg yolks, and beat until a smooth mixture is obtained. Add a pinch of salt and pepper, and the mustard, beating and mashing all the time. Add the vinegar gradually, and blend very carefully. Then add the oil drop by drop, as for a mayonnaise. When all is used up, taste and adjust seasoning. It should be quite strongly flavoured with mustard and vinegar. Stir in the sour cream, pour it over the celery and mix well, reserving a little to pour over the top in the serving dish. Chop the green leaves, and scatter over the top or mix with the salad as you prefer. Serves 4–6. This classic French hors-d'oeuvre should, strictly speaking, be made with celeriac, but I prefer to use celery. If using celeriac, first pare it, then shred it coarsely. Some people par-boil it for 5 minutes, others use it raw.

Broccoli salad; a simple tomato salad.

Cucumber with Yoghurt

1 large carton (1½ pt) yoghurt
2 large cloves garlic
salt and black pepper
1 cucumber
2 Tbs chopped mint *or* chives

Empty the yoghurt into a large bowl and beat with a wooden spoon until smooth. Crush 2 large cloves garlic and mix into the yoghurt with salt and black pepper to taste. Peel the cucumber and chop or cut into thin slices. Mix into the yoghurt. Chill for several hours before serving, then sprinkle with the chopped herbs at the last minute. A very popular Middle-Eastern dish, this salad is served sprinkled with dried mint, which most families make themselves. Instead of the commercial varieties, I prefer to use fresh mint, or chives. These quantities can easily be doubled for a buffet supper, or halved for a side dish to eat with curry, in which case the herbs should be omitted. A very delicious cooling dish that goes well with rich beef stews, roast lamb, or any hot spicy dishes. Serves 4.

A simple tomato salad; a mixed bean salad.

Cucumber and Tomato Ring

1 cucumber
½ lb tomatoes
1 packet (½ oz) gelatine
2 Tbs lemon juice
1 Tbs white wine vinegar
⅛ tsp chilli sauce
¼ tsp sugar

Filling
4 Tbs cream
¼ lb cream cheese
4 Tbs chopped parsley, chives, chervil, dill

Grate the peeled cucumber and chop the peeled and de-seeded tomatoes, reserving any juice you can. Dissolve the gelatine in ¼ pt cold water for 10 minutes, pour on ½ pt boiling water and mix. Add the lemon juice, vinegar, chilli sauce, sugar and the juice from the cucumber and tomatoes. When cool add the cucumber and tomato, mix well, and pour into a ring mould and chill. To make the filling, mix the cream and cream cheese and stir in the herbs. Chill in the ice compartment and then form into balls. Turn out the jelly on to a flat dish and fill the centre with the cream cheese balls. Serves 4–6.

Serve alone.

Cauliflower and Egg Mayonnaise

½ pt mayonnaise
curry powder
1 cauliflower
6 eggs
4 Tbs thin cream
cayenne pepper

Make the mayonnaise with a small pinch of a light curry powder (instead of mustard) added to the yolks at the very beginning. Divide the cauliflower into sprigs and cook in boiling salted water until only just tender. Drain well and allow to cool slightly. Cook the eggs for 12–15 minutes, then cool and shell them. Arrange the cauliflower round the outside of a flat dish with the halved hard-boiled eggs in the centre. Thin the mayonnaise with the cream and pour over all. Sprinkle with cayenne. Serves 4. Alternatively substitute a sauce vinaigrette for the mayonnaise.

Cucumber and watercress salad; a simple tomato salad.

Egg Salad

6 hard-boiled eggs
1 lettuce, round *or* cos
1 bunch spring onions *or* 1 medium onion
4 tomatoes
½ cucumber
6 new potatoes
6 Tbs olive oil
2 Tbs white wine vinegar
salt and black pepper

Slice the eggs thickly. Take the heart of the lettuce and shred it. Slice the spring onions or onion thinly. Peel and slice the tomatoes and cucumber. Boil the potatoes in their skins, cool and peel them, then slice thickly. Make a bed of shredded lettuce on a flat dish. Arrange the sliced eggs, tomatoes, onions, cucumber and potatoes in rows. Make a dressing with oil and vinegar, salt and black pepper, and pour over the salad just before serving. Serves 4.

Serve alone.

Greek Salad

½ cucumber
½ lb tomatoes
1 large green pepper *or* 2 small ones
1 Spanish onion
6 Tbs olive oil
2 Tbs white wine vinegar
salt and black pepper
6 oz Feta cheese
1 tsp dried marjoram *or* oregano

Peel the cucumber and cut in slices, not too thin. Peel the tomatoes, and cut in quarters or eighths. De-seed the pepper and cut in strips. Slice the onion thinly. Mix all the vegetables in a bowl. Mix the oil and vinegar with salt and black pepper, and pour over the salad. Dice the cheese, and scatter over the salad. Sprinkle the marjoram over all and mix well. Alternatively serve 3–4 Tbs dried marjoram in a little bowl, and let each person add it according to their taste. Another version of this salad is made by crumbling the cheese into the dressing and mixing with the salad. In this case, $\frac{1}{4}$ lb cheese will be enough. Serves 4–5.

Serve alone.

Guacamole

2 large avocado pears
$\frac{1}{2}$ lb tomatoes
1 bunch spring onions
1 green pepper
2 green chillies
salt and black pepper
2 Tbs lemon juice
1 Tbs olive oil

Peel the avocado pears, cut them in half, remove the stones and chop the flesh in small dice. Skin the tomatoes and chop them finely. Chop the bulb part of the spring onions. Cut the pepper in half, remove the pith and seeds, and chop in small dice. Blanch the chillies for 2 minutes in boiling water and chop very finely indeed, removing all the seeds. Mix all together and season with salt and black pepper. Stir in the lemon juice and olive oil. Serves 4.

Serve alone as a first course or a salad, or as a filling for cold pancakes, the centre of a tomato jelly ring or a filling for stuffed eggs, adding some of the chopped egg yolks.

Homus or Hummus

1 lb chick peas
salt and black pepper
$\frac{1}{2}$ pt *tahini* (sesame seed paste)
approximately $\frac{1}{2}$ pt lemon juice
3 large cloves garlic
approximately 2 Tbs olive oil *or* sesame seed
   oil
1 Tbs finely chopped parsley

Soak the chick peas overnight, then cover them with fresh cold water in a deep pan. Bring very slowly to the boil and simmer until soft when crushed between the fingers. This should take about 2 hours, but it may be longer. Replenish the water as necessary. When ready, drain the peas and put through the medium mesh of a vegetable mill. Stir in *tahini* and lemon juice alternately thinning with a little of the cooking liquid. (*Tahini* can be bought from shops specializing in Greek or Middle Eastern foods, or health food shops.) Crush the garlic and stir in, and add salt and black pepper to taste. When all is smooth, pour onto a large flat dish and pour a film of olive or sesame seed oil over it. Sprinkle with a little finely chopped parsley. Serves 10–12. This makes a large amount, but as it is a lengthy business it is not worth making in small quantities. It keeps well in the refrigerator, covered with an oiled piece of saran-wrap. Serve with hot Arab or Greek bread, sold in Greek or Cypriot shops as *pitta*.

Serve alone as an hors-d'oeuvre.

A Mixed Salad

1 lettuce
4 new potatoes
$\frac{1}{4}$ lb French beans
2 large tomatoes
2 hard-boiled eggs
salt and black pepper
$\frac{1}{4}$ tsp French mustard
5 Tbs olive oil
1$\frac{1}{2}$ Tbs white wine vinegar
1 clove garlic (optional)

Wash and dry the lettuce and put the leaves in a large bowl. Boil the potatoes in their skins, and skin them as soon as they are cool enough to handle. Cook the beans and cut in 1-inch pieces. Cut the (unskinned) tomatoes in wedges. Cut the eggs in quarters. Arrange all the ingredients on top of the lettuce and make the dressing. Put a pinch of salt and pepper in a cup with a $\frac{1}{4}$ teaspoonful mustard. Stir on the oil, then blend with the vinegar. Put a whole peeled clove of garlic in the cup and leave until time to serve. Then remove the garlic, pour the dressing over the salad and mix well. Serves 4. With the addition of an 8-oz tin of tunny fish, drained of its oil and broken into flakes; 6 anchovy fillets, drained of their oil and chopped; and 8 black olives, stoned, this becomes SALADE NIÇOISE.

Spanish Salad

1 cucumber
1 lb tomatoes
1 Spanish onion
1 small French loaf, 1–2 days old *or* cut in half
    and left in sun to dry
4 salad spoons olive oil
1½ salad spoons white wine vinegar
salt, black pepper and sugar

Wash the cucumber but do not peel it. Slice it thinly. Peel the tomatoes and slice them thinly. Slice the onion finely and divide each slice into rings. Cut the dry bread in cubes. Arrange the sliced vegetables and bread in layers in a glass bowl. Make the dressing and pour it over all. Chill in the refrigerator for several hours before serving. Serves 4. This is like a more solid version of *Gazpacho*, the iced Spanish soup. For a less substantial salad, the bread can be omitted.

Serve alone.

A Summer Salad

1 round lettuce, a soft leaved variety
1 cucumber
1½ lb green peas in the pod *or* ¼ lb shelled or
    frozen peas
½ tsp sugar
salt and black pepper
1 Tbs white wine vinegar
2 Tbs thin cream
2 Tbs olive oil

Wash the lettuce leaves and drain; pat dry in a soft cloth.

Cook the peas and drain; moisten with a little olive oil while still hot. Peel the cucumber and cut it in *bâtons* (2-inch slices, each cut into 9 stick-shaped pieces). To make the dressing, put the sugar, salt and black pepper in a small bowl, pour on the vinegar and mix to dissolve the seasonings. Add the cream and the olive oil and beat well. Arrange the lettuce leaves in a salad bowl. Put the cucumber on top and scatter the peas over all, or pile them in the centre. Pour over the dressing at the last moment and mix well. Serves 6. An excellent accompaniment to cold salmon trout.

Rice salad with herbs; a simple tomato salad.

Sweet Pepper Salad

2 large red peppers
2 large green peppers
salt and black pepper
2 Tbs olive oil
1 Tbs lemon juice *or* white wine vinegar

Put the peppers under a hot grill and turn until all sides are blackened and blistered. Remove from heat and cool slightly. When they are cool enough to handle, remove the skin with a small sharp knife. Cut away the stalk and remove the inner pith and all the seeds. Cut in thin strips. Mix the two coloured peppers in a dish and sprinkle with salt and black pepper. Pour over oil and lemon juice or vinegar, according to taste. Leave for 30 minutes, then serve. Serves 4 as an accompaniment to other dishes. Peeling peppers is a lengthy business, so do not attempt it in large quantities. In any case this excellent salad is one to be eaten in small amounts, with either one or two other hors-d'oeuvres, or other salads.

Saffron rice with peas; French bean vinaigrette.

Tonno e Fagioli

½ lb dried haricot beans *(soissons or cannellini)*
1 carrot
1 stalk celery
½ bay leaf
8 oz tinned tunny fish
1 Spanish onion
salt and black pepper
olive oil
white wine vinegar
2 Tbs chopped parsley

Soak the beans for 3 hours then cook them until tender in gently simmering water, with a sliced carrot, ½ an onion, 1 stalk celery and ½ bay leaf. Add salt towards the end of the cooking. When they are just tender but not yet broken, drain them and throw away the flavouring vegetables. Put them in a large bowl and add salt and black pepper, and pour over as much olive oil and vinegar as is necessary to moisten the beans well without making a pool in the bottom of the bowl; it is difficult to give exact quantities. Slice the remaining half onion thinly, divide into rings, and mix with the beans. Pile the beans onto a flat dish and put the tunny fish, drained of its oil, on the top. Pour a little fresh olive oil over the tunny, and sprinkle all with the chopped parsley. Serves 4–5.

Serve alone.

Haricot Beans Vinaigrette

As above, but omit the tunny fish.

Celery rémoulade; cucumber and watercress salad.

Tomato Aspic Ring

about ¾ lb tomatoes
1 clove garlic
½ small onion
1 clove
½ bay leaf
1 Tbs chopped basil, when available
a shake Tabasco *or* other chilli sauce
salt and black pepper
1 packet (½ oz) gelatine

Skin the raw tomatoes and put them in the blender until the seeds have disintegrated. You will need ¾ pt pulp. Pour into a small pan and add all the other ingredients except the gelatine. Bring slowly to the boil, then cover and leave at the side of the fire to infuse the flavours. Leave for 20 minutes. Melt the gelatine in ½ gill hot water. Add to the tomato mixture and stir over a gentle heat until melted. Pour through a strainer into a ring mould. Cool, then place in the refrigerator for 3–4 hours, or overnight. Turn out on a flat platter to serve, and fill the centre with cucumber and cheese salad, cold scrambled egg mixed with herbs, cold flaked fish in mayonnaise, or shredded lettuce with shelled prawns and a mayonnaise handed separately. Serves 4–5.

Serve alone.

Tomato and Mushroom Mousse

2 lb tomatoes
1 small onion
¼ lb mushrooms
1½ oz butter
1 tsp sugar
salt and black pepper
a few fresh leaves of marjoram *or* basil, when
    available
1 packet (½ oz) gelatine
¼ pt thick cream

Peel the tomatoes and chop them coarsely. Discard the juice

154

and seeds. Chop the onion finely and the mushrooms. Cook
the tomatoes, onion and mushrooms in the butter in a frying
pan, adding a pinch of sugar and salt and black pepper to
taste. Add the marjoram or basil, if available. After about
10 minutes, discard the herbs and put the vegetables through
the fine mesh of a vegetable mill or a sieve. Measure the
resulting purée and add gelatine dissolved in a little hot
water – $\frac{1}{2}$ oz gelatine to each pint of purée. Leave to cool,
stirring occasionally. When almost set, whip the cream and
fold in. Pour into a ring mould, or individual moulds. If
using a ring mould, turn out after 3–4 hours in the refrigerator, and fill the centre with diced cucumber moistened
with a French dressing. If using individual moulds, turn out
after about 2 hours onto small crisp lettuce leaves. Serves
4–5.

Serve alone or with a green salad.

Aubergine Purée

    3 large aubergines
    1 clove garlic
    1 Tbs onion juice
    2 Tbs olive oil
    1 Tbs lemon juice
    salt and black pepper
    $\frac{1}{2}$ Tbs very finely chopped parsley

Bake the aubergines at 350° for about 45 minutes. When they
are soft, cut them in half and scoop out the flesh. Put it
through the medium mesh of a vegetable mill. Add the
crushed garlic and the onion juice. Stir in the olive oil and
add about half as much lemon juice, enough to sharpen the
purée. Add salt and black pepper to taste, put in a dish and
chill. Sprinkle with a little very finely chopped parsley before
serving. Serve with toast or home-made bread. Serves 4.

Serve alone as an hors-d'oeuvre.

Aubergine Salad

2 aubergines
1 Spanish onion
4 tomatoes
salt and black pepper
olive oil and vinegar

Cook the aubergines in boiling water for 20 minutes, then drain and cool. Chop the onion and skin and chop the tomatoes. When cool enough to handle, peel the aubergines and chop the flesh. Mix all the vegetables together, season with salt and black pepper, and stir in enough oil and vinegar to moisten thoroughly, allowing roughly 3 parts oil to 1 part of vinegar. Serves 4. Also good as a stuffing for cold vegetables, such as hollowed-out cucumbers, green peppers or large courgettes. The vegetable shells must first be cooked in the oven until tender, then allowed to cool.

Cucumber and watercress salad; spinach and yoghurt salad.

Mixed Bean Salad I

½ lb dried haricot beans *(cannellini or soissons)*
¾ lb French beans
olive oil
white wine vinegar
salt and black pepper
1 onion

Soak the dried beans for 1 hour, then cook until tender in simmering unsalted water. Add salt when the cooking is almost over. Cook the French beans until only just tender, drain them and cut into 1-inch pieces. Mix the two lots of beans together while still hot, and stir in enough oil to moisten thoroughly without making a pool in the bottom of the bowl. Add white wine vinegar to taste, or in the proportion of 3 parts oil to 1 part vinegar, and season with plenty of salt and black pepper. Cut the onion in half, slice finely and divide each slice into rings. Mix with the beans and serve as soon as it has cooled. Serves 6.

Tomato salad; celery rémoulade.

Mixed Bean Salad II

$\frac{1}{4}$ lb dried haricot beans *(cannellini or soissons)*
$\frac{1}{2}$ lb string beans
$\frac{1}{2}$ lb shelled broad beans
olive oil
white wine vinegar
salt and black pepper
1 onion

Make as above, adding broad beans, cooked until they are just tender. Serves 6.

Fennel and tomato salad; radish and cucumber salad.

Red Bean Salad

$\frac{1}{2}$ lb red kidney beans, cooked *or* tinned
1 head celery
1 heart of cos lettuce
6 Tbs olive oil
2 Tbs white wine vinegar
2 Tbs chopped chives

If using tinned beans, rinse them well in a colander under a running tap. Drain and put them in a large bowl. Slice the celery heart and mix with the beans. Slice the lettuce heart in $\frac{1}{2}$-inch pieces and add to the salad. Mix the oil and vinegar with salt and black pepper and pour over. Scatter the chopped chives over all. Serves 4–5.

Cucumber with yoghurt; fennel and radish salad.

Beetroot Salad

1 lb small beetroot
salt and black pepper
olive oil
white wine vinegar

Cut the leaves off the beetroot and reserve them. Scrub the beetroot and put in cold water to cover. Add salt and boil until tender. Chop the leaves and cook separately in a little boiling salted water. Drain. When the beetroot are cooked, drain them and slice quite thickly. Lay on a flat dish, sprinkle with salt and black pepper, lay the chopped leaves over the top, and pour over olive oil and vinegar (3 parts oil to 1 part vinegar). Serve before it has completely cooled. Serves 4. Beetroot is also good covered with a cream dressing.

Rice salad with herbs; cucumber in sour cream.

Beetroot and Chicory Salad

3 small beetroot, cooked
½ lb chicory
salt and black pepper
olive oil
lemon juice *or* white wine vinegar

Cut each beetroot in quarters, then in slices. Cut the chicory in 1-inch slices, then divide into rings. Mix lightly, add salt and black pepper to taste, and moisten with olive oil and lemon juice or vinegar. Serves 4.

Carrot salad; broccoli salad.

Broccoli Salad

1 lb broccoli
olive oil
lemon juice
salt and black pepper

Cook the broccoli in boiling salted water, or steam it, until just tender. Drain it and lay on a flat dish. While it is still hot, pour over it olive oil and lemon juice – roughly 3 parts oil to 1 part lemon – and sprinkle with salt and coarse black pepper. Serves 4.

Sweet corn mayonnaise; potato salad with bacon.

Carrot Salad

½ lb new carrots
¼ pt yoghurt
2 Tbs orange juice

Shred or grate the carrots as finely as possible. Mix the yoghurt in a small bowl, beating until smooth. Mix with the carrots, and stir in the orange juice. Do not try using old carrots for this dish, as they are too coarse. Serves 4.

Broccoli salad; radish and cucumber salad.

Mixed Chicory Salad

2 heads chicory
1 endive
½ bunch watercress
olive oil
white wine vinegar
salt and black pepper

Remove the outer leaves of the chicory, wash and drain. Cut each head across in 1-inch slices. Separate the endive into leaves, wash, drain, and tear in pieces. Pinch the best leaves off the watercress, wash and drain them. Mix all together with a well-flavoured vinaigrette. Slices of peeled orange can be added to eat with cold roast duck. Serves 4. For a nutty salad use half walnut oil and half sunflower-seed oil, adding a handful of chopped walnuts when mixing the salad. Wet green walnuts are also delicious.

Lentil vinaigrette; fennel and radish salad.

Cucumber and Cheese Salad

½ lb curd cheese *or* cream cheese
3 Tbs lemon juice
2 Tbs sunflower-seed oil
½ cucumber, diced
salt and black pepper
4 Tbs chopped chives

Curd cheese is best for this dish – Sainsbury's make an excellent one – but if unobtainable get a cream cheese with as low a fat content as possible; Philadelphia is suitable. Mash the cheese with the lemon juice until it forms a smooth cream, then beat in the oil. Peel the cucumber and cut in very small dice. Mix into the cheese and season with salt and black pepper to taste, and more lemon juice if necessary. Mix in the chives and chill. To serve, pile on crisp lettuce leaves, or use as a stuffing for tomatoes or a filling for a tomato aspic ring. Serves 4.

Tomato and onion salad; mixed chicory salad.

Black Radish and Cucumber Salad

1 black radish
1 cucumber
salt and black pepper
3 Tbs sunflower-seed oil
1 Tbs white wine vinegar

Skin the radish and the cucumber, and grate both coarsely. Mix in a bowl, season with salt and black pepper, and pour over the oil and vinegar. Serve soon after making. Serves 4.

Broccoli salad; carrot salad.

Radish and Cucumber Salad

1 bunch (about ¼ lb) radishes
½ cucumber
salt and black pepper
¼ tsp sugar
½ gill thin cream
½ gill yoghurt
2–3 Tbs lemon juice

Trim the radishes, peel the cucumber, and slice both very thinly. Mix the two together. Put the salt, black pepper and sugar in a small bowl and mix with the cream and yoghurt. Add lemon juice to taste and pour over the radishes and cucumber. Mix well. Serves 4.

Egg and tomato salad; chick pea salad.

Cucumber Mousse

¼ lb Philadelphia cream cheese
¼ pt cream, sour cream *or* yoghurt
1 packet (½ oz) gelatine
¼ pt chicken stock
1 cucumber
1 dessertspoonful lemon juice
salt and black pepper

Beat together the cream cheese and the cream, sour cream or yoghurt until smooth. (Use cream for a richer dish, yoghurt for a simple unfattening one.) Melt the gelatine in the stock. Grate the peeled cucumber and mix it into the cheese mixture. Add the lemon juice, salt and black pepper to taste. Pour the melted gelatine through a strainer into the mixture and stir thoroughly. When well mixed, pour into a soufflé dish or mould and chill. Serves 4.

A simple tomato salad or egg and tomato salad; sweet pepper salad; beetroot salad.

Cucumber and Sour Cream Salad

1 cucumber
½ pt sour cream
2 Tbs tarragon vinegar
1 tsp sugar
½ tsp salt
2 Tbs chopped chives *or* dill *or* spring onions

Peel and slice the cucumber, or cut into sticks by cutting first into 1-inch slices, then cutting each slice downwards into 9 pieces. Sprinkle with salt and leave to drain. Pat dry in a cloth. Mix the other ingredients, beating until smooth. Combine with the cucumber and sprinkle the chives (or alternative) over the top. Chill. Serves 4–6.

Fennel and tomato salad; cauliflower vinaigrette.

Cucumber and Watercress Salad

1 cucumber
1 bunch watercress
olive oil
white wine vinegar
salt and black pepper

Peel the cucumber and cut into thick slices. Wash and drain the watercress; chop it coarsely, stalks and all. Mix both in a good vinaigrette. Delicious served with a crumbly white cheese such as the Greek Feta, or a cream cheese. Serves 4.

Egg and tomato salad; spinach and yoghurt.

Chick Pea Salad

$\frac{1}{2}$ lb chick peas
1 lemon
1 clove garlic
salt and black pepper
approximately $\frac{1}{4}$ pt olive oil
2 Tbs finely chopped parsley

Soak the peas overnight. Put them in a saucepan and cover generously with cold water. Bring slowly to the boil and simmer gently until tender – about 2 hours. Add salt only towards the end of the cooking. Drain them when they are soft enough to crush between the fingers, put them in a bowl and add salt and black pepper to taste. Stir in the juice of 1 lemon, a crushed clove of garlic and about $\frac{1}{4}$ pt olive oil. Sprinkle with chopped parsley and if possible serve before they have completely cooled. Serves 4–5.

Leek vinaigrette; fennel and tomato salad.

Sweet Corn Mayonnaise

approximately ¾ lb corn, fresh, frozen *or*
    tinned (whole kernel)
¼ pt mayonnaise
¼ pt sour cream
salt and black pepper
lemon juice (optional)
2 rashers streaky bacon

If using fresh corn, allow 6 ears. Cut off the kernels with a
sharp knife and cook in a very little lightly salted water until
tender, about 4 minutes. Drain and cool. Mix the mayonnaise (made with lemon juice if possible) with the sour
cream, and stir into the corn when it has cooled. Add salt
and black pepper to taste, also a little more lemon juice if
necessary. Fry the bacon rashers gently until crisp, drain and
crumble. Scatter over the corn when cool. Serves 4.

Leek vinaigrette; beetroot salad.

Egg and Tomato Salad

6 hard-boiled eggs
4 large tomatoes *or* 6 medium ones
½ Spanish onion
olive oil
vinegar
salt and black pepper
finely chopped parsley *or* chives

Chop the eggs. Peel the tomatoes and cut them in similar
sized pieces, discarding seeds and juice. Slice the half onion
very finely and divide each slice into rings. Mix the three
together with enough olive oil and vinegar to moisten – 3
parts oil to 1 part vinegar. Season to taste with salt and black
pepper, and serve in a bowl. Sprinkle with fresh herbs, when
available. Serves 4.

Cucumber in sour cream; broccoli salad.

Fennel and Tomato Salad

2 heads fennel
¾ lb tomatoes
salt and black pepper
olive oil
lemon juice

Put the fennel in iced water for half an hour to become crisp.
Peel the tomatoes. Slice the fennel thinly, and mix with the
sliced tomatoes on a flat dish. Sprinkle salt and freshly
ground black pepper over them, then pour over 4 tablespoons of olive oil to ½ tablespoon lemon juice. Serves 6.
FENNEL AND RADISH SALAD can be made as above substituting 2 bunches radishes for the tomatoes.

Lentil vinaigrette ; cucumber in sour cream.

Lentil Vinaigrette

½ lb freshly cooked brown lentils
1 small onion
2 oz streaky bacon rashers
black pepper
3 Tbs olive oil
1 Tbs white wine vinegar

Chop the onion finely and mix with the lentils. Fry the bacon
until crisp, then drain and crumble into small pieces, or
chop. Mix with the lentils. Season with freshly ground black
pepper and pour over the oil and vinegar. The bacon can be
omitted or replaced by slices of *peperoni*, or warm sliced
frankfurters. The whole salad is better served warm than
cold when possible. Serves 4.

Spinach and yoghurt ; French beans and tomatoes.

A Simple Lettuce Salad

1 round lettuce
lemon juice
sugar

Simply pile the dried lettuce leaves in a bowl and sprinkle with lemon juice and sugar to taste. A delicious light salad for a summer meal. Serves 4.

Saffron rice with peas; fennel and tomato salad.

Lettuce, Bacon and Mushroom Salad

4 oz streaky bacon rashers
4 oz raw mushrooms
1 lettuce
salt and black pepper
3 Tbs olive oil
1 Tbs white wine vinegar

Fry the bacon rashers until crisp; drain. Chop or break into small pieces. Slice the mushrooms; tear the lettuce leaves into pieces. Mix the three ingredients in a bowl. Make a dressing with the oil and vinegar and salt and black pepper, and pour over the salad. Serves 4. The lettuce can be replaced by sorrel or dandelions.

Lentil vinaigrette; radish and cucumber salad.

Sorrel and Lettuce Salad with Bacon

1 bunch sorrel (about 2 oz)
1 cos lettuce
4 rashers streaky bacon
1 Tbs white wine vinegar
black pepper

Cut the sorrel in thin strips with scissors. Cut the lettuce in 2-inch chunks. Mix the sorrel and the lettuce together in a bowl. Chop the bacon and fry very slowly until crisp. Lift out the chopped bacon and throw over the salad. Pour the vinegar into the hot fat carefully as it may froth up. Grind some black pepper over it and as soon as it is hot pour it over the salad and serve immediately. Serves 4.

Serve alone.

Mixed Green Salad I

1 lettuce
1 bunch corn salad (lamb's lettuce)
1 batavia *or* escarole
1 avocado
salt and black pepper
4 Tbs olive oil
½ Tbs lemon juice
1 Tbs orange juice
1 clove garlic

Wash the lettuce leaves, the corn salad, and the inner pale green leaves of the batavia. Dry well and arrange in a bowl. Peel and stone the avocado and cut in slices; scatter over the salad. Make the dressing by mixing the oil with the salt and black pepper, stirring in the fruit juices, and leaving until ready to serve with a whole peeled clove of garlic in the mixture. Discard the garlic before dressing the salad. Serves 4–6.

Mixed Green Salad II

1 lettuce
1 curly endive
2 chicory
1 green pepper
salt and black pepper
4 Tbs olive oil
1 Tbs white wine vinegar

Wash the lettuce and the inner pale green part of the curly endive. Remove the outer leaves of the chicory and trim the stalk. Cut in 1-inch pieces. Put the lettuce, curly endive and chicory in a bowl. Cut the pepper in strips, discarding seeds and stalk, and scatter over the salad. Make the dressing and pour over the salad. Mix well. Serves 4–6.

Mixed Green Salad III

1 lettuce
1 bunch watercress
½ cucumber
1 small root fennel
1 small green pepper
salt and black pepper
3 Tbs olive oil
1 Tbs walnut oil
1½ Tbs white wine vinegar

Wash the lettuce and dry well. Divide the watercress into sprigs and wash and dry. Peel the cucumber and slice or cut in sticks (cut in 1-inch slices, then cut each slice downwards into 9 *bâtons*). Slice the fennel finely and divide each slice into sections. Cut the green pepper into strips. Mix all together in a bowl. Make the dressing: put the salt and black pepper in a cup. Pour in the olive oil and mix. Add the walnut oil and mix again. Stir in the vinegar. Pour over the salad, mix and serve. Serves 4.

Mixed American Salad

1 crisp lettuce, Webb's *or* Iceberg
4 tomatoes
¼ lb cooked ham, in one thick slice
¼ lb Gruyère
2 thick slices white toast
salt and black pepper
5 Tbs olive oil
1½ Tbs white wine vinegar

Wash and dry the lettuce, and put the leaves in a bowl. Cut the unskinned tomatoes in wedges and lay on the lettuce. Cut the ham and cheese in cubes. Scatter both over the lettuce and tomatoes. Cut the toast in small squares and throw over the salad. Make the dressing in the usual way, pour over the salad and mix. Serves 4.

Orange and Watercress Salad

3 oranges
2 bunches watercress
salt and black pepper
4 Tbs sunflower-seed oil
1½ Tbs lemon juice

Peel the oranges removing all the white pith. Cut in thin slices. Divide the watercress into sprigs; wash and dry well. Mix the two together, seasoning with salt and black pepper. Pour over the oil and lemon juice and mix well. Good with cold duck. Serves 3–4.

Rice salad with peppers and peas; raw mushroom salad.

Hot Potato Salad

1½ lb new *or* waxy potatoes
1 medium onion
salt and black pepper
¼ lb streaky bacon rashers
2 Tbs white wine vinegar
2 Tbs finely chopped parsley

Boil the potatoes in their skins until tender and drain. Remove the skins as soon as possible and slice the potatoes quite thickly into a warm bowl. Chop the onion finely and mix with the potatoes, seasoning with salt and black pepper. Dice the bacon and fry slowly until crisp. Drain on soft paper, then mix with the salad. Pour the vinegar into the bacon fat remaining in the pan, re-heat carefully (it may froth up), and pour over the salad. Mix well and serve at once. Serves 4.

French beans Provençale; grilled mushrooms.

Potato Salad I

1½ lb new *or* waxy potatoes
1 bunch spring onions *or* 1 small onion
3 Tbs chopped chives
3 Tbs chopped chervil *or* parsley
salt and black pepper
4 Tbs olive oil
1 Tbs white wine vinegar

Boil the potatoes in their skins and drain. Remove the skins as soon as possible, and cut the potatoes in fairly thick slices, trying not to break them. Put in a bowl and scatter the finely sliced spring onions and the herbs over them. Season with salt and black pepper and pour over the oil and vinegar. Serves 4. Do not make this dish too long in advance; it is best made quickly and eaten within the hour, for if it is left too long, the oil will be absorbed and more must be added.

Cucumber and sour cream; broccoli salad.

Potato Salad II

1½ lb new *or* waxy potatoes
¼ pt cream
salt and black pepper
1 bunch spring onions
4–6 Tbs chopped parsley and chives

Boil the potatoes in their skins and drain. Remove the skins as soon as possible and slice the potatoes into a shallow bowl. Beat the cream with the salt and black pepper and pour over the sliced potatoes. Lift carefully with a spatula trying not to break them. Mix in half the herbs and scatter the rest over the top. Serve within the hour if possible. Serves 4.

Tomato and onion salad; radish and cucumber salad.

Rice Salad with Peppers and Peas

½ lb Patna rice
salt and black pepper
grated nutmeg
½ pt thin cream
juice of ½ lemon
1 large red pepper
½ lb shelled green peas *or* ½ lb frozen *petits pois*

Cook the rice, drain and season while still hot with salt, black pepper and grated nutmeg. Add the cream and lemon juice. Grill the pepper until the skin has blackened on all sides. Remove the skin and dice the flesh, discarding the seeds. Cook the peas until just tender, and drain. Mix the chopped pepper and the peas with the rice. Serves 6.

Tomato and onion salad; beetroot salad.

Rice Salad with Herbs

½ lb Patna rice
salt and black pepper
grated nutmeg
3 Tbs olive oil
1½ tsp white wine vinegar
1½ tsp tarragon vinegar
4–6 Tbs chopped fresh herbs
1½ oz pine kernels

Cook the rice in boiling salted water until just tender. Drain well. While still hot, add salt, black pepper, and grated nutmeg to taste. Stir in the oil and vinegars. When cool, stir in the chopped herbs (e.g. chives, chervil, dill, tarragon, parsley) and the pine nuts, keeping back a little of each to scatter over the top. Serves 6. This makes a very pretty green and white dish.

Stuffed mushrooms; broccoli salad.

Saffron Rice with Peas

½ lb Patna rice
2 packets (½ tsp) saffron
chicken stock
½ pt thin cream
½ lb shelled green peas *or* ½ lb frozen *petits pois*
lemon juice
salt and black pepper

Cook the rice in the stock with half the saffron. Drain when tender and put in a large bowl. Heat half the cream with the remaining saffron; when well flavoured, mix with the rest of the cream, and sharpen with lemon juice. Cook the peas and drain. Mix the rice and peas while still hot and pour over the saffron cream. Mix well and adjust seasoning, adding more lemon juice, salt and black pepper to taste. Leave to cool. A pretty dish for a buffet supper. Do not prepare too long in advance or it will become rather thick and solid. Serves 6.

Stuffed tomatoes; raw mushroom salad.

Spinach and Yoghurt Salad

1 lb spinach
¼ pt yoghurt
1 clove garlic
salt and black pepper

Cook the spinach in a little boiling salted water. Drain well, squeezing out excess moisture with the hands as soon as it is cool enough to handle. Chop with a long knife on a board. Beat the yoghurt with a wooden spoon until smooth; crush the garlic in a press and mix into the yoghurt. Add salt and black pepper to taste. Mix the yoghurt with the chopped spinach; chill slightly before serving. Serves 3–4.

Carrot salad; cauliflower vinaigrette.

Spinach and Bacon Salad I

½ lb spinach (only tender summer spinach will
  do)
¼ lb streaky bacon, cut in thin slices
3 Tbs best olive oil
1 Tbs white wine vinegar
black pepper

Cut the stalks off the spinach with scissors. Wash the leaves
very well indeed, and drain. Toss in a soft cloth to get rid of
as much moisture as possible then cut them in thin strips.
Fry the bacon rashers and drain on soft paper. When cool,
chop or crumble them into small pieces. Mix the spinach
and bacon in a bowl, and pour over the vinaigrette made
with the olive oil and vinegar. Season with black pepper. No
extra flavouring is needed. Sorrel or dandelion leaves can be
substituted for the spinach. Serves 4.

Raw mushroom salad; tomato salad.

Spinach and Bacon Salad II

Same ingredients as above, but omit the oil. Prepare the
spinach beforehand, but only fry the bacon at the last
moment. After removing the bacon from the pan, crumble
it quickly and mix with the spinach while still hot. Pour
1 Tbs wine vinegar into the pan containing the bacon fat,
being careful as it may flare up, stir for a moment, then pour
it over the salad, mix and serve immediately. This salad
must not be allowed to wait, or the fat will cool and congeal.

Serve alone.

Salad San Lorenzo

½ lb young spinach
1 avocado
¼ lb streaky bacon rashers
1 Mozzarella cheese
salt and black pepper
6 Tbs olive oil
2 Tbs white wine vinegar

Wash the spinach well, remove the stalks and cut the leaves across in ½-inch strips. Peel and stone the avocado and cut in slices. Fry the bacon and drain on soft paper. When cool, crumble or chop it. Slice the Mozzarella. Mix the spinach, avocado, bacon and cheese together. Make the dressing and pour over all. Serve immediately. Serves 4.

Serve alone.

Tomato Ice

about ¾ lb raw tomatoes
¼ pt mayonnaise
¼ pt sour cream
1 clove garlic
1 tsp onion juice (put through garlic press)
salt and black pepper
1–2 Tbs lemon juice

Skin the tomatoes and put them, whole, in the blender. Blend until smooth and seeds are disintegrated. You will need ½–¾ pt pulp. Mix the sour cream into the mayonnaise. Stir in the pulped tomatoes. Add the garlic, put through the press, and the onion juice. Add salt, black pepper and lemon juice to taste. When well mixed and flavoured, pour into a ring mould, shallow dish or ice trays, and freeze. Turn out to serve. Serves 6. This light and refreshing dish is particularly delicious served after a hot main course, especially a curry.

Serve alone.

A Simple Tomato Salad

1 lb tomatoes
salt and black pepper
sugar

Skin the tomatoes and leave them whole. Cut with an X-shaped incision in the top, and pull out the central core with the fingers. Leave upside down for a little while to allow all the juice and seeds to drain away. Arrange right side up on a flat dish and sprinkle lightly with salt, sugar and black pepper. Do not add any dressing, but serve quite plainly. They make an excellent accompaniment to a series of dishes dressed with olive oil or cream dressings. Serves 4.

Rice salad with herbs; cucumber and sour cream salad.

Tomato and Avocado Salad

$\frac{3}{4}$ lb tomatoes
2 avocado pears
1 orange
$\frac{1}{2}$ lemon

Skin the tomatoes, cut them in half vertically, then slice with the cut half flat on the board. Skin the avocado pears, cut in half and remove the stones. Slice each half to the same thickness as the tomatoes. Mix the two together in a dish. Squeeze the juice of the orange and the half lemon. Pour over the salad and mix. Serves 4. Alternatively this salad can be dressed with oil and lemon juice, but I like the freshness of the fruit juices alone.

Cucumber and cheese salad; Arabic parsley salad; a watercress salad.

Whole Tomatoes in Horseradish Sauce

1½ lb small, ripe tomatoes

Horseradish sauce
¼ pt mayonnaise
¼ pt sour cream
4 Tbs grated horseradish, fresh if possible
lemon juice to taste

Skin the tomatoes and leave them whole. Chill in the refrigerator while making the sauce. Mix the mayonnaise (made with lemon juice if possible) and the cream in a bowl, beating until smooth. Stir in the horseradish and add lemon juice to taste. Pile the tomatoes in a pyramid on a flat dish and spoon the sauce over. Chill in the refrigerator until time to serve. Serves 6. This makes an excellent accompaniment to cold beef dishes.

Cucumber and radish salad; broccoli vinaigrette.

Sauces

A Light Curry Sauce

¾ pt milk *or* half milk and half vegetable stock
¼ bay leaf
½ small onion
1 clove
½ tsp salt
6 black peppercorns
1 oz butter
1½ Tbs flour
1–1½ Tbs light curry powder
1 packet saffron
½ gill cream
lemon juice
cayenne pepper

Put the milk in a small pan with the bay leaf, onion, clove, salt and peppercorns. Bring to the boil, cover, and leave by the side of the fire for 20 minutes to infuse. Melt the butter, stir in the flour and curry powder, and pour on the strained milk. Stir until smooth and well blended, then add the saffron. (If using saffron threads, infuse them in the hot milk after straining for 5 minutes, before adding to the roux.) Simmer for 4 minutes, then add the cream and lemon juice to taste. Add more seasonings as required: cayenne pepper, more curry powder, salt, etc. If you have a sweet fruit juice or syrup add 1 dessertspoon and some more lemon juice. Makes just under ½ pt, serves 4. This is a light curry sauce in the French manner, so do not be tempted to add too much curry powder; a strong curry would overpower the vegetables it is to be served with.

Sauce Hollandaise

4 oz butter
3 egg yolks
1 Tbs white wine vinegar *or* lemon juice
$\frac{1}{4}$ bay leaf
4 black peppercorns
salt

This sauce must be made in a double boiler. I use a small china bowl which fits securely inside a tall saucepan; the water in the pan must not touch the bowl. Cut the butter in small pieces and put in a small bowl over hot water until it has half melted. Put the vinegar in a small pan with 3 Tbs water, the bay leaf and peppercorns. Heat slowly. Break the egg yolks into the top half of your double boiler (not yet set in its pan) and remove the threads. Have the water in the pan heating while you beat the yolks for 3 minutes. When the water reaches boiling point, turn down the heat so that it is a few degrees below boiling. Set the bowl with the eggs in the pan and continue to beat until they have thickened very slightly. Pour on the hot vinegar very, very slowly, having removed the bay leaf and peppercorns. Continue to beat all the time and maintain an even heat. When all the vinegar is added, start to add the semi-melted butter, beating continuously. This must all be done very slowly. When all the butter is absorbed, taste and add a little salt. The sauce will never become very thick, nor should it be made very hot. It should be served warm, and can be kept warm for a little while by covering the bowl, and leaving it over the hot water, after first adding a couple of spoons of cold water to the pan to lower the temperature and stop the cooking. Serves 4. This most delicious of sauces makes the perfect accompaniment for delicate green vegetables, such as asparagus, seakale, artichokes and broccoli; it is also excellent with Jerusalem artichokes, leeks and salsify.

Mayonnaise

2 egg yolks
salt
½ tsp French mustard *or* a pinch dry mustard
    powder
½ pt olive oil
1–2 Tbs white wine vinegar *or* lemon juice

Have the eggs at room temperature, also the oil. Break the
yolks into a mortar or heavy bowl of generous size. Add a
pinch of salt and the mustard. Beat thoroughly and steadily
with a wooden spoon or the pestle (if using a mortar) for a
few moments before starting to add the oil. Have the oil in
a light jug that is easy to handle with your left hand. While
still beating steadily, start to add the oil, drop by drop. Continue very slowly indeed, until about ⅓ of the oil has been
amalgamated, when you can start to add it more quickly. If
the mayonnaise gets too thick to work easily, thin it down by
adding a little of the vinegar – about ½ a tablespoonful, drop
by drop. When all the oil is used up, add more vinegar
gradually until it suits your taste. Some people prefer to use
lemon juice, but I like a good vinegar best of all. Failing the
best French wine vinegar, however, lemon juice makes a
perfectly good mayonnaise, and better than a coarse vinegar.
Keep in a covered jar in the refrigerator or cool larder until
needed. If at any point it curdles, break another egg yolk
into a clean bowl and add the curdled mayonnaise to it
gradually, drop by drop, then the remaining oil, then an
extra ¼ pt oil to allow for the extra yolk. Mayonnaise is
easier to make in large quantities; 1 egg yolk to ¼ pt olive
oil is the hardest of all to achieve.

Skordalia

4–5 large cloves garlic (about half a head)
1 large potato, boiled, peeled, and diced
2 slices stale bread, crusts removed
about ¼ pt olive oil
1–2 Tbs lemon juice
approximately 1 Tbs milk *or* thin cream

Peel the garlic and chop finely. Put in a mortar and pound until reduced to a mash. Add the potato and pound again until amalgamated. Add the bread (use brown, for taste, or white for appearance), which you have soaked in water and squeezed between your hands until all the water has been expressed. Pound again until reduced to a smooth pulp. Start to add the oil drop by drop, as you would for a mayonnaise, beating with the pestle or a wooden spoon. It can separate as easily as a mayonnaise, so you must be very careful. If it shows signs of separating, beat in 1 Tbs tepid water. Add lemon juice to taste, and beat in a little milk or cream, to improve the colour. It should be very pale, almost white, not grey like porridge. Makes enough for 4–6. Serve with courgette or aubergine fritters, hard-boiled eggs, boiled potatoes, fried fillets of fish, etc.

Aïolli

4 cloves garlic
2 egg yolks
salt
½ pt olive oil
1–2 Tbs white wine vinegar *or* lemon juice

Crush the garlic in a mortar. Break in the egg yolks and pound into the garlic with the pestle. Add a pinch of salt. Beat continuously with the pestle adding the oil drop by drop. When about ⅓ of the oil has been amalgamated, add it more quickly. If it gets too thick, add a little of the vinegar or lemon juice to thin it. When all the oil is used up, add more vinegar or lemon to taste. Serves 4. A delicious accompaniment to dishes of plainly boiled vegetables, still warm, such as French beans, courgettes, carrots, broad beans or peas, also hard-boiled eggs, boiled cod or poached chicken; this sauce can be the basis of a whole meal. It is equally good with raw tomatoes, lettuce leaves, cucumber, etc. This is the genuine Provençal proportion of garlic and is very pungent; for those who prefer a milder version, cut down the garlic to 2 cloves.

Arabian Sauce

4 oz Philadelphia cream cheese
¼ pt buttermilk
approximately 1 tsp lemon juice
½–1 tsp *harissa*
salt and black pepper

Cut the cheese in small pieces and put in the blender with the buttermilk. Stir in the lemon juice and the *harissa* (a paste made from hot red peppers obtainable in tins from Eastern shops). Add salt and black pepper. Heat for a hot sauce, or chill in the refrigerator. A very hot sauce to serve with grilled chicken, *cous-cous*, or grilled lamb kebabs.

Celery Sauce

1 celery heart (about 6 oz)
¾ pt chicken stock
1 oz butter
1½ Tbs flour
½ gill cream
salt and black pepper
mace

Slice the celery and put in a saucepan with the stock. Bring to the boil, cover and simmer for 30 minutes. Cool slightly and put in the blender. Melt the butter in a cleaned pan, add the flour and pour on the blended celery and stock. Blend and simmer for 4 minutes. Add the cream and season to taste with salt, black pepper and a pinch of mace. Serves 4. Serve with poached chicken or roast lamb.

Cheese Soufflé Sauce

2 oz butter
3 Tbs flour
½ pt milk
3 oz grated Gruyère
salt and black pepper
2 eggs

Melt the butter, stir in the flour and cook for 3 minutes, stirring continuously. Add the heated milk, and stir until smooth. Simmer for 5 minutes, stirring now and then, then add the grated cheese. Stir over gentle heat until smooth and melted. Season well with salt and black pepper. Remove from the heat and beat in the beaten egg yolks. Whip the whites and fold in. Pour over cooked vegetables and bake for 12 minutes at 400°. This sauce is good with boiled asparagus, broccoli or leeks. It should be less solid than a soufflé – more like a foamy sauce.

Cream Cheese Sauce

4 oz Philadelphia cream cheese
¼ pt buttermilk
1–2 tsp lemon juice
salt and black pepper

Dice the cheese and put in the blender with the buttermilk. Blend until smooth. Add lemon juice to taste. Season with salt and black pepper. Serve chilled, or heat gently without boiling. Makes a scant ½ pt. I use this as a base for many cold sauces; it is quickly made and combines well with herbs, garlic or horseradish, and makes a good light dressing for cooked vegetable salads without being rich or fattening. It is equally quickly made in double quantities.

Cream Dressing

salt and black pepper
½ tsp sugar
1 Tbs white wine vinegar
2 Tbs thin cream
2 Tbs olive oil

Put a pinch of salt, a few turns of the peppermill and the sugar in a small bowl. Pour on the vinegar and leave for a few moments to dissolve the seasonings. Add the cream and beat to blend. Pour on the oil and beat again. Excellent over lettuce salad or a mixture of cold cooked vegetables.

Cream Sauce

½ oz butter
1 Tbs flour
¼ pt chicken stock
¼ pt thin cream
3 Tbs grated Gruyère
salt and black pepper

Melt the butter, stir in the flour and cook for 3 minutes. Heat the stock and the cream together, pour onto the roux and blend. Simmer for 4 minutes, then stir in the cheese until smooth. Season with salt and black pepper to taste. Serves 4. This sauce is used as the accompaniment for dishes like Eggs St Germain, and poached eggs on spinach purée.

Cucumber Mayonnaise

½ pt mayonnaise (see p. 179)
½ cucumber

Make the mayonnaise (see p. 179). Grate the unpeeled cucumber and squeeze out most of the moisture with the hands. Stir the cucumber into the mayonnaise. Taste for seasoning and add extra lemon juice if needed. Serves 5–6. Serve with fried *goujons* of sole.

Cold Cucumber Sauce I

½ cucumber
1 Tbs finely chopped onion
3 Tbs sour cream
2 Tbs mayonnaise
chilli sauce *or* anchovy essence to taste
    (about ½ tsp)
salt, black pepper and cayenne

Peel the cucumber and cut in small dice. Mix with the finely chopped onion. Beat the sour cream and the mayonnaise together and flavour to taste with chilli sauce – Sea Isle or Tabasco – or anchovy essence. Season with salt and black pepper and a pinch of cayenne. Mix with the cucumber and onion and chill. Sprinkle with cayenne before serving. Serves 3–4. Serve with grilled or fried sole.

Hot or Cold Cucumber Sauce II

4 oz Philadelphia cream cheese
¼ pt buttermilk
approximately 2 tsp lemon juice *or* white wine
    vinegar
salt and black pepper
½ cucumber

Cut the cheese in small pieces and put in the blender with the buttermilk. Blend until smooth. Add lemon juice and salt and black pepper to taste. Grate the cucumber – I prefer to leave the peel on, but this is a matter of choice – and squeeze out the juice in the hands. Stir into the sauce and taste. Add more lemon juice as required. Heat gently in a small pan, or chill in the refrigerator for a cold sauce. Makes ½ pt. A useful sauce, particularly for those on a diet. Good with poached fish, a dish of skinned tomatoes, a salad of hard-boiled eggs and tomatoes, etc.

Dill Sauce

¾ oz butter
1 Tbs flour
¼ pt stock: chicken, beef *or* veal
¼ pt thin cream
salt and black pepper
3–4 Tbs chopped dill
1 egg yolk (optional)

Melt the butter, stir in the flour and cook for 1 minute. Heat the stock and the cream together and pour onto the roux. Stir until blended, and simmer for 4 minutes. Season with salt and black pepper and stir in the chopped dill. For a richer sauce beat the egg yolk in a cup and add a spoonful of the simmering sauce to it, then return to the pan and stir without boiling for 1 minute. Otherwise serve as it is. Good with boiled beef.

Garlic Sauce with Yoghurt

1 large clove garlic
salt
¼ pt yoghurt
2 Tbs chopped herbs: chives, chervil, mint *or* dill

Mince the garlic, then pound it to a pulp in a mortar, adding a good pinch of salt. When reduced to a smooth paste add the yoghurt gradually, pounding after each addition to make a really smooth sauce. When all the yoghurt is amalgamated, add more salt to taste, and stir in the chopped herbs. Chill until ready to serve. Serves 3–4. Excellent with roast lamb, roast chicken, aubergine or courgette fritters, grilled or fried aubergines and courgettes, grilled tomatoes, a spinach soufflé or a steamed broccoli mould.

Herb Sauce

4 oz Philadelphia cream cheese
¼ pt buttermilk
approximately 2 tsp lemon juice
salt and black pepper
4 Tbs chopped mixed herbs *or*
    2 Tbs chopped tarragon *or* basil

Cut the cheese in pieces and put in the blender with the buttermilk. Blend until smooth. Add lemon juice, salt and black pepper to taste. Stir in the chopped herbs. The quantities must vary according to the strength of the herb: tarragon and basil are so strong that less is needed. Serve chilled, or heat gently without allowing to boil. Makes ½ pt. Serve over soft-boiled eggs, sliced cucumber, or a mixed salad.

Horseradish Sauce I

¼ pt sour cream
3–4 Tbs grated horseradish
1–2 tsp white wine vinegar
salt and black pepper

Stir the grated horseradish into the cream; add enough vinegar to flavour well. Season with salt and black pepper. Makes ¼ pt, serves 3–4. Good with roast or boiled beef, smoked fish and beef stews.

Horseradish Sauce II

¼ pt mayonnaise made with lemon juice
¼ pt sour cream
4 Tbs grated horseradish
lemon juice

Mix the mayonnaise and the sour cream together. Beat in the grated horseradish and add lemon juice to taste. Makes ½ pt, serves 6. This makes a creamier, richer sauce to serve with vegetable dishes like tomatoes; the simpler version above is best with beef.

Horseradish Sauce III

¼ lb Philadelphia cream cheese
¼ pt buttermilk
approximately 1 Tbs lemon juice *or*
 white wine vinegar
salt and black pepper
about 3 Tbs grated horseradish

Cut the cheese in small pieces and put in the blender with the buttermilk. Blend until smooth, then pour into a bowl. Add ½ Tbs lemon juice or vinegar, then stir in grated horseradish to taste. Add more lemon juice or vinegar if necessary, salt and black pepper. Make some hours before needed to allow the flavour to develop. Chill in the refrigerator. Makes a scant ½ pt, serves 4–6. This is good poured over a dish of small peeled tomatoes, an excellent accompaniment to cold roast beef.

Horseradish and Apple Sauce

¼ pt unsweetened apple purée (2 large cooking
 apples)
2 Tbs grated horseradish *or* more according to
 taste
2 Tbs mayonnaise
2 Tbs sour cream
lemon juice

Stir the horseradish into the apple purée. (I use an excellent German grated horseradish called *Koch-brand*, to be found in the frozen food compartments of good delicatessens.) Stir in the mayonnaise and sour cream, and add a little lemon juice to sharpen it. This sauce should be a perfect blending of the two flavours, so add enough horseradish to flavour it well, without obscuring the taste of the apples. Makes ½ pt, serves 6. Excellent with cold duck, cold roast beef and cold pork.

Hot Sauce

1 tsp ground cumin
1 tsp ground coriander
½ tsp ground chilli *or* chilli powder
½ tsp celery salt
2 Tbs condensed tomato purée
2 Tbs stock

Put the spices and tomato purée into a small bowl, pour on the hot stock and mix to a paste. A hot sauce to serve with dishes of *cous-cous*.

Mushroom Sauce

¼ lb mushrooms
¾ pt chicken stock
1 oz butter
1½ Tbs flour
salt and black pepper
½ gill cream

Chop the mushrooms and cook in the stock for 20 minutes. Cool slightly, then put in the blender. Melt the butter in a cleaned pan, stir in the flour and blend. Cook for 2 minutes, then pour on the blended mushroom mixture. Simmer for 4 minutes, then add the cream and season to taste with salt and black pepper. Serves 4. Good with spinach pancakes; stuffed tomatoes.

Mushroom and Tomato Sauce

6 oz mushrooms, flat for preference
2 oz butter
1 8-oz tin Italian peeled tomatoes *or* ½ lb fresh
    tomatoes
¼ tsp celery salt
¼ tsp sugar
2 Tbs lemon juice
¼ pt sour cream

188

Chop the mushrooms and toss in the butter until soft. Drain and cool. Put the tinned tomatoes in a blender (if using fresh ones, peel and chop them, keeping the juice, and toss in butter until slightly softened), with the mushrooms, seasonings, lemon juice and sour cream. Blend until smooth, then taste and adjust seasoning if necessary. Pour into a small pan and simmer gently for 10 minutes. An excellent smooth sauce for timbales, stuffed cabbage, soufflés, etc.

Sauce Mornay I

¾ pt milk
¼ bay leaf
½ small onion
2 cloves
6 black peppercorns
½ tsp salt
1 oz butter
1½ Tbs flour
¼ pt cream
3 oz grated Gruyère

Put the milk in a small pan with the bay leaf, onion, cloves, peppercorns and salt. Bring to the boil, put to the side of the fire, cover and leave for 20 minutes to absorb the flavours. Melt the butter, stir in the flour and cook for 2 minutes, stirring constantly. Pour on the strained milk and blend. Simmer for 4 minutes, stirring often. Add the cheese by degrees, stirring over a very low heat until smooth. Add the cream and adjust seasoning to taste. Serves 4–6. This sauce is excellent poured over cooked vegetables, with some more grated cheese scattered over the top, and gratiné under a hot grill.

Mint Sauce

3 Tbs chopped fresh mint
1 Tbs sugar
3 Tbs lemon juice
¼ pt boiling water

Put the chopped mint in a mortar and pound. Add the sugar and pound again. Pour on the lemon juice, then the boiling water. Leave until cool. The traditional accompaniment to roast lamb.

Sauce Mornay II

¾ oz butter
1 Tbs flour
¼ pt chicken *or* vegetable stock
¼ pt thin cream
salt and black pepper
3 oz grated Gruyère
1 egg yolk (optional)

Melt the butter, stir in the flour, and cook for 1 minute. Heat the stock and cream in a small pan and pour onto the roux. Blend and simmer for 4 minutes, stirring often. Stir in the grated cheese, and cook until melted and smooth. Season with salt and black pepper to taste. Add 1 egg yolk for a richer version. Serves 4.

Onion Sauce

½ lb onions
¾ pt chicken, game *or* beef stock
1 oz butter
1½ Tbs flour
salt and black pepper
½ gill cream

Chop the onions coarsely and put in a pan with the stock. Bring to the boil, cover and simmer for 30 minutes. Cool slightly, then put in the blender. Melt the butter in a clean pan, stir in the flour and cook for 2 minutes. Pour on the blended onion mixture and simmer for 4 minutes. Add the cream, and season to taste with salt and freshly ground black pepper. Serves 4. Serve with boiled chicken, boiled mutton or grilled lamb chops.

Parsley Sauce

½ pt milk
½ onion
1 clove; ¼ bay leaf
¼ tsp celery salt
4–5 black peppercorns
1 oz butter
1½ Tbs flour
4 Tbs freshly chopped parsley

Put the milk in a small pan with the onion, clove, bay leaf, celery salt and the peppercorns. Bring to simmering point, then cover the pan and leave at the side of the fire for 20 minutes. Melt the butter, stir in the flour and cook for 1 minute, stirring constantly. Pour in the strained milk, stir until blended and simmer for 3–4 minutes. Season well with black pepper. Stir in the parsley and mix well. Serves 4–6.

Pistou or Pesto

¾ pt fresh basil leaves
2 cloves garlic
4 Tbs pine kernels
2 oz grated Parmesan
approximately ½ pt olive oil

Chop the basil and pound in a mortar. Add the chopped garlic and the chopped nuts. Pound all together, then add the cheese. Continue to pound until smooth and well blended, then beat in the oil, drop by drop, as for a mayonnaise. It should be the consistency of creamed butter. Serves 6. An excellent sauce for gnocchi and spaghetti. The nuts can be omitted.

Sauce Rémoulade

2 hard-boiled egg yolks
2 raw egg yolks
salt and black pepper
1 Tbs *Moutarde de Dijon* (*Grey Poupon* for
    preference)
2 Tbs white wine vinegar
2 Tbs tarragon vinegar
½ pt olive oil
6–8 Tbs sour cream (optional)

Mash the hard-boiled egg yolks in a mortar, and beat in the
raw egg yolks. Pound until a smooth creamy mixture, then
add a pinch of salt and black pepper and the mustard. Continue to beat while you add the vinegar gradually, then the
oil, drop by drop, as for a mayonnaise. When all is finished,
taste and adjust seasoning (it should taste quite strongly of
mustard and vinegar). Beat in the sour cream if you want a
lighter sauce, or omit. Serves 4–6. Serve with shredded
celeriac; hard-boiled eggs; or vegetable salads.

Cold Sour Cream Sauce

¼ pt carton sour cream
½ gill tinned *vichysoisse*
2 Tbs tomato ketchup
2 shakes Tabasco
lemon juice (about ½ lemon)

Mix all the ingredients together, beat until smooth with an
electric beater or rotary whisk, and adjust seasoning to taste.
Chill. Makes enough for 3–4. An excellent sauce for salads
of raw or cooked vegetables; also good with shellfish.

Sauce Vinaigrette I

salt and black pepper
3 Tbs olive oil
1 Tbs white wine vinegar

Put a pinch of salt and three or four turns of the peppermill in a small bowl and add the oil and vinegar. Beat well to amalgamate. This simplest form of vinaigrette is also known as French dressing.

Sauce Vinaigrette II

2 Tbs finely chopped onion
2 Tbs finely chopped parsley
1 Tbs finely chopped chives, when available
salt and black pepper
1 clove garlic
½ tsp sugar
½ tsp French mustard
2 Tbs white wine vinegar *or* 1 Tbs wine
    vinegar and 1 Tbs tarragon vinegar
5 Tbs olive oil

Put the chopped onion and herbs, a pinch of salt, about four turns of the peppermill, the crushed garlic, the sugar and the mustard in a bowl and add the vinegar slowly, beating with a wooden spoon. Add the oil gradually, beating until well mixed with the vinegar. Serves 6. This delicious sauce should be thick with onion and herbs; it is very good with boiled beef, either hot or cold. With the addition of a few chopped capers, it becomes the Italian *salsa verde*. Another good addition is one or two hard-boiled eggs, finely chopped.

Sauce Vinaigrette III

2 eggs
salt and black pepper
mustard
5 Tbs olive oil
2 Tbs white wine vinegar

Cook the eggs exactly 5 minutes in boiling salted water, and cool immediately in cold water. When cold, shell them carefully. Cut them in half and tip the yolks into a small bowl (do this over the bowl as they should still be runny).

Stir with a wooden spoon and mix in a pinch of salt, black pepper and mustard. Add the oil gradually, stirring all the time. Then add the vinegar. Taste for seasoning, chop the egg whites and mix those into the sauce also. Good with a green salad.

Sauce Vinaigrette IV

1 hard-boiled egg
salt and black pepper
½ tsp made mustard
1 Tbs finely chopped parsley
4 Tbs olive oil
1 Tbs white wine vinegar

Mash the yolk of the hard-boiled egg, and beat it with a pinch of salt, black pepper, mustard and parsley. Add the oil gradually, then the vinegar. Beat until smooth, then add the finely chopped white of egg. Serves 4. Serve poured over a green salad.

Spinach Sauce

½ lb spinach *or* ½ lb frozen chopped spinach
1 oz butter
1 Tbs flour
¼ pt milk
¼ pt thin cream
salt and black pepper
nutmeg

Cook the spinach, drain very well and chop. Melt the butter, stir in the flour, add the heated milk and the cream, stir until smooth and season well. Add a pinch of grated nutmeg. Stir in the chopped spinach. Put in the blender, then return to the cleaned pan to re-heat. Taste for seasoning, and add a little extra milk if too thick. This sauce is a pretty pale green, and ideally should be served in a white bowl. Serve over soft-boiled eggs or stuffed pancakes.

Cold Tomato Sauce

¾ lb tomatoes
¼ pt mayonnaise, made with lemon juice if
   possible
¼ pt sour cream
1 clove garlic
1 tsp onion juice (put through garlic press)
salt and black pepper
lemon juice

Make as for TOMATO ICE (see p. 173), but chill instead of freezing. Serve with cold shellfish, cold stuffed vegetables, cold mousses and aspics, etc.

Frozen Tomato Sauce

Make as above, and put in freezer until semi-frozen. (About 1½–2 hours.) Then beat with a fork until mushy and serve in a chilled sauce-boat. Good with fried *goujons* of sole, hot cucumber or courgette fritters, hot spinach soufflé, steamed spinach or broccoli rings, hot timbales, etc. An iced sauce can be excellent when served with very hot dry food, like fritters, but both foods must be at the extremes of temperature for a complete contrast, and they must be served quickly.

Quick Tomato Sauce (Hot or Cold)

½ lb tomatoes
¼ pt sour cream
salt and black pepper

Skin the tomatoes and put them in the blender with the sour cream. Purée and add salt and black pepper to taste. For a hot sauce, heat gently without allowing to reach boiling point. For a cold sauce, serve as it is, or chill in the refrigerator. Serves 4–6. Good with stuffed vegetables, rice dishes, green timbales or soufflés.

Thick Tomato Sauce

¾ lb tomatoes
1 small onion
1 oz butter
salt and black pepper
sugar

Melt the butter and cook the chopped onion until golden. Skin the tomatoes and chop coarsely. Add to the onion and cook gently for 8 minutes. Season with salt, black pepper and a pinch of sugar. Serves 3–4. This sauce can be served with a timbale of green peas.

Spicy Tomato Sauce

4 oz Philadelphia cream cheese
¼ pt buttermilk
1–2 tsp lemon juice
salt and black pepper
1 Tbs condensed tomato purée
a few drops Tabasco *or* other chilli sauce

Cut the cheese in small pieces and put in the blender with the buttermilk. Blend until smooth then add lemon juice, salt and black pepper, and tomato purée to taste and blend again. Add a few drops Tabasco and taste. When seasoning is correct, heat in a small pan without allowing to boil, or chill in the refrigerator, depending on whether you want a hot or cold sauce. Makes a scant ½ pt. Good as a cold sauce for shellfish, cucumber dishes or salads of white fish.

Smooth Tomato Sauce

½ pt tomato purée (not condensed)
1 oz butter
2 Tbs flour
¼ pt chicken stock
¼ pt thin cream
salt and black pepper

To make the tomato purée, either drain a 14-oz can of
tomatoes and put through the medium mesh of a vegetable
mill, or peel and chop 1½ lb fresh tomatoes, stew in butter
for 20 minutes and sieve. Melt the butter and stir in the
flour. Heat the stock and pour on; stir until smooth and well
blended. Add the tomato purée and bring to the boil. Simmer for 5 minutes, then add the cream and season to taste
with salt and black pepper.

Watercress Sauce

1 bunch watercress
½ pt chicken stock
½ oz butter
1 Tbs flour
½ gill cream (*or* more according to taste)
salt and black pepper

Chop the watercress coarsely and simmer in the stock for
5 minutes. Pour into the blender, or push through the fine
mesh of a vegetable mill. Melt the butter, stir in the flour
and cook for 2–3 minutes, stirring constantly. Pour in the
watercress and stock mixture, and stir until blended. Simmer gently for a few minutes, then add the cream. Season
with salt and black pepper. Serves 4–6. This pretty green
sauce is excellent poured over a dish of *oeufs mollets* or
poached eggs.

Yoghurt and Cream Dressing

¼ pt yoghurt
¼ pt thin cream
½ tsp salt
black pepper
¼ tsp sugar
4–6 Tbs lemon juice

Beat the yoghurt and the cream together until blended. Add
the seasonings and lemon juice to taste. Serves 6. A useful
dressing for salads, as it is not too rich.

Vegetable Encyclopedia

Agar-Agar

A gelatinous substance derived from various seaweeds; until
recently this was eaten as food only in the Far East, while in
Europe it has been used in chemical laboratories. However
it is now sold in health food shops as a substitute for gelatine.
It has a natural gelatinous quality and, like all seaweeds, but
unlike gelatine, is full of iron and other minerals. Another
advantage over gelatine is that the liquid to be jellified does
not need to be heated to a high temperature so the vitamin
content of, say, fruit or vegetable juices need not be lost. It
has no taste of its own, so can be put to any purpose. In the
East it is used by swallows for building their nests, thus is
one of the ingredients of birds' nest soup.

Artichoke, Globe
[Lat. *Cynara scolymus*, Fr. *Artichaut*]

This succulent vegetable is the flower of a decorative thistle.
Although a native of North Africa, it grows happily in
Europe and North America. It is a very handsome plant of
delicate greyish-green, with spiky leaves, thick stems and
flower heads of differing shapes according to the variety.
Even from a purely visual point of view, it is an asset to any
garden, but it demands a lot of space. In Europe it is in
season throughout the summer. There are numerous different varieties, some producing flat round heads with
smooth-edged leaves, like the Brittany artichoke; others with
more pointed heads and sharp spiky leaves, like the Paris
artichoke. A good choice for most gardens is the French
Gros Vert de Laon. Interesting varieties not to be found in
England are the small Florence artichoke, the Venice artichoke, and the variety known as *Violet du Midi*. The tender
little flower heads of the Florence artichoke can be boiled
and eaten whole, as is often done in restaurants in Rome and
other Italian cities. But it is useless to attempt this with our
own garden artichokes by picking them while still very

small; the flowers must be allowed to mature in order for the fleshy edible base of the leaves to form.

In many recipes only the delicate *fond d'artichaut* is called for. This may seem wasteful to city dwellers who have to pay shop prices, but it is a different matter for those who grow their own. The term refers in fact to the actual bottom of the artichoke, while *coeur d'artichaut* means the bottom with the innermost tender leaves still adhering to it, the choke having been removed. The bottoms alone can be used for a number of elegant dishes such as tiny soufflés, bases for purées of chopped vegetables, *Eggs Sardou*, scrambled eggs with chopped truffles, as part of the French dish *Filets de Sole Murat*, as garnishes, or as one of the ingredients of a salad. Whole artichokes are always served at the start of a meal. Usually simply boiled, they are served either hot, with melted butter, or cold, with a sauce vinaigrette or mayonnaise. Rich in iron and other minerals, they are very sustaining and the large ones practically make a meal in themselves.

To prepare: Trim the stalks of the artichoke, remove any discoloured outer leaves, wash well under a running tap, and leave to soak for 15 minutes in cold water. Drain upside down in a colander before cooking. Some people trim off the sharp ends of the leaves with sharp scissors; this has the advantage of reducing them in size if you do not have a large enough pot in which to cook them.

There are two ways to prepare the *fond d'artichaut*. I find it easier to cook the artichoke first, then discard the leaves and choke when they are cool enough to handle. Some people prefer to cut off all the leaves and most of the stem before cooking, leaving only the choke to be removed afterwards. To cook either whole artichokes or the bases alone, bring a very large pan of salted water to the boil and throw in the drained artichokes. Bring back to the boil and cook briskly for 35–50 minutes, according to size. Test to see if they are cooked by pulling away one of the outer leaves; if it comes away from the head without undue pressure, they are ready. If still in doubt you can pierce the centre of the base with a fine skewer. As soon as they are cooked, lift them out and drain upside down in a colander. If cooking the choke alone the timing will probably be about 30–35 minutes; test with a skewer.

If the artichokes are to be eaten hot, they should be served on a flat dish with the sauce in a separate bowl. They look elegant wrapped in a white linen napkin. In restaurants the choke is sometimes removed with a narrow spoon and some of the sauce poured into the centre of the artichoke, but I prefer the simpler method. If they are to be eaten cold, they are at their best when they have only just cooled, about one hour after cooking. They are also good eaten tepid. If you are using only the bottoms, they must be sprinkled with lemon juice to prevent them discolouring.

Artichoke, Japanese
[Lat. *Stachys affinis*, Fr. *Crosnes*]

Also known as the Chinese artichoke, this curious bulbous root used to be quite common in England, but I have not been able to discover any trace of it in recent times. Nonetheless it is still a popular winter vegetable in France. A root vegetable with a delicate flavour, it is best eaten soon after being lifted from the ground. Like Jerusalem artichokes, they are difficult to clean; perhaps this led to their decline in popularity.
To prepare: Scrub the artichokes well before cooking to remove all earth. Do not attempt to peel them until after cooking. To cook cover with cold water, add salt, bring to the boil and cook for 15–20 minutes. Drain and rub in a coarse cloth with some coarse salt to remove the skins. Toss in melted butter to reheat, sprinkle with chopped parsley and serve. Alternatively, cover with a cream sauce, or a sauce mornay and gratiné under a hot grill (this only in the case of the sauce mornay).

Artichoke, Jerusalem
[Lat. *Helianthus tuberosus*, Fr. *Topinambour*]

The Jerusalem artichoke is a native of North America where it was first recorded as having been seen in Massachusetts in 1605. It was taken to France shortly afterwards, then to England. The name has remained something of a mystery; 'artichoke' is taken to refer to the slight similarity in flavour between this root and the bottom of the globe artichoke, while 'Jerusalem' is believed to be a corruption of the Italian word for sunflower, *girasole*. It is an annual, each year producing tall stems, and curious misshapen tuberous growths on the roots, which are the edible part. It makes a useful winter vegetable, as the tubers can be lifted any time from October until February. They should be left in the ground until they are needed, as they quickly become dry and shrivelled. They are not affected by frost as long as they are left in the ground, so it is pointless to lift and store them. They are very nourishing and rich in carbohydrates.

To prepare: Jerusalem artichokes are extremely difficult to clean, some varieties being even more uneven and knobbly in shape than others. I find the best way is to wash and scrub them well before cooking, and peel them afterwards. Just cover with cold salted water, and boil until tender, which will take about 15 minutes. Drain them and rub off the skins as soon as they are cool enough to handle. They are then ready to be served in a variety of different ways. They make an excellent purée, either alone, or mixed with an equal part of mashed potatoes, or other root vegetables: carrots, turnips, swedes, etc. They can also be made into an excellent soup in this way, in which case you should preserve the water in which they cooked. They also make a delicious first course, cut in thick slices and covered with a sauce hollandaise. They can also be dressed with a sauce mornay, or simply cut in chunks and tossed in butter with chopped parsley.

Asparagus
[Lat. *Asparagus officinalis*, Fr. *Asperge*]

Asparagus has been esteemed as one of the greatest delicacies of the table since Roman times. There are a great many different varieties, each prized in its own country. The French and Belgians like the thick white stalks ending in pale purple tips, known as Argenteuil, while in England the thinner green variety, closer to the wild one, is preferred. Both are in fact excellent in their own ways. It is a difficult plant to grow successfully and it will only tolerate light sandy soils. If you are lucky enough to grow your own, or to live near an asparagus farm, the misshapen stalks, and the thinnings, known as 'sprue', can be obtained cheaply and made into excellent dishes. Imported asparagus can be

202

bought in the shops from early spring onwards, but it quickly loses its flavour once cut, and it is better to wait for native asparagus to appear in June and July. It is rich in minerals and vitamins, and should be cooked in the minimum of water in order to preserve these as well as the flavour.

To prepare: Trim the asparagus stalks to an equal length, wash the green tips under running water, and using a sharp knife scrape the woody white part of the stem. Then tie the asparagus in bundles with fine string, leaving long ends with which to lower them in and out of the water. Ideally, asparagus should be cooked upright, with water coming halfway up the stems. Special pans are made for this purpose, but an alternative method can be devised using a double boiler, with the top half inverted over the bottom, so that only the stems are in water, while the tender tips cook more gently in the steam. Failing this they can be cooked horizontally in a rectangular pan with a strainer which makes it easier to lift them out of the water without breaking any of the tips. They should be put into already boiling, lightly salted water, and will take about 10–20 minutes to cook, depending on the thickness. The best way to test them is to hold one stalk upright: the tip should start to bend over about two thirds of the way up. Alternatively, pierce the stalk halfway up with a skewer, but do not expect the very bottom of the stalk to become soft. Lift them out of the water and drain well.

Asparagus is almost always served, either hot or cold, at the start of a meal, but the tips are also used as a garnish for many main dishes.

When at its best asparagus should be served as simply as possible, that is to say, well drained, laid on a flat dish or wrapped in a white linen napkin, with a jug of melted butter handed separately and a bowl of salt. For a more elaborate dish, it can be served with a sauce hollandaise, or a sauce maltaise (a sauce hollandaise with the juice of a blood orange squeezed into it). In Belgium it is often served with melted butter and a plate of halved hard-boiled eggs; each person takes half an egg, and mashes the yolk into some of the melted butter on their plate, which gives a delicious slightly thicker sauce. They are also good served cold, with a sauce vinaigrette, or covered with a sauce mornay and gratiné under the grill. Another good dish is to beat a couple of egg whites into the sauce mornay and put the dish in a hot oven until the sauce has risen slightly and set like a soufflé. When the tips alone are used as garnishes the English green variety is the best.

Aubergine
[Lat. *Solanum melongena*, Fr. *Aubergine*]

Although we connect the aubergine with Mediterranean cookery, it was originally a native of India and parts of Asia. It was introduced to England in the late sixteenth century, but did not become popular until after the Second World War, when a great vogue for Mediterranean cooking swept our shores. It is virtually impossible to grow in England, as it demands much sunshine, and is grown extensively all around the shores of the Mediterranean, from Spain, through Southern France, Italy, Greece, Turkey and the countries of the Middle East, and along the northern coast of Africa. It produces a fruit of rare beauty, purple in colour and varying in shape from round to oval and globular forms. There is also a white variety, which must have given rise to its American name (egg-plant), as it is curiously like the egg of some gigantic exotic bird, with its translucent glow, but it is more often used for decorative purposes than for cooking. As they are generally imported, they are almost always available. They are one of the main ingredients of Mediterranean cuisine, usually cooked in oil, either alone, or combined with tomatoes, peppers, onions or courgettes.

To prepare: The stalks should be removed with a sharp knife, and the aubergine washed or wiped with a damp cloth. According to how they are to be cooked, they are then cut in halves or quarters, sliced or chopped, usually with the peel left on. They are then sprinkled with salt and left to drain in a colander for about half an hour; this gets rid of the slightly bitter taste they sometimes have. If possible choose fairly young ones, before the seeds have had time to form. Before cooking rinse off the salt and pat dry in a cloth or soft paper.

Aubergines can be cooked whole, baked in the oven like potatoes. They will take about 45 minutes at a moderate temperature, and can be tested with a skewer. This is usually done when only the inner pulp is wanted for a purée, as in

the Middle Eastern hors-d'oeuvre *Melanzata* (see p. 144).
They can also be boiled, whole or cut in half, and cooked
under the grill. But in most cases they are cut in slices, unpeeled, and fried in oil in a frying pan. They have to be done
in batches, a few at a time, as they must all be in one layer,
so they take some time to do, and consume huge quantities
of oil. After cooking drain them on soft paper and keep in a
warm place until needed. They are one of the main ingredients of ratatouille, stewed in oil with tomatoes, onions,
peppers and courgettes, and also make a delicious gratin
mixed with sliced tomatoes and cooked in the oven. They
are an extremely versatile vegetable and can be used for
stuffing or alternatively, since they look pretty and can be
eaten equally well hot or cold, they can be stuffed with
mixtures of meat and rice, or rice and pine nuts.

Avocado Pears
[Lat. *Persea gratissima*, Fr. *Avocat*]

Although this is strictly speaking the fruit of the avocado
tree, it is usually treated as a vegetable and I am therefore
including it as such. A native of South America, it has a
strange flesh of soft texture and subtle flavour. It is full of
vitamins and minerals, and an extremely nourishing food.
High in calories, it should be avoided by those on diets.
Avocados should be chosen with care, held gently in the
hand and only the lightest pressure applied to determine
the degree of ripeness. They should be slightly soft at the
end, and have an all-over feeling that is hard to describe –
a mixture of firmness approaching softness – and be
without bruises or black marks, when they are ready to
eat. They can be bought while still unripe, and allowed to
ripen on a sunny window-sill. The stone can be grown into
an attractive plant by suspending it in the neck of a bottle
with two toothpicks, so that the base is in water. When the
stone has germinated and the root grown down some inches
into the water, it should be planted in a pot.

To prepare: Avocado pears are almost always eaten raw, and
are best when served in conjunction with a sharp taste to
contrast with their own blandness. I think they are best
eaten quite simply, cut in half, the stone removed and the
cavity filled with a French dressing, or cut up in slices and

added to a green salad. They can be made into a purée by pushing through a sieve or blender, and incorporated into more elaborate dishes, such as cold soups, mousses, jellies and moulds. They are sometimes combined with mayonnaise, but I find this a mistake as they are already rich. However they are to be used, they should be sprinkled with lemon juice as soon as they are cut if not to be consumed immediately, or the flesh will discolour. This also applies to dishes made from avocado flesh.

Bamboo Shoots
[Lat. *Phyllostachys pubescens*]

These are the tender young shoots of the bamboo cane, or bambusa. A native of Malaya, it can be grown in temperate parts of England and the United States. The shoots form one of the main ingredients of Chinese cooking, where they are used in their fresh state, but they are also canned and sold extensively throughout England and America.
To prepare: Bamboo shoots can be sautéed or steamed like any other tender vegetable such as asparagus or seakale, or eaten raw in salads.

Batavia
[Lat. *Cichorium endivia*, Fr. *Escarole*]

Also known as escarole, batavia is a variety of endive. The shape and the colour are similar, with pale yellow leaves in the centre surrounded by darker green leaves, but the leaves are broader and rounder in shape, and less curly. It is in season at the same time as the endive, and has a similar though less bitter taste.
To prepare: Batavia can be treated in exactly the same way as endive, and eaten either raw, as is most often done, or cooked.

Bean Curd
[Lat. *Glycine max*]

Bean curd is made from the soya bean, and has the same high vitamin content. It is extremely cheap and nourishing, and forms one of the basic foods for the Chinese. It can be bought in Chinese shops and is easy to cook and very versatile, combining well with most other foods – fish, meat or other vegetables.

To prepare: Bean curd is usually deep fried. It should be cut in cubes about 1 inch square, dropped into hot oil and fried until crisp and golden brown on the outside and soft on the inside. It can also be boiled.

Bean Sprouts
[Lat. *Glycine max*]

These are the young shoots of a variety of soya bean, and are used extensively in Chinese cookery. They can be bought in tins or packets throughout most parts of England, or they can easily be grown at home after the fashion of mustard and cress, as any waiter in a Chinese restaurant will tell you. In fact what are often given in Chinese restaurants as bean sprouts, are pea sprouts, which are even more tender and quickly cooked.

To prepare: Bean sprouts can be steamed in a matter of 4–5 minutes over boiling stock or water, or simmered for 4–5 minutes in liquid. Alternatively they can be cooked in a sauté pan in a very little hot oil for 5 minutes, stirred now and then.

Beans, Azuki

A native of Japan, this tiny hard red bean is grown extensively throughout China and Japan. In the East the beans are cooked in both their fresh and dried states, but we only ever find them dried, in health food or Oriental shops.

To prepare: The dried azuki beans take an extremely long time to cook, and should be soaked beforehand for several hours, or overnight. After soaking they will probably take about 2 hours to become soft.

Beans, Broad
[Lat. *Faba vulgaris*, Fr. *Fève*]

Broad beans came originally from the East, but they have been grown in England for hundreds of years. They are frequently referred to in the earliest English cookery books in existence, published in the fourteenth century.

To prepare: If they are picked while still very young, broad beans can be eaten raw, as part of a selection of crudités; they should be left in their pods and served with a bowl of salt. At this stage they can also be cooked in their pods, which are still tender enough to be eaten. A little later they should be podded and cooked as simply and quickly as possible, that is to say thrown into a pan of lightly salted boiling water, just enough to cover them, and cooked for only a few moments until just tender, then drained and served with a knob of melting butter. At this stage I prefer not to add any extra flavouring in the way of herbs. When they are fully grown but still young, they can either be tossed, after boiling, in parsley butter, served in a parsley sauce, or sprinkled with chopped chervil, parsley or summer savory. The latter is the classic French accompaniment to broad beans, but I prefer chervil. When older, they should be skinned either before or after cooking. Alternatively they can be pushed through a vegetable mill, which holds back the tough outer skin, to make a delicious light green purée. Stir in butter or cream, salt and black pepper. This makes the perfect accompaniment to dishes of hot boiled ham or bacon.

Beans, Coco

An excellent variety of French bean, the coco bean is also a decorative plant. It has small purple flowers, and the bean pods are a dark purplish-black which turns to green when they are cooked. It can be grown as a climbing bean, or in a dwarf variety; there is also a white coco bean but I think much of its charm lies in its unusual colour.

To prepare: If picked while still young, the whole pods can be cooked and eaten like string beans; later, the beans can be podded and cooked like broad beans; the third crop can be dried and stored for winter use, like haricot beans.

Beans, French
[Lat. *Phaseolus vulgaris*, Fr. *Haricots verts*]

Also known as string beans, these are grown for their pods rather than their seeds. They originated in South America, and did not appear in Europe until the sixteenth century. Originally a climbing plant, dwarf forms have now been introduced which save space and labour in the garden. As they are generally grown for the sake of the pod, they should be gathered while still young, before the seeds have had time to grow.

To prepare: At an early stage French beans are best cooked whole; the only preparation necessary is to nip off the ends before throwing them into a pot of lightly salted boiling water, just enough to cover, and cooking briskly for the short time – 5–10 minutes – needed to leave them still crisp but tender. They should be quickly drained and tossed in melting butter. Young beans are also good when steamed. If, however, you have too many in the garden to eat at one time, they can be treated like haricot beans and left until the inner bean is grown, then either cooked like broad beans, or dried and kept for winter use. (See Haricot Beans, below.) In England they are usually served as an accompaniment to the main course, but in France and Italy they are often served as a dish in their own right, either after the main course, or as an hors-d'oeuvre. They can be garnished with chopped onion or bacon, or mixed in equal quantities with fresh haricot beans. They also make a delicious cold dish, dressed while still hot in an oily vinaigrette, and served before completely cold. They are quite high in mineral content and in vitamin B; when dried the beans become even more valuable as a source of vitamins.

Beans, Haricot

Although these are usually thought of in their dried state, they can also be eaten fresh, as they are in France and Italy, and are quite delicious. Every vegetable garden should include a few of these versatile beans – such as 'granda' in England, or 'white half runner' in the United States – as they are so useful. Firstly, the pods can be picked while very young and used as string beans. Later, when the seeds have matured, they can be cooked and eaten fresh, while a third crop can be picked and dried for winter use. They are in fact essential for making that excellent Provençal soup, *Soupe au pistou*, when for a few weeks only the two sorts of beans overlap, and one can pick both the pods and the white beans,

209

both of which are needed. Unless we dry our own beans, we are very much at the mercy of the shopkeeper, for the quality of dried vegetables depends greatly on their age and the length of time they have been in store. It is well worth stocking up from a reliable foreign shop in the autumn, when the fresh crops come in. My favourites are the medium-sized kidney-shaped beans, called *soissons*, or *cannellini*, depending on whether they come from France or Italy. I much prefer them to the English varieties, the tiny 'haricot' or the giant 'butter bean'. I also love the pale green flageolet, and sometimes make a pretty dish of mixed green and white beans.

To prepare: There are two schools of thought about the cooking of dried beans: some people soak them for hours beforehand, others cook them in two stages. For years I soaked them for three or four hours, but recently I have changed to the other method. I first wash them well in a colander, throwing away any wrinkled or discoloured beans, then put them in a large pan well covered with cold water, unsalted. I bring it slowly to the boil, then cover the pan and turn off the heat. After one hour they are ready for the final cooking, either in the same liquid, with an onion, a carrot, a stalk of celery, a bay leaf and a few stalks of parsley, or in stock. Bring them back to the boil and simmer gently until they are tender; another hour's cooking should be enough unless they are old. Do not add salt until they are nearly done as it makes them tough. They are extremely useful as a source of vitamins during the winter; for some reason they gain in nutritional value through the drying process. They are also cheap and filling food for cold weather. They make an excellent soup (see p. 19) and a delicious accompaniment to roast lamb, when tossed in a tomato and onion sauce with plenty of garlic. In summer, I use them for the Italian hors-d'oeuvre, *tonno e fagioli*, mixed with a sauce vinaigrette and slices of raw onion, with chunks of tunny fish piled on top.

Beans, Kidney

In England this can be taken to mean the runner bean, but in America it would usually mean the dried red bean that forms a central part of Mexican cookery.

Beans, Lima

[Lat. *Phaseolus lunatus*, Fr. *Haricot de Lima*]

As their name suggests, these are a native of South America, and have never been successfully grown in England, or in most parts of Europe for that matter. They require a great deal of sun to ripen fully, and are the nearest American equivalent to the English broad bean, which will not grow in the United States. Originally a tall climbing plant like the English runner bean, they have now been developed in dwarf bush varieties, taking less space in the garden. Excellent varieties are 'Fordhook', or 'Henderson's Dwarf', a small bean that is becoming more popular than the old-fashioned larger bean. Some varieties, such as 'Fordhook', or 'Baby Fordhook', produce a round potato-shaped bean; others, such as 'Improved Bush Lima', give a flatter bean that some people prefer.

To prepare: Bring a little lightly salted water to the boil in a saucepan, throw in the beans and cover the pan. Simmer until tender – about 30 minutes – then drain off the water and add a knob of butter, or some cream, or sour cream. Season well with salt and black pepper and serve immediately.

To make the Indian dish succotash, mix the cooked beans with an equal amount of freshly cooked corn. Add butter, salt and black pepper, and serve. Do not attempt to substitute canned lima beans for fresh ones, as they are too starchy to mix with the already starchy corn.

Beans, Runner

[Lat. *Phaseolus multiflorus*, Fr. *Haricot d'Espagne*]

This must be the most commonly grown vegetable in England; not only does every cottage garden seem to have a crop lasting all summer long but every village shop has an excess for sale, while country folk are continually making presents of them to their neighbours. They are extremely easy to grow, and make a very decorative plant, covered with red flowers, but they demand a lot of space and regular attention in tying them to their supports as they grow so very quickly. City dwellers returning from a visit to the country are wise to bring back a stock of freshly picked beans with them. If recently picked, they can be kept successfully for up to a week in the refrigerator without losing their crispness. Outside England they are not very popular. I have certainly never seen them in France or Italy, where the so-called 'French bean' is preferred.

To prepare: If the pods are picked while still very young they can be cooked whole like string beans, with only the ends removed. When older they must have the strings running along each side pulled off before being cut into square chunks. The traditional English habit of cutting the bean into thin shreds is completely unnecessary; not only does it make them taste watery, it reduces their vitamin content to almost nil. The chunks should be thrown into a little fast boiling salted water, and cooked until only just tender, about 8 minutes. Then they should be quickly drained, tossed in a knob of melting butter and seasoned with salt and black pepper.

Beans, Soya
[Lat. *Glycine max*]

This plant is a native of China, where it is still grown extensively with almost as many varieties as we have climbing and bush beans. In recent years it has become extremely popular in the United States, but it will not grow in England, as the climate is not suitable. It is the most nutritious and easily digested of all the beans, and has become one of the favourite foods of 'health food' addicts. It contains large amounts of vitamins B and E, plus a very high degree of minerals, especially calcium and iron. It is richer in protein and fat than almost any other food, including meat, yet is low in starch, and thus it is ideal for certain diets. It is the basis of soya sauce, and is also made into a flour and an oil.

To prepare: The plant is similar to the French or runner bean, and the beans themselves can be eaten either fresh or dried, in exactly the same manner as haricot beans.

Beans, String

See BEANS, FRENCH.

Beetroot
[Lat. *Beta vulgaris*, Fr. *Betterave*]

A native of Southern Europe, the beetroot plays an important part in the cuisine of Poland and Russia. There are an amazing number of different varieties: one reference book illustrates eighteen totally different plants, ranging in shape and size from a giant carrot-shaped root to a flat squat object like a tiny turnip, and lists many more. More popular in the United States than in England, where it is hard to buy raw beetroot in the shops (they are usually sold already boiled), both countries seem to favour the round variety with dark red flesh. For those with gardens, it is possible to grow a beetroot with white flesh which I have never seen in any shop – 'white ball' in the United States, 'snowhite' in England – or yellow flesh – 'golden beet' in England – but the latter looks too much like a swede to have much appeal for me. The white variety does have the advantage of not bleeding and discolouring other foods, thus seeming more suitable for salads.

To prepare: Twist off the leaves carefully (if young and fresh, they can be cooked separately and served as a green vegetable; they are even richer in vitamins than the roots). Scrub the beetroot gently under a running tap to remove all the dirt, being careful not to puncture the skin. Buy small ones whenever possible, as large ones take forever to cook. One cannot cut them in pieces without losing the colour except by cooking in the minimum of water, so that it has all evaporated by the end of the cooking and the colour remains in the beetroot. This is quite tricky, however, as they still take a considerable time to cook, and the water has to be replenished to prevent it boiling away entirely. To cook in the normal fashion put in a large pan covered with cold water, add salt and bring to the boil. Cook until soft when pierced with a skewer – at this stage they will not bleed. Allow up to 2 hours for small roots. Alternatively, they can be baked in the oven like potatoes, taking 1½–2 hours. After cooking, the beetroot can be cut in thick slices or chunks and tossed in melted butter or thick cream. Serve these with a handful of chopped fresh herbs – dill is particularly good with beetroot – thrown over them and seasoned well with salt and black pepper. Already cooked beetroot can be cut in slices or coarsely grated and re-heated in a sauté pan, with cream and herbs, or butter, or sour cream, and plenty of salt and black pepper. Be careful they do not stick to the pan as they have a high sugar content and 'catch' easily. Beetroot makes an excellent soup, not only the well-known *bortsch*, the classic soup of Russia, but also delicate summer consommés, to serve hot, chilled or jellied.

Borecole
See KALE.

Bracken
[Lat. *Pteris aquilina*, Fr. *Fougère a l'aigle*]

The proper name, pteris, comes from the Greek word meaning feather, or wing. Bracken is the common fern, growing wild over huge areas of the British Isles and North America. If the shoots are picked while still very young, not more than two or three inches high, the tightly curled heads, known as 'fiddleheads', can be cooked and eaten. They are rich in potash, and have a curious, slightly bitter taste that is quite pleasant.
To prepare: The heads should be flung into a pan of boiling lightly salted water and cooked for about 7 minutes, then drained, tossed in butter and eaten immediately. If they are kept waiting, the bitter taste becomes more pronounced and they lose their texture.

Broccoli
[Lat. *Brassica oleracea botrytis*, Fr. *Brocoli*]

Broccoli is a form of cauliflower, in season during the winter and early spring, unlike the cauliflower proper which is not available in England until the summer. Both vegetables are cultivated from the wild cabbage; broccoli was the earlier of the two, and grew originally in Italy, where it is still enormously popular. It is rich in vitamin C, and has a more delicate flavour than the cauliflower; it is also easier to grow for the amateur gardener. There are two main types, each comprising many different varieties. The earlier form was the sprouting variety, each individual shoot bearing dark

214

green leaves and a flowering head. The green sprouting one is also known by its Italian name *calabrese*, while the purple sprouting variety is sometimes called 'asparagus broccoli'. Later developments produced a large-headed variety with a compact flower, like a small cauliflower except in colour, the flower being usually purple or green, although there are also white varieties.

To prepare: Sprouting broccoli is not easy to cook to perfection, as the tough stalks take far longer to cook than the delicate head. I find the best method is to cook it in two stages: chop the stalks and put them in a fairly broad pan containing just enough lightly salted boiling water to barely cover them, replace the lid and cook for 5 minutes. Then lay the flower heads whole on the top and leave them to cook in the steam. After another 6–7 minutes both parts of the vegetable should be tender; if the heads are ready first, they can be lifted out carefully and kept warm while the stalks finish cooking. They should then be drained and arranged round the edges of the serving dish with the flower heads in the middle. Melted butter seasoned with salt and black pepper should then be poured over all. Alternatively, broccoli can be very successfully cooked by steaming, allowing twice as long for the stalks as for the flower heads.

The large-headed sort is much easier to cook, and should be treated like a small cauliflower. Leave it whole, just trimming off the end of the stalk and the outer leaves, and choose a pan that fits it neatly. Measure enough water to come half-way up the broccoli, then remove it while you bring the salted water to the boil. Put the broccoli in stalk downwards, cover the pan and cook until the stalk is just tender. Drain carefully and lay in a round serving dish. Melt some butter with salt and black pepper and pour over it, or have a sauce hollandaise in a separate bowl. Broccoli has a special affinity with eggs and butter, and is delicious served with sauces of this type, or with scrambled eggs.

Brussels Sprouts
[Lat. *Brassica oleracea bullata gemmifera*, Fr. *Chou de Bruxelles*]

This ungainly member of the cabbage family is not a decorative plant, unlike most varieties of cabbage, but is an extremely useful winter vegetable, in season from October until March. It was first developed in Belgium, as the name suggests, and did not come to England until the nineteenth century. It is rich in vitamins B and C, and has a good nutty flavour. The sprouts are borne along the length of the stems, which grow to a height of 1½–2 feet. Dwarf varieties have recently been developed to save space in smaller gardens. Unlike most other members of the same family, it does not form a head, but only a loose rosette of leaves at the top of the stem, which should be left until all the sprouts – there are usually two crops – have been picked. They should always be picked and eaten while still small and tight. All too often they are allowed to grow into small cabbages.

To prepare: Very small sprouts need little or no preparation beyond washing; the slightly larger ones should have the stem trimmed and cut with an X-shaped cross, so that the stalk will cook more quickly. Bring a large pan of salted water to the boil, and throw the sprouts in. Bring back to the boil as quickly as possible and cook briskly until tender, about 10 minutes. Drain well, and return to the pan to dry out over gentle heat. When all excess moisture has evaporated, add a generous knob of butter and grind plenty of salt and black pepper over them. Brussels sprouts are excellent if after draining they are quickly chopped with a long knife, returned to the pan and tossed in melting butter and salt and black pepper. They go particularly well with dishes of roast or grilled lamb.

Cabbage
[Lat. *Brassica oleracea*, Fr. *Chou*]

The name 'cabbage' covers an enormous family of plants that have been cultivated throughout Europe and western Asia since the earliest records. They were much used by the Romans, as much for their supposed medicinal qualities as for their nourishment. They include the cauliflower, broccoli, kale, Brussels sprout and kohlrabi, as well as the many different varieties of cabbage. Some have been developed for their leaves, others for their flower, root or sprouts, and some even for the stem of their leaves. There is also an ornamental cabbage with beautiful coloured leaves used for winter bedding out in flower gardens. Most of the cabbages are decorative plants, except the leggy Brussels sprout and

216

the swollen-rooted kohlrabi. I have divided the cabbages as we know them into the following categories to avoid confusion: green, white and red. (There is also the Chinese cabbage, which is a quite separate species.)

Cabbage, Green

This is the best-known of the cabbages; it grows particularly well in England as it favours a moist cool climate. It is rich in vitamins C, E and K, and in mineral salts which are all too often lost in the cooking. There are two main subdivisions of green cabbage: the smooth-leaved, and the curly-leaved, or Savoy, cabbage. The former is the more widely grown, but the Savoy is generally considered to have the more delicate flavour.

To prepare: Both types of green cabbage should be treated in the same way. Remove the leaves from the stem and wash carefully. Only the inner tender leaves should be used in my opinion, but if the tougher ones are to be included the stems should be cut out at their largest part (the base of the leaf), in the shape of a V. The leaves can then be left whole, torn into pieces 4 or 5 inches across, or chopped. Put a couple of inches of lightly salted water in a large pan and bring to the boil. When it bubbles, throw in the drained cabbage and cover the pan. Cook fairly rapidly, turning over the cabbage from time to time, and making sure the water does not boil away. As soon as the stems are tender but still crisp when pierced with a skewer, drain away the water, shaking the pan well to get rid of every drop. Return the pan with the cabbage still in it to a low heat, and stir about for a few minutes, to evaporate as much moisture as possible. When the cabbage is more or less dry, add a good lump of butter and plenty of salt and black pepper. Alternatively turn out onto a board and chop, returning to the pan with butter and seasonings. It can also be made into a purée by pushing through the coarse mesh of a vegetable mill, but this tends to become watery by forcing out the inevitable remaining liquid. It can also be simmered very gently in milk, then the milk reserved and thickened with a beaten egg yolk in the manner of a custard, seasoned with salt and black pepper, and poured back over the cabbage. This, surrounded with croûtons of toast or bread fried in butter, makes an excellent dish. For a more substantial dish such as is often seen in Central European cuisine, the whole cabbage or the individual leaves can be stuffed with a variety of different fillings. This makes a pretty and sustaining main course for a vegetable meal, especially when served with a contrasting sauce.

Cabbage, Red

A useful winter vegetable, the red cabbage is rich in vitamin C, especially when eaten raw. It forms a central part of the cuisine of Poland, Hungary, Austria and neighbouring central European countries, where it is often served as an accompaniment to game. It is also very good served with pork or boiled bacon, and with sausages.

To prepare: Red cabbage can be shredded finely and eaten raw in salads. Some people par-boil it to make it more digestible, but vinegar or lemon juice must be added to the water to preserve the colour, or it will turn an ugly mauve. I find boiling it makes such an unpleasant smell which quickly fills the house that I prefer to eat it raw, or not at all. In any case it should first be cut in quarters, and the outer leaves and central core removed. After washing and draining, the quarters can be thinly sliced with a sharp knife; I find this more satisfactory than using an electric shredder. It is now ready to be eaten raw or cooked, according to your recipe. The red cabbage responds to long slow cooking in the oven or on top of the stove, moistened with fat and some good stock. It is excellent with the addition of other flavours: chopped apples, crushed juniper berries, garlic and caraway seeds are good, as are a little wine vinegar, some sugar, or some yoghurt or sour cream added at the end of the cooking. (Yoghurt must be first mixed with a little flour to prevent it separating.) (For exact recipe, see p. 88.) Like *sauerkraut*, it improves by being made in advance and re-heated.

Cabbage, White

This is usually shredded, or very thinly sliced, and eaten raw. It makes the classic American dish, cole slaw, and is also good mixed with other grated raw vegetables, fruit and nuts. It goes a surprisingly long way, and a quarter of a head makes quite a substantial dish as it is very filling. It is rich in vitamin C. It is also made into the classic German dish, *sauerkraut* [Fr. *choucroute*], made from finely shredded white cabbage which has been pickled in brine. It is the national dish of Alsace, and many of the central European countries, such as Germany, Austria and Poland. Most families prepare their own version each year in a barrel, and consume it during the winter months. The pickling process makes it more easily digested than it would otherwise be; it can be well drained and rinsed and eaten raw as a salad. The most usual way of cooking it is a slow lengthy process in a heavy casserole in the oven, with additions of fat, stock, and juniper berries or caraway seeds. It is usually served with a variety of smoked and fresh meat, mostly pork: boiled ham or bacon, pigs' feet, sausages, either fresh or smoked, pork chops; any or all of these can be served on a huge platter of *sauerkraut*, surrounded with boiled potatoes. This extremely hearty meal is the speciality of many of the Paris brasseries, served with a variety of mustards. *Sauerkraut* also goes well with game, and is often served in Austria as an accompaniment to venison, wild boar or pheasant. It can be bought straight from the barrel in some foreign delicatessens, or in tins.

Cabbage, Chinese
[Lat. *Brassica pekinensis*]

This unusual vegetable is really more like a cos lettuce than a cabbage, and can be used in place of either.

To prepare: The crisp leaves can be shredded and eaten raw, as in cole slaw, or cooked quickly in the minimum of boiling salted water for only a few moments, and well drained. They can also be steamed or sautéed, as they are generally treated in Chinese restaurants. The leaves are also well suited to stuffing, being a more convenient shape than the round cabbage, and of a stronger consistency than the lettuce. They make a welcome appearance in the late summer, when the best of the early vegetables are over, and the autumn ones have not yet come.

Calabrese

The Italian name for green sprouting broccoli. See BROCCOLI.

Cardoon

[Lat. *Cynara cardunculus*, Fr. *Cardon*]

Like the globe artichoke, the cardoon is a member of the thistle family, and is a native of southern Europe. It was popular in England some two hundred years ago but is now rarely seen, although it is still much prized on the Continent, and quite common in the United States. The plants grow to an even larger size than the artichoke, and resemble a giant form of celery. Like celery, they need to be earthed up and tied in the autumn for winter eating. The variety most popular in France, the *Tours cardoon*, has very prickly leaves which makes it difficult to cultivate; the Spanish cardoon with spineless leaves is more popular. Like celery, both the stalks and the roots are edible.

To prepare: Cut the stalks into pieces of equal length and scrape off the outer skin, sprinkling lemon juice over the white flesh to prevent it discolouring. Cut off the outer covering of the root and rub lemon juice over it. The cardoon is best cooked like celery, only allow much more time. The stalks should be braised, or stewed slowly in stock or salted water. They may take 1½–2 hours to become tender. Some of the stock can then be used to make a sauce, the whole sprinkled with chopped parsley. They are also good served with a well-flavoured cream sauce, or a sauce mornay; alternatively they may be made into a purée by pushing through a sieve or vegetable mill, and mixing with an equal quantity of potato purée. Beat in some butter, a little cream, and season well with salt and black pepper.

Carrageen

[Lat. *Chondrus crispus*, Fr. *Mousse perlée d'Irlande*]

Also known as 'Irish Moss', this seaweed grows on the coasts of the British Isles, and parts of North America. Like all edible seaweeds, it is extremely rich in minerals, especially iodine. It has strong gelatinous qualities, and a commercially prepared form is sold in health food shops as a 'vegetable gelatine'. It is a dark purple or green in colour, and has many branches. It must be gathered in April and May, and very well washed, preferably in a running stream or rock pools, rinsed in fresh water and spread out in the sun to dry. It should be left out for several days, to be moistened by the rain and dew and dried and bleached by the sun. (If there is no rain during this period, it should have a bucket of fresh water poured over it every day.) When ready for use, it should have bleached a pale whitish colour, and the tough stems and ends should be trimmed off with kitchen scissors. Take it into the house to finish drying, and when it is quite brittle, it should be cut or broken in small pieces and stored in a dry place.

To prepare: The dried seaweed should be soaked for at least 30 minutes then put in a pan with three times its own bulk of water or milk. Simmer gently for 30 minutes, stirring occasionally. A pinch of salt should be added during the cooking, and a flavouring such as lemon rind, ginger or vanilla, if desired. After the cooking it should be strained to get rid of any pieces that have not dissolved, then it will set to a jelly. Sugar can be added to taste, while a beaten egg white or whipped cream can be folded in before it has set.

Carrots
[Lat. *Daucus carota*, Fr. *Carotte*]

A native of Europe, the wild carrot must have been growing in the British Isles for hundreds of years before the first cultivated variety was introduced during the seventeenth century. Carrots are in season all the year round, but the most delicious are the new carrots in the early summer. There are many different varieties of carrot, ranging from long thin tapering roots to short stumpy turnip-shaped ones. The colour also varies from a pale yellow to a dark reddish orange. The most popular in England and the United States is a medium-length orange root. A good all-round choice for the garden is the French 'Early Nantes' variety, which produces a 5–6 inch long root of a good colour and flavour. A more unusual one is the English 'Altringham' strain. Now more often seen in France than in England, it has an extremely long thin root growing up to 20 inches, with the unusual feature of growing about two inches of its root above the surface of the ground. Carrots are immensely rich in vitamin A, and possess quantities of vitamin C and minerals. All these precious nutrients are stored close to the surface of the root, which must be treated with care to conserve them. New carrots need only a light brushing under a running tap, while older ones should be scraped with a sharp knife, being careful to remove only the minimum of skin.

To prepare: When new, carrots are best cooked whole, in which case they should be covered with cold lightly salted water, brought to the boil, and cooked until tender, about 15–20 minutes. Drain and return to the pan with a knob of butter, a sprinkling of sugar, and serve with chopped parsley sprinkled over them. Older carrots are best cut in thin slices, or little matchstick-shaped pieces for really large ones. These pieces should be put in a pan with a very little cold water, just enough to cover the bottom of the pan, and a pinch of salt and sugar. Bring to the boil, cover the pan and cook gently for about 15 minutes, shaking the pan from time to time. Check now and again to see that all the water has not boiled away. After 10 minutes put in a knob of butter; after another 5 minutes the carrots should be tender or nearly so, while the cooking liquid should have reduced to a couple of spoonfuls of buttery juice. If there is still too much liquid, remove the carrots with a slotted spoon, and reduce by fast boiling until slightly thickened and syrupy. Taste to make sure it does not get too salty. Serve in their juice.

Raw carrots are the most rich in vitamins; they can either be made into a delicious juice with a juice extractor, or grated and served as a salad, either alone or mixed with other grated raw vegetables, such as celery, white cabbage, hard fruits like apples, and chopped nuts. The juice also can be drunk alone, or mixed with others like spinach, watercress or tomato. Carrots are also one of the most valuable flavouring vegetables for stocks and stews, while a sliced carrot is almost always included in a *court-bouillon* for poaching fish. They make excellent soups and purées, either alone, or mixed with other root vegetables. One of my favourite winter soups is made with an equal mixture of carrots, parsnips and turnips.

Cauliflower
[Lat. *Brassica oleracea botrytis*, Fr. *Chou-fleur*]

The cauliflower is a member of the cabbage family which has been developed for the sake of its flower, a compact white head surrounded by tender pale green leaves, with a delicate flavour which requires careful treatment in the kitchen.

To prepare: There are a choice of methods of cooking the cauliflower; the plant can be left whole, which looks pretty, or it can be divided into sprigs, which facilitates the cooking. If left whole, the stalk should be cut with a deep X, to hasten the cooking of the toughest part. Choose a pan just large enough to contain it, and measure enough water to come half-way up the vegetable. Remove the cauliflower while you bring the salted water to the boil, then put it in and cover the pan. Cook briskly for about 10 minutes, then start testing it with a fine skewer every two minutes, and remove it as soon as the stalk is reasonably tender. It must never be allowed to cook for a moment longer than is necessary to become tender, as it very quickly turns into a watery mass of an unappetizing pallor. It should be removed from the cooking water while it is still definitely crisp and firm, drained well in a colander and dressed with melting butter. A careful seasoning with salt and black pepper is essential; an additional garnish of chopped hard-boiled egg, parsley and/or browned breadcrumbs can be added if desired. Alternatively, make a cheese sauce with some of the cooking water reduced and mixed in equal quantities with thin cream, and flavoured with grated cheese, Parmesan for preference. If you put flavour above appearance, it is probably better to divide the cauliflower into sprigs before cooking. This is certainly a simpler method as the pieces are all roughly equal in size, and are cooked at the same time. Bring just enough lightly salted water to cover them to the boil, throw in the washed sprigs, and cook for 8–10 minutes, removing from the fire as soon as they are beginning to soften. Drain well, tip them into a shallow dish, and serve with melted butter seasoned with salt and black pepper, or a cream sauce, or a cheese sauce, poured over all.

Cauliflower also makes a delicious cold dish, the sprigs mixed with quartered hard-boiled eggs and dressed with a sauce vinaigrette flavoured with finely chopped fresh herbs. A thin mayonnaise can replace the vinaigrette, and the eggs can be omitted. To be at its best, the cauliflower should be only just cooked, and dressed immediately with the sauce, then allowed to cool just before eating. It is much better to eat it while still slightly warm than completely cold. It is also delicious eaten raw, and extremely healthy, as it is full of vitamins (A, B and C) and mineral salts which are best preserved in this way. To eat raw, it should be finely chopped or grated; the stalks can be finely chopped and the flowers grated over the top.

Celeriac
[Lat. *Apium graveolens rapaceum*, Fr. *Céleri-rave*]

Celeriac is an extremely useful winter vegetable which has only recently become popular in England. Not only does it contain more iron than almost any other food, it has the flavour of celery without its stringy texture, which makes it better suited for cooking. The swollen root is shaped like a turnip, and can be eaten raw or cooked. The classic French hors-d'oeuvre, *Céleri rémoulade*, is made with raw shredded celeriac mixed with a well-seasoned sauce remoulade. It can also be grated or shredded and sprinkled over a salad, but must first be pared quite thickly.

To prepare: The peeled celeriac should be cut in slices or chunky pieces and covered with cold salted water. Bring to the boil and simmer until it is soft, about 30 minutes, depending on the size of the pieces. Drain well, and make into a purée with an equal quantity of freshly-boiled potatoes. Beat in a little butter or cream, season carefully with salt and black pepper, and serve. A thinner version, cooked in stock instead of water, then puréed with the stock, makes an excellent and very nourishing soup. The pallor needs a sprinkling of chopped parsley for contrast. The flavour goes particularly well with all sorts of game. Slices of celeriac, par-boiled, can be made into fritters by dipping in batter and deep-frying.

Celery
[Lat. *Apium graveolens*, Fr. *Céleri*]

A native of Britain, celery can be found growing wild in fields and marshes. The cultivated variety is quite hard to grow, needing trenching and blanching. It has ridged concave stalks which have a delicious crisp texture and cleansing taste when eaten raw.

To prepare : The best method of cooking celery is to braise it, otherwise I prefer to use its turnip-rooted cousin, the celeriac. It contains valuable quantities of minerals, and vitamin C, but not as much iron as celeriac. In England, it has long been a custom to serve stalks of celery whole with cheese, as they have a particular affinity. One can find beautiful goblet-shaped glasses, in which it was served, dating from early Georgian times. Nowadays it is often used as part of a mixed raw vegetable salad, chopped in small pieces. The pale green leaves are also good, and should be chopped and used as a garnish, or mixed with the salad, while the root has an excellent flavour also. A dish of braised celery makes the classic accompaniment to roast pheasant; it is also indispensable for flavouring soups, stews and stocks. A celery stalk forms part of the classic bouquet garni, the other ingredients, the bay leaf, two or three stalks of parsley and thyme, being wrapped in the hollow of the celery stalk and tied with thread.

Cèpes
[Lat. *Boletus edulis*, Fr. *Cèpe*]

Cèpe is the French name for an edible mushroom of the Boletus family. They are to be found growing wild in England, on the fringes of beech woods, or under larch trees; they appear during the early autumn, especially after a damp summer, and they are easily recognized by their brilliant golden brown colour, like the top of a crème caramel. They have a porous spongy substance in place of gills, and a stem that bulges near the base. They are highly thought of in France where a superior variety can be bought in shops, but in England and the United States we have to fall back on the dried cèpes, imported from France, Italy and Germany. These are very good for certain dishes, and have a better flavour than the cultivated mushroom.

To prepare : If you find some cèpes growing wild, wipe them with a damp cloth and remove the spongy part. Heat some butter or oil in a pan and cook a finely sliced onion until soft. Add the sliced cèpes and a minced clove of garlic. Cook gently until softened, about 10 minutes, then sprinkle with chopped herbs and serve. Alternatively, omit the garlic and add a teaspoon of flour at the end of the cooking, then mix in $\frac{1}{4}$ pt cream coloured with $\frac{1}{2}$ teaspoon paprika. Season with salt, stir until well blended, and serve. They can also be cooked whole in the oven or under the grill, moistened with oil and seasoned with salt and black pepper. They emit a slightly gluey juice whose consistency is not liked by all, but the flavour is good. I am convinced they have a strange exhilarating effect on one, having studied my reactions carefully the first few times I ate them, more than a little apprehensive in case I had mistaken them for some poisonous variety of fungi, but I cannot find any of my friends who will agree, most of them being too nervous even to try.

Chanterelle
[Lat. *Cantharellus cibarius*, Fr. *Chanterelle*]

This is the French name for a species of wild mushroom much prized in France, and sometimes found growing wild in Southern England. It should be looked for at the end of the summer and the early autumn, in woods where it is easily spotted by its bright golden yellow and strange trumpet shape.

To prepare: Chanterelles should be cooked like most mushrooms in butter or oil, with a flavouring of chopped onion and garlic, and served with a sprinkling of fresh herbs when possible.

Chard
[Lat. *Beta vulgaris*, Fr. *Bette* or *Blette*]

Also known as seakale beet, white beet or spinach beet, this is a variety of beetroot grown for the sake of the central rib of the leaf, which is called the 'chard'. Easy to grow, and rich in vitamin C, this useful vegetable is not as popular in England or the United States as it is in France.

To prepare: Both the leaf and the stem are nutritious and have a delicate flavour, but they are best cooked separately. The leaf should be cut away from the chard and cooked like spinach, that is to say in the absolute minimum of water. Put a couple of tablespoons of water in a heavy pan and pack in the leaves. Bring the water to the boil and cook gently, turning the leaves over as the bottom ones release their moisture, until all are wilted and tender. Drain well, pressing out excess liquid, and serve with a little melted butter seasoned with salt and black pepper. The ribs should be left whole and cooked like seakale. Bring enough lightly salted water just to cover them to the boil in a broad pan, or in a steamer, and cook them gently until tender. Drain them well, and serve them on a dish with melted butter poured over them. If very large, they can be cut into pieces after cooking. Some varieties (spinach beet, for instance), do not produce such large ribs to their leaves, and can be cooked together. Cut the leaves across, including the chard, in $\frac{1}{2}$-inch pieces, and cook in already boiling lightly salted water until just tender, drain and re-heat in seasoned melted butter.

Chick Peas
[Lat. *Cicer arictinum*, Fr. *Pois chiches*]

These rock-like objects are much used in the Middle East, Spain, Morocco and parts of France and Italy. Like all dried vegetables they are rich in vitamins, but they take an extremely long time to cook. They have a curious flavour which is not liked by all, but once one has acquired a taste for them, as in the Arab dish, *Hummus*, made with sesame seed paste, one can't live for long without them. They are also one of the ingredients of the classic *cous-cous*, and are made into nourishing soups and stews, or eaten cold as salads.

To prepare: Chick peas should be soaked overnight, then brought very slowly to the boil in a large pan. Simmer gently for one hour, adding flavouring vegetables. Then add salt, and cook for another hour, or until soft. If for a cold dish, they should be dressed with olive oil while still hot. As they take so long to cook, it is sensible to cook enough for two dishes at one time. Half the peas can be kept in their cooking liquid until the following day, then made into an excellent soup.

Chicory
[Lat. *Cichorium intybus*, Fr. *Endive*]

Like many other English people, I live in a state of permanent confusion over the difference between chicory and endives. This arises from the fact that in France what we call 'chicory' is called 'endives', and vice-versa. I still have to think twice before I know which I mean, having at some stage adopted the French form of naming them. Chicory in England is a long thin vegetable with overlapping white leaves edged with pale green, and a curious slightly bitter taste. It is a native of Europe, and has been used for hundreds of years in salads and medicinally. The cultivated variety is blanched to achieve the desired white leaf, and the bitterness is greatly reduced. It is in season from November to March.

To prepare: Chicory is generally used raw as part of a mixed salad, either with the leaves left whole or torn into pieces, or the whole plant cut across in thick slices. It also combines well with beetroot. If cooked, they should be placed whole in a heavy casserole, arranged in layers with a little stock or water, a generous piece of butter, a little lemon juice and a pinch of salt. Cover and cook in the oven for 45 minutes. They also make a delicious filling for a pastry quiche, or can be served as a dish on their own if after braising they are covered with a good cheese sauce and lightly gratinéed.

Cocozelle

An Italian strain of courgette with dark green fruit of a delicate flavour. See COURGETTE.

Colewort

A term that is no longer in use, colewort was often mentioned in early English cookery books as a green vegetable, probably a form of cabbage that does not form a head. It seems probable that the term 'collards' was a corruption of the word, as it is used in the southern States of America to describe a form of greens. See COLLARDS and KALE.

Collards
[Lat. *Brassica oleracea*]

Collards is a general term which covers all sorts of greens that do not form a head, such as kale, turnip tops, 'spring greens' or chard. They were frequently mentioned in medi-

eval English cookery books, and they are still a familiar
term in 'soul-food' cookery – the cooking tradition formed
by the black slaves in the southern States of America. I have
a theory that many English dishes common in the early
seventeenth century were taken to America by the first
settlers and preserved there, while in their native country
they were forgotten, or superseded by newer fashions
brought from other European countries.

Collards have no special distinction of flavour, but form a
source of vitamins during the winter months. Like all ingredients of soul food, they are basically a poor man's food.
It is on foods like these that soul food was based – the left-
overs from the white man's table. Other basic ingredients
were the odds and ends of the pig that no one else wanted –
chitlings, heads and tails – which together with 'collard
greens' of various sorts the black women managed to trans-
form with loving care into cheery satisfying meals.

Corn-on-the-Cob
See SWEET CORN.

Corn Salad
[Lat. *Valerianella olitoria*, Fr. *Mâche*]

Also known as Lamb's Lettuce, this salad vegetable is much
more popular in France and Italy than in England or the
United States, but it is easily grown and should be more
widely cultivated. It is rich in sodium and vitamin C, and
being in season from early autumn until the spring is invaluable for adding variety to winter salads. A native of
Europe, the wild form can be found growing in the fields,
but the cultivated form has larger leaves and a better
flavour. It combines well with beetroot and with celery, also
with all green salad vegetables.

Courgette

There is no English name for these miniature vegetable
marrows; in England we use the French word courgette,
while in the United States the Italian term zucchini has
been adopted. The courgette is a cultivated form of vege-

table marrow specially developed to give a succession of tiny fruits, rather than one mammoth exhibit. For best results they should be picked while still very young, no longer than one's middle finger, although larger plants are still perfectly edible.

To prepare: Courgettes can be cooked in a variety of different ways, fried whole, or in slices, in butter or oil, poached, stewed in their own juice, or baked in the oven. They combine well with tomatoes, and herbs such as basil, dill and chervil. They also go well with other Mediterranean vegetables like aubergines, sweet peppers, onions and garlic, as in the classic ratatouille. They are good flavoured with cheese, but it should be a subtle and delicate one such as Parmesan or Gruyère, rather than a strong English Cheddar. They can be peeled or not, left whole, or cut in slices. Many books tell one to slice them and sprinkle them with salt, leaving them to drain for 30 minutes, but with young courgettes I do not think this necessary. The male flowers of the plant can also be cooked, and make a very pretty dish. They can either be dipped in batter and deep fried, or stuffed with a light stuffing and fried or baked in the oven.

Cress
[Lat. *Lepidium sativum*, Fr. *Cresson alénois*]

A native of Persia, this tiny plant must be the easiest of all to grow. It germinates very quickly, and can be grown anywhere in the garden in summertime, and indoors during the winter. One of the easiest ways to grow it is in a shallow box filled three-quarters full with a fine light soil, and covered with a pane of glass. Set in a sunny place, the cress will be ready for picking in about twelve days. Children like to grow it on a piece of damp flannel; it is one of the easiest ways to learn how seeds sprout, as the process is so quick.

To prepare: Cress is rarely seen nowadays, unless in a mixed salad. But in the early years of the century, its main use was in sandwiches, either alone or mixed with mustard whose hot taste complements it. Made with very thinly sliced brown bread and butter, these tiny sandwiches were a classic part of the English tea table in the 1920s and 1930s, a more elegant form of brown bread and butter to serve with dressed crab, plovers' eggs or a lobster salad.

Cucumber
[Lat. *Cucumis sativus*, Fr. *Concombre*]

A native of Asia and Egypt, the cucumber was not introduced into England until the late sixteenth century. Part of a large family which includes the marrow, gourd and melon, the cucumber is borne on a creeping plant with herbaceous stems. Although there are many different varieties, such as the white or yellow cucumber, and a range of sizes and shapes, the most popular in England and the United States is the familiar long straight fruit, with pale green flesh enclosed in dark green smooth or slightly ridged skin. There are also some varieties grown specially for pickling, which are smaller than the normal cucumber. Pickled cucumbers are sold under the name of gherkins [Fr. *cornichons*]. Recent developments have made the cucumber more digestible; it was long considered indigestible, and one was advised to slice and salt it for some time before eating. This makes it limp, which some people prefer, but I like to keep its crisp texture and I don't bother to salt it any more. However I do prefer to cut it in fairly thick slices, rather than the paper thin ones of old which were often swallowed whole, without chewing, making it even more hard to digest. Many people leave the skin on for the same reason, but in some varieties this is too tough to be much appreciated.

Full of vitamins B and C, the cucumber has no fat content or carbohydrate, which makes it ideal for those on slimming diets. It has a cool refreshing quality that makes it delicious for summer meals, or as an accompaniment to curries and other hot dishes. It makes a good summer soup, either hot or chilled, and an excellent Middle Eastern salad, mixed with yoghurt, garlic, and chopped mint. For many years, cucumber sandwiches were one of the most loved items on the English tea table, and it is also one of the most versatile of salad vegetables.

To prepare: The cucumber can be cooked in the manner of a courgette; although usually eaten raw, it is delicious hot, and very quick and easy to prepare. It can be left unpeeled, cut in thick slices (about ¾ inch), and gently fried on each side in butter. To serve, sprinkle with chopped chervil or dill. It can also be cut in very thin slices and coated in flour, or dipped in batter and fried in deep fat. It can be cut in oval shapes, or small balls, and tossed in butter as a garnish for a sole or trout, or a fillet of veal. It makes a pretty aspic ring, either alone or mixed with diced tomato, or a variety of excellent sauces – hot, cold or semi-frozen – to accompany fish or vegetable dishes.

Custard Marrow

A variety of vegetable marrow best suited for stuffing with a highly seasoned mixture, due to its rather tasteless bland flesh, but practical and pleasing shape. See VEGETABLE MARROW.

Dandelion
[Lat. *Leontodon taraxacum*, Fr. *Pissenlit*]

The dandelion is a weed that grows all over Europe and North America. In France and Italy the young leaves that appear in the spring are much prized as a salad vegetable and cultivated as such, but in England and the United States we have to look for it growing wild in the fields. It is rich in iron and minerals, and in vitamins A and C. It is believed to have medicinal qualities by many, but is worth searching for in any case, because of its refreshing sharp taste. It is much improved by being blanched, which can be done by covering the plant with an inverted flower pot or two slates for ten days before using. The leaves lose some of their bitterness when treated in this way, and are more easily digested, but only the very young leaves should be used.
To prepare: The leaves can be eaten raw as a salad, either alone or with other salad vegetables, or they can be cooked like spinach. They make an excellent salad mixed with diced bacon fried crisp, like the American raw spinach salad. The root can also be eaten, cut in thin slices and cooked gently in a little oil in a covered sauté pan, adding a pinch of salt and a little soy sauce at the last. The flowers have been used in England for hundreds of years to make dandelion wine.

Dulce or Dulse
[Lat. *Rhodymenia palmata*]

A bright red seaweed, with deeply divided leaves, dulce is found on parts of the western coast of the British Isles.

To prepare: In *Food in England* (Macdonald & Co. 1954), Dorothy Hartley advises cooking it for about 5 hours. After draining, add butter, salt and black pepper. Like all edible seaweeds, dulce is rich in iron.

Elder Flower

Although it is not strictly speaking a vegetable, I cannot resist including the flower of the elder tree, as it can be put to such delicious use in the kitchen, but very rarely is. The berries have been used in England for hundreds of years to make elderberry wine, but the flowers have been for the most part neglected although they too make a good wine. In central Europe, Poland and Austria, they are much loved as a flavouring, but in England I have only once come across them, in the form of a delicious sorbet at The Wife of Bath, a small restaurant in Wye, Kent. They have a most delicious and unusual flavour, subtle and very hard to place. In an old cookery book, I read that their aroma is so strong that a bunch of the flowers drawn through a fine jam just before bottling will be enough to scent it deliciously.

To prepare: The flowers can be cooked as they are in Austria, dipped into a batter and deep fried, the fritters being sprinkled with fine sugar and eaten as a dessert.

Endive
[Lat. *Cichorium endivia*, Fr. *Chicorée frisée*]

A native of the East, the endive was brought to England in the sixteenth century, where it was highly thought of as a salad vegetable. It is a green vegetable, rather like a round lettuce in shape, with very curly leaves, pale yellow in the centre and darker green around the edges. Only the pale leaves should be used, as the green parts are bitter. It is extremely rich in vitamins B and C and minerals, including iron.

To prepare: Endive is delicious mixed with watercress and

233

chicory, or batavia and corn salad. As it is in season during the winter, it makes a good substitute for lettuce. The leaves can also be cooked, in which case the darker ones are also used. Cook for 12 minutes in lightly salted boiling water and drain very well. Chop the leaves and return to the pan. Mix with a good cream sauce, season carefully and serve.

Escarole

See BATAVIA.

Fennel

There are three main varieties of fennel, which I have listed separately to avoid confusion.

WILD, OR BITTER, FENNEL [Lat. *Foeniculum vulgare*, Fr. *Fenouil*] This is the original wild plant, a weed which grows all over southern Europe, especially France and Spain. It is in fact a herb, and the feathery leaves have been used in England since earliest known records for culinary and medicinal purposes. It was supposed to have marvellous powers for restoring eyesight and curing headaches. The stems have a very bitter taste, so for the kitchen the cultivated varieties are preferable.

GARDEN, OR SWEET, FENNEL [Lat. *Foeniculum officinale*, Fr. *Fenouil doux*] Cultivated as an annual, this relative of the wild fennel has thicker stems with a less bitter flavour. It is very popular in Italy, where it is called *carosella*, and eaten raw as a salad.

FINOCCHIO, OR FLORENCE, FENNEL [Lat. *Foeniculum dulce*] This variety, also enormously popular in Italy, is the one we usually find in shops in England and the United States. It has a bulbous root base, with a strange taste, like celery with overtones of anise, which is much liked by some.

To prepare: When young and tender, the roots can be thinly sliced and eaten raw, dressed with olive oil and lemon juice, either alone or mixed with tomatoes, radishes or other salad vegetables. When cooked it is best cut in half and braised in the manner of celery. It can be cooked either on top of the stove, in a shallow-lidded sauté pan, or in the oven, in a large shallow dish covered with a piece of aluminium foil. It should be dotted with butter, and sprinkled with a little lemon juice and chicken or vegetable stock, then cooked gently, turning over now and then, for about $1\frac{1}{2}$ hours. It is also good cooked in this fashion, then drained and covered with a sauce mornay.

Flageolet

A pale green dried bean, much liked in France and Italy, flageolets can be used as a hot vegetable, particularly good with roast lamb, or as a salad, with olive oil and vinegar or lemon juice. See BEANS, HARICOT.

Garlic
[Lat. *Allium sativum*, Fr. *Ail*]

A relative of the onion, garlic is a bulbous root which is a native of southern Europe. It was grown extensively in England about four hundred years ago, when it was highly thought of both for cooking and for medicinal purposes, but it was later forgotten, and did not regain its popularity until after the Second World War. Now it is to be found in every English greengrocer and is widely used. It is much less popular in the United States, where less strong flavours are preferred. It can easily be grown by the amateur; the outer cloves should be separated and planted in a sunny position in well-drained soil. If planted under peach trees, it is supposed to keep away the dreaded disease leaf curl. It should be remembered, however, that garlic grown in the north is stronger than when cultivated in its natural habitat, like the South of France. It is still thought to be healthy, but its pungent flavour is not liked by all. When eaten raw, as in salads or aïolli, the French garlic mayonnaise, its taste is exceptionally strong; in long cooking it becomes milder.

Good King Henry
[Lat. *Chenopidium bonus-henricus*, Fr. *Ansérine*]

A native of Europe, this hardy vegetable is rarely seen in England or the United States. It was widely cultivated in England hundreds of years ago, when it was known as mercury, or goosefoot. (Seed can still be bought from The

Old Rectory Herb Farm, Ightham, Kent.) It grows between 2 and 3 feet high, with thick central ribs and arrow-shaped dark green leaves, not unlike a chard. It is very easy to grow, and has a good flavour similar to spinach.

To prepare: If the plants are earthed up like asparagus, the first shoots can be blanched and eaten in the same way. They should be tied in bundles, lowered into boiling salted water, and cooked rapidly until tender. They are then drained and served with melted butter. Later the leaves can be cooked like spinach: throw them into boiling salted water, cook quickly until tender and then drain them well in a colander. Chop them coarsely and toss in melting butter with salt and black pepper.

Gourds
[Lat. *Cucurbita*, Fr. *Courge*]

An enormous family of vegetables, the gourds include among their cultivated forms pumpkins and marrows, courgettes, cucumbers and melons. However, all these are covered under their own names, and I will only mention here the decorative gourds which are grown solely for the sake of their appearance. They are useful in the vegetable garden for covering an unsightly corner; they grow extremely well on a mound of earth heaped over a pile of manure. There are many different gourds, of all shapes and colours, and after picking they can be dried and kept as decorations for the winter, when flowers are scarce. Although they are edible, they are not worth cooking, and are only of interest for their amazing colours and unusual forms.

Gumbo or Gombo

See OKRA.

Hop Shoots
[Lat. *Humulus lupulus*, Fr. *Jets d'houblon*]

Hops were not introduced into England until the sixteenth century as before that beer was made from malt, and known as ale. The first thinnings from the hops are taken in April or May and they make a most delicious vegetable. It is however essential to make sure that they have not yet been sprayed.

To prepare: The tender hop shoots are cooked like asparagus, tied in bundles and lowered into boiling salted water for 12 to 15 minutes, then drained and served with melted butter. A little lemon juice should be added to the cooking water. They are much esteemed in Belgium, where I saw them for the first time in a restaurant, with poached eggs laid on top, the whole covered with a sauce hollandaise.

Horseradish
[Lat. *Cochlearia armoracia*, Fr. *Raifort*]

As the classic accompaniment to roast beef, horseradish has been grown in England since the sixteenth century. It is also popular in the United States. In England it has become hard to find in its natural state, most people seeming to prefer the ready-made sauce, or bottled grated horseradich. The latter is in fact very good, but it is a pity not to have it fresh, and as it is easily grown, every garden should include a few roots. It can be propagated from a short piece of its own root, planted vertically or at an angle, in very well-dug manured soil. The root grows to a great length and tends to spread over the garden.

To prepare: The root needs to be well scrubbed under a running tap, then scraped or grated. I like it very well as it is, piled in little mounds on slices of rare beef, but it can also be made into an excellent sauce mixed with cream and lemon juice, or added to a mayonnaise. (For recipes, see pp. 186 and 187.)

There is an excellent German brand of finely grated horseradish, so fine as to be almost a purée, called Koch-brand, to be found in the deepfreeze of good delicatessens. It can be eaten as it is, or stirred into lightly whipped cream with a little lemon juice or vinegar added.

Kale
[Lat. *Brassica oleracea acephala*, Fr. *Chou vert*]

Also known as borecole, Scotch kale, curly kail, colewort, and in the southern States of America as collards, kale is the earliest form of cabbage. It is a beautiful vegetable, with tightly curled leaves of a dark bluish-green, which do not form a heart. They are full of vitamins. It is basically a poor man's food, which explains its popularity in Scotland, Ireland and the southern States where the negro slaves made it one of the main ingredients of soul-food cookery.

To prepare: Bring a large pan of lightly salted water to the boil, throw in the leaves, either whole or torn in pieces, and boil rapidly until tender. Drain very well, chop on a flat board with a long knife, return to the pan and re-heat with a knob of butter and plenty of salt and black pepper. In Scotland it is traditionally cooked with oatmeal in a dish called kail brose, a sort of thick soup. It is also good boiled as above and served with egg sauce, or it can be made into a purée mixed with equal parts of potato, and with hot milk and butter added. Season well.

Kohlrabi
[Lat. *Brassica oleracea caulo-rapa*, Fr. *Chou-rave*]

This vegetable is better known on the Continent than in England or the United States, although it can occasionally be found in shops, and most good nurseries sell seeds. It is not unlike a turnip in flavour and appearance although it is not in fact a root, but a swelling of the stem near the base.

To prepare: Kohlrabi can be cooked in any of the ways used for turnips, but has a rather more delicate flavour. It is best sliced and cooked for a few minutes in fat, then covered with stock and simmered until tender, about 30 minutes. The leaves can be chopped and used as garnish, or cooked separately. It can also be made into purées or fritters, or grated and eaten raw in salads.

Lamb's Lettuce

See CORN SALAD.

Laver
[Lat. *Porphyria laciniata*]

The purple seaweed known as 'sloke' in England is called 'laver' in Ireland and Wales where it is mixed with oatmeal and made into flat cakes known as 'laverbread'. See SLOKE.

Leeks
[Lat. *Allium porrum*, Fr. *Poireau*]

Native to Europe, the leek is one of the most versatile and useful vegetables in the kitchen; it is valuable both as a flavouring agent for other food, and as a vegetable in its own right. It is good combined with carrots, or with tomatoes, it goes exceptionally well with lamb, and is delicious in cheese dishes, or cooked with cream. It makes exquisite soups, such as the American favourite vichysoisse, and the French *Soupe à la bonne femme*, and is excellent in pastry dishes. When young, leeks are good eaten cold dressed with a sauce vinaigrette. When older, I like to cut them in thick slices before cooking, as this avoids possible stringiness.

To prepare: A simple way to cook leeks is as follows: after washing, cut them in slices one inch thick. Bring an inch of lightly salted water to the boil in a broad heavy pan and throw in the leeks. Cover the pan and cook briskly for 10 minutes, shaking the pan from side to side occasionally. Check to make sure that the water is not boiling away. When the time is up, they should be perfectly tender, and only a minimum of water left to throw away. Toss them over a gentle heat to dry them out, then add a knob of butter, some salt and plenty of black pepper.

Lentils
[Lat. *Ervum lens*, Fr. *Lentille*]

The lentil is the seed of a small bushy plant, which grows not more than 1½ ft high. It is a native of the Mediterranean shores, and has been cultivated since Roman times. It is one of the most nutritious foods of all, being full of iron and vitamin B, and is therefore an extremely useful addition to our winter diet. The seeds are borne in tiny pods, and should be stored in the pods until they are to be marketed. The lentils vary in colour from an orangy-yellow, to green, to brown. In England the orange ones are most commonly seen but these are the least satisfactory from the point of view of cooking. They have very little flavour, and quickly disintegrate into a mush. Both the green and brown ones are a great improvement, and can be found in foreign shops; I like the Egyptian brown lentils.

To prepare: Lentils do not need soaking, but careful washing and picking over in a colander to remove any little stones and discoloured seeds. They can then be covered with cold water with an inch or two to spare and brought very slowly to the boil. Simmer them for 50 minutes to 1 hour, until they are soft, adding salt towards the end of the cooking. Drain them, reserving the liquid for soup, and add some butter and seasoning of salt and black pepper. I sometimes also add a little soy sauce. Alternatively, they can with advantage be first cooked in butter with a chopped onion and clove of garlic, then hot water or stock can be added, and the lentils simmered until tender. If they are to be eaten as a vegetable this is the better way, but for adding to other dishes the first is better.

Lentils make marvellous soups, either alone or mixed with other vegetables, which should be thick and unsieved. They are also good as a dish in their own right, garnished with hard-boiled eggs or croûtons, and strips of bacon. They make a very good cold dish, dressed with oil and vinegar while still hot, and eaten before they have completely cooled. They are good with sausage dishes of all kinds; they have a comforting warming quality that is especially welcome in cold weather. There is also a well-known Indian dish called dhal, which is composed of orange lentils cooked almost to a mush and served with curry.

Lettuce
[Lat. *Lactuca sativa*, Fr. *Laitue*]

The lettuce comes from the East, probably from India or parts of Asia. Its origins are so ancient that they are inevitably rather obscure. It was cultivated in Greek or Roman times, probably even earlier. There are innumerable different varieties which fall into three main categories: the round, or cabbage, lettuce; the cos lettuce; and the cutting lettuce. The first two are universally known; the latter is a useful salad vegetable as it does not form a head, but continues to grow new leaves after each cutting, thus giving a successive supply of salads for some time.

'All the year round' is a favourite round lettuce, easily grown by the amateur, and good for both summer and winter. The American 'Buttercrunch', now available in England also, is well worth growing as it produces a crisp head which is unusually slow to bolt, and does not develop a bitter taste when not picked soon after maturing. 'Iceberg' is an excellent crunchy type of lettuce very popular in the United States, as is also 'Bibb' lettuce, which produces a small loose head with a particularly good flavour. Both of these can now be bought from English seed specialists. 'Webbs wonderful' is an old favourite that has not been improved on.

Even the smallest garden can afford to have a selection of different lettuces, so that one can vary one's summer salads. By using cloches, and by planting crops in succession, one can have a supply of lettuces starting from early summer right through to the autumn. When there are more than are needed for salads, lettuces can be braised as a hot vegetable, or made into excellent summer soups.

Mange-touts

Also known as sugar peas, or snow peas, these are an edible podded variety of pea that has long been used in Chinese cookery, and recently become popular in England and the United States. They are to be found in enterprising greengrocers and in Chinese shops, and they can also be grown quite easily in the garden and as they are best eaten soon after picking, this is in fact preferable to buying them.

To prepare: The mange-touts simply need the ends pinched off; if they are gathered while still young there should be no stringy parts at all. Cook them in a broad heavy pan, either whole or cut across in squares, with just enough water to cover the bottom of the pan. Put a lump of butter on the top, and a sprinkling of salt and sugar. Bring to the boil and cook for 4–6 minutes, by which time they should be tender but still crisp. Put them in a serving dish, boil up the juice for a few moments to reduce it to a couple of spoonfuls, and pour it over them.

Marrow

See VEGETABLE MARROW.

Mushroom

[Lat. *Agaricus campestris*, Fr. *Champignon*]

The field mushroom is an edible fungi which is found growing wild in meadows in the late summer and early autumn,
particularly after a spell of damp weather. The same variety
is grown commercially in England and the United States,
and can be bought all the year round. It is sold at two
stages; first, as button mushrooms, and later when it has
developed a larger flat cap. When freshly picked the gills
on the underside of the cap are a delicate shade of buff pink;
by the time they reach the shops this has turned to brown.
The flavour of the forced variety is not so fine as that of the
wild one, which also benefits from being cooked shortly
after picking. They should never be kept for any length of
time as they quickly deteriorate.

To prepare: When young and very fresh, mushrooms can be
eaten raw; sliced and dressed with oil and lemon juice they
make a delicious salad. They can also be cooked, in a variety
of different ways: fried, grilled, baked, stewed in their own
juice or cooked *sous cloche*. They are invaluable not only as
a vegetable in their own right, but as a flavour to enhance
other foods. They make an excellent sauce, and are a favourite ingredient of the classic French dishes, as an accompaniment to fish, meat, and poultry.

Dried mushrooms, obtainable in delicatessens from
France, Italy and Germany, are a useful stand-by for the
larder. The flavour is in fact better than our own forced
mushrooms, but they are only suitable for certain dishes.
They need half an hour's soaking before cooking, and are
excellent for adding to stews and casserole dishes, or a
sauce for spaghetti. They are usually a form of *boletus*, or
cèpes, rather than the field mushroom, which is not so highly
thought of on the Continent as in England and the United
States.

Mustard, White

[Lat. *Sinapis alba*, Fr. *Moutarde blanche*]

This tiny plant is amazingly quick to germinate; it can be
picked within a week of sowing. The leaf, with its hot tangy
taste, is usually mixed with cress in sandwiches, or used as a

garnish for cold dishes. It is more often grown for the sake of its seed, which is made into table mustard. The seeds were used as a condiment in England as early as the thirteenth century, but it was not for another five hundred years that they were ground to make a fine flour, similar to our mustard powder. It has always appealed to the English love for strong and fiery condiments, although I personally far prefer the milder French mustards, such as *Moutarde de Dijon Grey Poupon*.

In recent years a number of French mustards have appeared on the market with the mustard seeds incorporated whole. I find these absolutely delicious; one of the best known is *Moutarde de Meaux Pommery*, but another less well-known one that I find even better is called *Moutarde de grains au vin blanc de Meursault*. Both these and the smooth mustards are invaluable for cooking as well as for use on the table. I like to add mustard to most cheese dishes, and to a sauce with turnips, or tiny onions. A heaped teaspoonful of *Moutarde de grains* added to a frozen packet of onions in white sauce makes an easily prepared and excellent side dish to eat with sausages, pork or veal.

Mustard Greens

Popular in the southern States of America, where they are one of the main ingredients of soul-food cookery, mustard greens are similar to collards, but more tender and with a more delicate tangy flavour. They used to be mentioned frequently in English cookery books, but I have not found any mention of them after the seventeenth century.

To prepare: Mustard greens are cooked like kale or any other greens. See KALE.

Nettles
[Lat. *Urtica dioica*, Fr. *Ortie*]

The young shoots of nettles, picked in April and early May when they are not more than three or four inches high, make a pleasant and nutritious dish. They are much prized in Italy as a purifier of the blood after the winter, but in England few people bother to cook them. Gloves must be worn to pick them, but they lose their sting as soon as they are immersed in boiling water. They reduce greatly in cooking, so be sure to pick plenty.

To prepare: Throw the nettles into a large pan of boiling salted water and cook briskly for 8–10 minutes. As soon as they are tender, drain them well in a colander and return to the pan with a knob of butter, salt and black pepper. They should be served immediately. They can be made into soup in the same way as spinach, adding some cream at the end. They can also be mixed with spinach, lettuce or sorrel in a variety of dishes.

Okra
[Lat. *Hibiscus esculentus*, Fr. *Gombo*]

A native of the West Indies, okra is also grown extensively in South America where it is known as 'gombo'. In England it is sometimes called 'lady's fingers'. The word 'gumbo' is also used in the southern States of America to denote a soup or stew containing okra, for instance 'chicken gumbo'. Okra also figures in Middle Eastern cooking. It is easily bought in England in cities with a high immigrant population from the West Indies.

Okra is an annual plant growing to a height of 2 or 3 feet, with long narrow spherical pods. These are somewhat like chillies in appearance, but much longer.

To prepare: The pods are sliced or cooked whole; they are usually cooked in oil, and are often mixed with onions, tomatoes, aubergines and peppers.

Onion
[Lat. *Allium cepa*, Fr. *Oignon*]

The onion came originally from central Asia, and has been for many centuries the most important vegetable from the culinary point of view. It is hard to think of any country where it does not figure largely in the cuisine, while it would be almost impossible to re-create any dish of the classic *haute cuisine Française* without making use of the onion in one of its forms. (The family also includes the shallot, leek and garlic.) It has become accepted as a vital flavouring agent for so many dishes, whether they be of fish, poultry, game or meat, while there is hardly a savoury sauce that does not include some form of onion. Soups, stews, casseroles and *court-bouillons* all rely heavily on the onion, which is also used in vegetable dishes. It is useful in almost all its stages of growth: first, as seedlings, as a substitute for spring onions; later, the medium-sized bulb; and finally the giant Spanish onion. The flavour becomes milder as the size increases, which is why many people prefer the Spanish onion for most purposes, especially where it is to be eaten raw.

To prepare: Onions are easy to grow and store, and can be cooked in a variety of different ways. They can be steamed, boiled, baked in the oven like potatoes, sautéed in shallow fat or deep-fried in batter, stewed or cooked under the grill. When left whole they take a long time to become tender, so are usually sliced or chopped. Raw onions can be thinly sliced, minced or grated, and eaten in salads of raw or cooked vegetables. The juice can be extracted by squeezing, and used as a flavouring agent. They combine extremely well with potatoes and with tomatoes, and they go particularly well with lamb, mutton and beef.

Orache
[Lat. *Atriplex hortensis*, Fr. *Arroche*]

This plant is a hardy annual, similar to a coarse spinach, which is not often seen nowadays although it was popular in England many hundreds of years ago. (Seed can still be bought from The Old Rectory Herb Farm, Ightham, Kent.) It is sometimes called summer spinach, mountain spinach, or in the United States, French spinach. It grows 3 or 4 feet high, and has broad leaves of pale yellow, green or red, according to the variety.

To prepare: Orache can be cooked like spinach, and may be eaten alone, or mixed with spinach or sorrel. It can be made into a good soup or used as a base for poached or soft-boiled eggs.

Palm Tree Hearts
[Fr. *Coeur de Palmier*]

These delicacies, the tender young shoots of a variety of palm tree, can be bought tinned in foreign shops in England and the United States. They make an excellent hors-d'oeuvre in no time at all.

To prepare: Simply drain the hearts and cover with a good vinaigrette.

Parsnips
[Lat. *Pastinaca sativa*, Fr. *Panais*]

Parsnips do not seem too highly thought of in France; not only had I never seen the French word *panais*, but, on searching for some reference to it, I found no mention of them in Escoffier, while Larousse dismissed them curtly: 'for flavouring stock'. After many years of disfavour, they gradually seem to be coming back into fashion in England, while they have long been popular in the United States, whose appreciation of vegetables has always been higher than the English. I have always loved their nutty flavour, but they do tend to be watery and for this reason need careful cooking. They should never be plainly boiled, as was formerly done in England, or served in a white sauce, as this exaggerates their least attractive points. They have a great affinity with butter, and should always have fat added at some stage.

They are a useful winter vegetable, in season from November to February. Unlike most other vegetables, they are at their best after a frost, which improves their flavour. They can either be left in the ground until needed, or lifted and stored for winter use. They are a long knobbly white root, easy to grow and presenting few problems. They make a good substitute for potatoes, and are an excellent choice if only one vegetable dish is to be served.

To prepare: Parsnips should be pared thinly and cut in chunks; peel them only shortly before cooking and leave covered in cold water. To cook, cover with cold water, add a little salt and bring to the boil. Simmer until tender when pierced with a skewer – 20–30 minutes, depending on the size of the pieces. Drain them well and dry them out over a gentle fire. Add a generous knob of butter and a handful of chopped parsley, and season carefully with salt and black pepper. When all are well coated with hot fat, serve immediately. A little brown sugar can be added instead of the parsley, to bring out their sweetness. They can also be roasted in the oven, like potatoes, round a joint, or boiled and drained as above, then made into a purée, either alone or mixed with potatoes. Well beaten over the fire, with butter, a little cream and plenty of salt and black pepper added, they make a delicious accompaniment to grilled steaks. No other vegetable is needed.

I have devised a really excellent soup (see p. 30) made with parsnips and two other root vegetables – carrots and swedes or turnips. I think all root vegetables go well together and like to mix them. A purée of parsnips and carrots, or parsnips and turnips, is good, or one can make a dry purée of parsnips alone, mixed with a little chopped fried onion, shaped into little flat cakes and fried in butter. Slices of parsnip, after boiling, can be dipped in batter and deep fried. They also make the base for an unusual soufflé. (See p. 50).

Peas, Green
[Lat. *Pisum sativum*, Fr. *Pois*]

The pea is an annual that has been widely grown through-out the world, except for the tropics, since antiquity. It is thought to have been introduced into England in the six-teenth century, but its exact origins are unknown. It must be the most popular of English vegetables, and makes the best of all possible accompaniments to most English summer delicacies – salmon trout, spring chicken, the first of the young lamb from the salt marshes, still so young that a leg and saddle are cooked as one joint, river trout, grilled Dover sole, etc.

Peas are at their best in June and July, although the sea-son continues into early autumn during mild weather. The gardener will always have an advantage over the shopper with regard to peas, as they are a good example of a vege-table that is incomparably finer when picked really young and cooked shortly afterwards. When very fresh the pods also are valuable, and make a good soup. Peas are not difficult to grow, especially since the development of dwarf cultivars that eliminate staking and take less space in the garden. Varieties that are grown especially for the sake of their pods, which are picked before the peas have had time to grow, have recently become popular in Europe and America, under the name of 'mange-touts', or 'sugar peas', although they have long been used in Chinese cookery, where they are called 'snow peas'. (See MANGE-TOUTS.)

To prepare: As peas are only at their best for a short time, I think it is best to cook them as simply as possible, usually dispensing with any additional flavour, even the classic sprig of mint. When very young they need only 4–6 minutes cooking in already boiling very lightly salted water. Drain them quickly and serve in a hot dish with a knob of butter and a pinch of sugar.

During the late summer they lose their initial freshness and delicacy of flavour, and can then be treated differently, made into soups and purées, timbales and mousses, or cooked *à la Française*, with tiny onions and lettuce leaves. In old cookery books I often come across instructions to cook peas for 30–45 minutes, which makes me think they must have used them at a much later stage then we do, or perhaps the variety was much tougher. One rarely sees an old pea nowadays; I suppose we have become so conditioned to tiny peas by the frozen variety that they would not be acceptable. It is sad, though, that the manufacturers of frozen peas now get the pick of the market; this is just another reason for growing one's own crop whenever possible.

Peas, Split

These are dried peas, which are useful during the winter months as a source of vitamin B. They have been used in England for hundreds of years to make 'pease pudding', a traditional accompaniment to boiled bacon. The pudding is tied in a cloth, and cooked in the same pot as the bacon; it can also be made with fresh peas when they have become too old and floury for most other dishes. Dried peas have a special affinity for ham and bacon; an excellent winter soup can be made with split peas, using the bone and scraps of a ham for flavour. (See p. 37 for recipe.) Ham bones can often be bought cheaply from shops selling ham on the bone.

To prepare: Split peas are cooked in the same way as lentils; they do not require soaking, but should be well picked over and washed in a colander under a running tap. Put them in a pan, cover with plenty of cold water, add a sliced onion, carrot, leek, celery stalk or whatever is available in the way

248

of flavouring vegetables, and bring very slowly to the boil. Simmer gently until they are soft when crushed, but not reduced to a mush; only add salt towards the end of the cooking. They will probably take about 45 minutes to become tender. Drain them well, unless making a soup, and re-heat stirring in a lump of butter or a little cream, and plenty of salt and black pepper. They can be made into a good purée by pushing through a vegetable mill, then reheating as above. This is excellent with sausages.

Peppers, Green and Red
[Lat. *Capsicum annuum*, Fr. *Piment doux or Poivron*]

Also known as the sweet pepper, or bell pepper, the capsicum must not be confused with the Spanish pepper, or pimiento. It is a native of South America, and is a tender plant unable to withstand the cold. Recent developments have produced a more hardy variety which can be grown with care in England and most States in America, but it almost always needs some artificial heat to start growing. The green and red pepper are in fact the same plant; the flesh starts green and turns scarlet gradually as it ripens. They are widely grown in Mediterranean countries, particularly Spain, southern France, Italy and North Africa. They are also popular in central European countries, like Hungary. They are mainly used in Provençal-type dishes, stewed in oil with garlic, mixed with onions, tomatoes, or aubergines and courgettes. They are also found in stews like the Hungarian goulash, or in dishes of stuffed vegetables, either hot or cold. They are also much used in salads, as they can be eaten both raw and cooked.

To prepare: The seeds must always be discarded, along with the stalk and the fibrous interior. The seeds in particular have an unpleasant bitter taste. Many people find peppers hard to digest raw, in which case they can be peeled by placing under a hot grill until the skin has blackened, when it peels away easily. This totally alters their character; they lose their slightly bitter taste and crisp quality, and become sweet and of a meltingly soft consistency. In the latter way they make a delicious garnish for a dish of scrambled eggs, but on the whole I prefer them in their unpeeled state.

They combine well with eggs, as in *piperade*, or as a stuffing for an omelette (for which they should be peeled).

Pimiento
[Lat. *Capsicum annuum*, Fr. *Piment de Chili*]

Although closely related to the sweet pepper, the pimiento or chilli has a very different effect. It is a tiny tapering fruit, only a few inches long, in varying shades of green, yellow and red. It is not much used in its fresh state, because of its tremendous hotness, except in Indian and Oriental cookery, where it is also used in its dried form. We are more familiar with it in the form of red pepper (cayenne, paprika, or chilli powder), as the base of hot pepper sauces (Tabasco and other chilli sauces) or as the fiery paste called *harissa*, which is used in Morocco and Algeria to season *cous-cous*.

Potato
[Lat. *Solanum tuberosum*, Fr. *Pomme de terre*]

The potato was originally a native of South America, and it is generally believed to have been brought to England in the 1580s by Thomas Herriott. The first potatoes were planted in Ireland, where Herriott landed near Cork, and it is interesting to note that it is in Ireland that they are most valued. There are several hundred different types of potato, yet in the shops it is rare to find more than two varieties to choose from, if that. They fall into two main types: the firm-fleshed waxy variety, and the mealy floury-fleshed one. The former are ideal for dishes where the potato must keep its consistency, as in *gratins* and other dishes of sliced potatoes, while the latter are essential for purées. New potatoes are always waxy, and cannot be made into purées as they form a glutinous sticky paste.

If growing one's own, it is sensible to have a crop of each type; even in a small vegetable garden I think a few potatoes are well worth growing, if only for the pleasure of being able to pick them while they are still tiny. They also have the valuable property of cleansing the soil. Most of the vitamin content of the potato – vitamin C and various minerals – lies just beneath the surface of the skin. For this reason, they should be cooked in their skins whenever possible; if they must be peeled, this can be done after cooking without so much wastage. In Ireland, where potatoes are the staple diet and floury potatoes seem to be universally grown, they are cooked in the following way which makes them particularly delicious.

To prepare: Scrub the potatoes well, removing any eyes. Put them in a large pan with plenty of cold salted water. Bring to the boil uncovered, and boil gently until almost tender, about 15–20 minutes according to size. When they are still slightly firm when pierced with a skewer, and before they have started to fall to pieces, pour off all the water and cover the pan with a soft clean cloth. Replace over very gentle heat, or at the back of the stove, and leave for another 5–10 minutes, by which time they will be soft, but not yet disintegrated, with the skin split in a few places to show the delicious floury interior. Serve quite plain, with a dish of butter on the table.

To steam potatoes: peel them and cut in half, or quarters if large. Bring some water to the boil in the bottom half of a steamer, and place the potatoes over it when boiling point is reached. Sprinkle with salt, cover the pan, and cook until soft when pierced with a skewer. They will take slightly longer than when boiled. Do not add butter; the potatoes should be served quite plainly, and are particularly delicious with any dish in a rich sauce, or with fish.

To bake potatoes in their jackets scrub them well and dry in a cloth. Rub the skins lightly with oil or softened butter to prevent them bursting. Put the potatoes in an oven preheated to 400°, laying them on the rack. Cook for 1 hour, by which time all but the most gigantic will be soft. Test by squeezing them gently with a cloth, or piercing with a thin skewer. They should not be kept waiting too long or the skins will toughen. Cut a cross in the top to allow the steam to escape and serve as soon as possible, with plenty of butter, or a bowl of sour cream mixed with chopped chives. For more detailed recipes see pp. 127–130; 134–140.

As well as the innumerable ways of cooking potatoes, they can be used as the base for a large range of dishes by mixing a dry potato purée with eggs and flour to form a dough; this can be made into scones, pancakes, fritters, gnocchi, soufflés, pastry and bread. The potato adapts itself so well to so many flavours, without being over assertive, that one never seems to tire of it.

Pumpkin
[Lat. *Cucurbita maxima*, Fr. *Potiron*]

The pumpkin is one of a huge family of plants, some of which we classify as vegetables, others as fruits. They include the cucumber, the vegetable marrow and courgette, the melon and the whole range of ornamental gourds. The pumpkin itself is not much used for cooking nowadays in England, but is grown rather for decorative purposes, for harvest festivals and similar occasions. It can be made into a good soup, but is not often seen on English tables. In the United States, however, it is enormously popular as part of the classic American dessert, pumpkin pie. In this instance it is cooked with sugar and spices in a way that no longer appeals to the English, although it is curiously reminiscent of many medieval English dishes. But English tastes have changed over the centuries; they have grown to dislike, with a few exceptions, mixtures of sweet and savoury foods, and cook pumpkin only as a vegetable, with salt and black pepper.

Purslane
[Lat. *Portulaca oleracea*, Fr. *Pourpier*]

Purslane is a salad vegetable not much seen nowadays, except as a weed. It came originally from the East Indies, and was brought to England in the late sixteenth century. (Seed can still be bought from The Old Rectory Herb Farm, Ightham, Kent.)
To prepare: Purslane has a small leaf, usually eaten raw in salads, although it can also be cooked like spinach, only the leaves and tender tips of the shoots being used. It shrinks in the same way as spinach, so it must be cooked in large quantities very quickly in boiling salted water, then well drained and tossed in butter.

There is also a winter purslane [Lat. *Claytonia perfoliata*, Fr. *Claytone perfoliée*], which has trumpet-shaped leaves, as opposed to the oval-shaped leaves of the summer variety. It can be eaten either raw or cooked, in the same way as summer purslane.

Radish

[Lat. *Raphanus sativus*, Fr. *Radis*]

The radish is a native of southern Asia which has been popular in England since the sixteenth century, or even earlier. The most common sort is the red radish, but there is also a black radish, which should be peeled before eating, then treated exactly like the red one. A white-fleshed variety, and a yellow one, have recently been developed but as one of the most attractive things about the radish is its bright scarlet exterior and its snowy white flesh, I can see little to recommend them. Radishes come in varying shapes, from round to long and narrow. One variety, the 'Half long', has a long red oval shape with a white tip to the root; it is very pretty.

To prepare: Radishes are almost always eaten raw; they can in fact be cooked in boiling water for 5–6 minutes, but they lose their crisp texture which is their most appealing feature. In France, they are served as an hors-d'oeuvre, alone, with coarse salt and fresh unsalted butter. They should be well scrubbed, the root end trimmed, and a neat bunch of leaves left with which to hold them. They are also good sliced and scattered over a mixed salad, or grated and mixed with a sauce remoulade. They are easily grown, one of the best varieties having the attractive name of 'French breakfast'.

The leaves can also be eaten, and in a late nineteenth-century cookery book I have found a recipe for radish sandwiches, using the sliced flesh and the finely chopped leaves, moistened with French dressing. The radish is full of minerals, and vitamins A and C, and children should be encouraged to eat plenty of them. Their crunchy texture is generally popular; they also make a good cocktail snack for adults.

Rampion

[Lat. *Campanula rapunculus*, Fr. *Raiponce*]

Rampion is a native of Europe and can be found growing wild in the fields. It is a member of the *campanula*, or bell-flower family, which we are more familiar with in our herbaceous borders than the vegetable garden. This particular *campanula* produces an edible root, long and tapering like a carrot, but with white flesh. It was formerly grown in England, and is often mentioned in seventeenth-century cookery books, but is now generally neglected (although seed can still be bought from The Old Rectory Herb Farm, Ightham, Kent). It is still grown in France.

To prepare: Both the roots and the leaves are edible, and are generally eaten raw in salads. Nevertheless they can both be cooked: the roots like salsify and the leaves like spinach.

Rape
[Lat. *Brassica napus*, Fr. *Navette*]

Perhaps this is strictly speaking a herb rather than a vegetable, but as it is used as a salad vegetable I have included it in this section of the book. A native of Europe, rape grows wild in many parts of England. It was formerly cultivated as a salad vegetable, but is now mostly grown for feeding sheep. Its seed is made into an oil called 'colza' or 'coleseed oil'.

Rocket
[Lat. *Eruca sativa*, Fr. *Roquette*]

A native of southern Europe, rocket was introduced to England in the sixteenth century, and was very popular as a salad vegetable. It later fell into disuse, but is still widely grown in the United States, and to a lesser extent in France. I have been unable to find a nursery garden in England who stock the seed, which is a pity as it produces a small fresh-tasting leaf early in the summer which makes an excellent addition to a mixed green salad. Rocket is supposed to have spread rapidly among the ruins of London after the Great Fire.

Salsify
[Lat. *Tragopogon porrifolium*, Fr. *Salsifis*]

Also known as the oyster plant, or vegetable oyster, salsify is a biennial plant, a native of Europe, which produces a long tapering root whose white flesh has a subtle and unusual flavour. It is less popular now than formerly in England and the United States, although it is still eaten in France.

To prepare: Pare the roots and cut in chunks. Leave covered with cold water with a drop of vinegar or lemon juice until ready to cook, or they will discolour. To cook, cover the pieces of salsify with lightly salted cold water, bring to the boil and cook until tender, about 30–45 minutes. Drain, then toss in butter and sprinkle with finely chopped chervil or parsley before serving. The black-skinned variety of salsify called scorzonera actually has the better flavour, but is more troublesome to cook. See SCORZONERA.

Samphire

[Lat. *Crithmum maritimum*, Fr. *Perce-pierre*]

Samphire is not, as I first thought, a seaweed but a cliff plant resembling a herb. It grows on rocky coasts and shingle beaches, just above high water mark, where it is within reach of the spray but not the actual waves. It can be found on many shores of the British Isles, particularly in Cornwall. It resembles seaweed in that it has valuable contents of iron and other minerals, and like most seaweeds should be picked in May.

It can be grown in the garden by gathering seed from the wild plants and sowing it in the autumn in a seed-bed. It is susceptible to frost, and should be grown at the base of a wall for protection, or given some other form of shelter during the coldest months.

To prepare: Samphire was highly thought of in England in the seventeenth century; Shakespeare mentions it in King Lear, and there are many recipes for that period. It was generally eaten raw in salads, or pickled. It can also be steamed, like asparagus, and served with melted butter which seems more appealing to modern palates.

Savoy

A variety of cabbage. See CABBAGE, GREEN.

Scallions

This is another example of a word which was commonly used in England in Elizabethan times, but is now obsolete except in the United States where it is used to describe what the English now call 'spring onions'. In Wales these are called 'holtsers'. See SPRING ONIONS.

Scorzonera
[Lat. *Scorzonera hispanica*, Fr. *Scorsonère*]

This is the black-skinned variety of salsify; it differs slightly in that the roots are thicker and covered with a hard black skin, but the flesh is still white. It is generally thought to have the better flavour, but I find it troublesome to cook, as it must be peeled after cooking, when the soft white flesh tends to fall to pieces while one tries to remove every particle of black skin thereby scalding one's fingers. It is well worth the trouble to prepare in small quantities, but I would not attempt it for more than three or four people.

To prepare: Brush the roots well with a stiff brush and trim the ends with a sharp knife. If you have a long enough pan to accommodate them, do not cut the roots, but cook them whole. (An asparagus pan is ideal, if it is the sort to hold the asparagus horizontally, not an upright steamer. A small fish kettle will also do well.) Measure enough water to cover the roots, salt it lightly, and bring it to the boil. Drop in the scorzonera, bring back to the boil, and boil until they are tender – about 35–40 minutes. Lift them out and drain them. When they are cool enough to handle, scrape off the skin with a small knife and cut the roots in pieces about 1½ inches long. To serve re-heat by tossing in a little butter, and add a few drops of lemon juice or a couple of spoonfuls of chopped fresh herbs – chervil would be ideal. Alternatively, leave the scorzonera whole, lay in a shallow dish and cover with a sauce mornay (see p. 189), or a cheese soufflé sauce (see p. 182). Or the roots can be cut in pieces and dipped in any of the batters listed on pp. 78–80, and fried in deep fat. Serve with quarters of lemon.

Seakale

[Lat. *Crambe maritima*, Fr. *Chou-marin*]

A native of western Europe, seakale originally grew along the sea shores. It has been cultivated for hundreds of years in England, although it is much less often seen nowadays than formerly. It has never been very popular in France or other European countries apart from England, and is not well-known in the United States. It is sometimes forced for winter eating, but the flavour is better when allowed to grow naturally, and eaten in the early summer.

To prepare: The stems should be blanched, by growing through layers of pebbles, sand or seaweed; dried bracken or dead leaves can also be used. The part of the plant that is eaten is the stem: broad, white and curved, culminating in a tiny clump of leaves. Seakale should be cooked like asparagus, lowered into boiling lightly salted water, simmered until tender, then carefully drained and served on a white cloth. A bowl of melted butter should be handed separately.

Seakale Beet

See CHARD.

Seaweed

For edible seaweeds, see CARRAGEEN, DULCE, LAVER, and SLOKE.

Shallot

[Lat. *Allium ascalonicum*, Fr. *Échalote*]

The shallot is a native of Palestine, and is actually closer to garlic in its method of growth than the onion. The bulb divides itself into a number of cloves, as does garlic, and does not produce seed, as does the onion. It is used primarily as flavouring, and is considered more suitable than the onion for delicate sauces. It is much used in French cuisine in this manner.

To prepare: Shallots should always be finely minced or chopped, and they must be cooked gently without allowing them to brown, which gives a bitter taste to the finished dish.

Skirret

[Lat. *Sium sisarum*, Fr. *Chervis*]

The skirret is a very old vegetable, originally coming from China, and popular in England for hundreds of years. It was supposed to be a favourite food of the Roman Emperor Tiberius. Seventeenth- and eighteenth-century English cookery books abound in recipes for cooking skirret – stewed, fried, as fritters, soups, in pies, etc.

To prepare: The edible part of the skirret is the root, which grows in a swollen clump, not unlike a dahlia. They are cooked like salsify, carrots or other root plants; they should be peeled after cooking, and served with melted butter. (If they are peeled before cooking, they must be kept covered in water with a little vinegar or lemon juice in it, or they will discolour like salsify.) If they have a hard inner core, like an old carrot, it should be removed before serving.

Sloke

[Lat. *Porphyria laciniata*]

Also known as sea-spinach, sloke is a seaweed very similar to the purple laver found on the south and west coasts of England. In Ireland and Wales it is known as laver.

To prepare: Sloke needs very slow lengthy cooking, 4–5 hours, then add seasonings, butter and a little orange or lemon juice. It used to be served as an accompaniment to roast mutton.

Sorrel

[Lat. *Rumex*, Fr. *Oseille*]

There are several different varieties of sorrel; the one that grows wild in England *(rumex acetosa)* is rather bitter. The sort that is generally cultivated is the French broad-leafed sorrel *(rumex scutatus)*. Indeed it is much more generally used in France and Belgium than in England or the United States, and is very rarely found in English shops, though it can be easily grown from seed in the garden.

To prepare: Sorrel makes a most useful and unusual addition to many summer dishes, either alone, or mixed with other green leaves such as spinach, dandelion, watercress or lettuce. The young leaves are delicious sliced and eaten raw as a salad with the addition of crumbled fried bacon (for the recipe see p. 165). If you have only a small quantity it is better to use it in this way, as ½ lb will serve three or four people, while if it is cooked you must allow ½ lb per person, as it shrinks alarmingly, like spinach.

Sorrel is cooked like spinach. It then makes an excellent purée, which with cream and butter added is good served with *oeufs mollets*, or with poached eggs on top for a light luncheon dish. It can be mixed with spinach when making a spinach soufflé, or made into a delicate soup. Its slightly bitter taste goes well with the blandness of eggs, and it can be used to advantage as the filling for an omelette or as garnish for a dish of scrambled eggs.

Spinach
[Lat. *Spinacia oleracea*, Fr. *Épinard*]

A native of Persia, spinach has been grown in France since the fourteenth century, and in England since the sixteenth. It has always been popular, and is a very valuable source of iron, and vitamins B and C. There are two sorts, the winter and the summer spinach, and between them it is in season almost all the year, excepting the autumn. The summer spinach is far the more delicate of the two, with soft green leaves and stalks, and a lighter flavour, while the winter variety is coarser both in texture and in flavour. It is usually better to discard the stalks of the winter spinach before cooking.

To prepare: In the United States, and in France and Italy, spinach is often eaten raw as a salad. Only the summer variety should be used in this way but it makes an excellent and unusual salad that should be more widely known in England. In cooking it must be remembered that spinach shrinks amazingly, and at least ½ lb per person should be allowed. It must be very well washed, in three or four different waters. There are two schools of thought about the best way to cook spinach; I use the English way, which is to rub a heavy pan with a piece of butter and pile in the spinach leaves with only the drops of water left on the leaves after washing. They must be cooked over very gentle heat until the water has started to emerge from the leaves, when the heat can be turned up and the cooking accelerated. The leaves should be turned over from time to time with a wooden spoon.

The French method is to throw the leaves into a large pan of boiling water and cook until just tender. In either case the spinach must be very well drained in a colander, pressing out the water with the back of a spoon. If left to cool slightly, it can be squeezed between the hands. After draining it can be served *en branches*, tossed in a knob of butter with salt and black pepper, or it can be chopped and returned to the pan with the same additions, or sieved to make a very fine purée with cream and a pinch of grated nutmeg. A creamy purée of spinach is delicious with poached eggs or *oeufs mollets*, and the best accompaniment to veal. It is one of the few vegetables that goes well with fish, and it also has an affinity with cheese and cream cheese. A little puréed spinach can be added to many basic mixtures to make an unusual dish, green gnocchi, for example, or spinach dumplings, or green pancakes, as well as sauce verte, where chopped spinach and herbs are added to mayonnaise to make a pretty pale green summery sauce to serve with salmon trout or soft-boiled eggs.

Spinach Beet

See CHARD.

Spring Onions
[Lat. *Allium cepa*]

Spring onions or scallions (known as holtsers in Wales) are not the thinnings from the larger onions, although these are sometimes used as such, but a special variety of onion that matures while still very small. One of the best seeds is 'white Lisbon'. Spring onions are almost always used raw, either whole, with other crudités or cheese, or in salads. They can be cooked, but usually as an addition and flavouring to another dish, as in the Irish potato dish called 'champ', rather than in their own right.

Sprue

This is the technical name for the thinnings from the asparagus beds, which can often be bought cheaply either directly from asparagus farms or in the shops. These thin green stalks can be made into many delicious dishes for very reasonable cost.

To prepare: Cooked like asparagus, but more briefly, they are delicious served as a bed for poached eggs, covered with sauce hollandaise. They can also be used for asparagus soups, or any of the dishes requiring asparagus tips as a garnish.

Squash
[Lat. *Cucurbita*, Fr. *Courge*]

The squash is an enormously popular American vegetable, available in varying forms all the year round. It includes a number of varieties never seen in England, as well as some similar to the English courgette and marrow. The summer squashes come in all shapes and colours, and have a delicate thin skin which can be pierced with the finger nail. They include 'straight neck' squash, 'crooked neck' squash, cymling (like the English custard marrow), cocozelle and zucchini (like the English courgette).

To prepare: The summer squash should be cooked while still young, before the seeds have had time to form. They do not store well, but should be cooked soon after picking. They are best cooked like courgettes, left whole if small enough, or else cut in chunks or slices. Peel or not as you wish, then steam, poach, sauté or stew gently in their own juice until tender. Season well before serving.

The winter squash come into season in the autumn and are available until early spring. With the exception of the 'butternut' squash, they have hard skins. They include 'golden delicious', 'acorn', 'buttercup' or 'turban', and 'Hubbard' squash, and store well, especially the Hubbard squash. Before cooking, the seeds should be removed, after which they can be peeled and cut in pieces; or they can be baked in the oven for 30–45 minutes and the flesh removed from the shell after cooking. They lend themselves well to stuffing with mixtures of rice, meat or vegetables.

Swede
[Lat. *Brassica napus*]

Although much despised in France, where it is grown as food for cattle, the swede has been popular in England since the eighteenth century. It is also liked in the United States, where it is known as 'rutabaga'. Originally called the 'Swedish turnip', it is a member of the huge cabbage family similar to the kohlrabi, in that the edible part is an underground swelling of the stem rather than an actual root. Its flesh is yellow, as opposed to the white flesh of the turnip.

To prepare: The swede is prepared and cooked exactly like a turnip. The tops also make an excellent green vegetable if picked while still young and tender. They should be cooked until just tender in boiling salted water, well drained, chopped and tossed in melted butter with salt and black pepper. Ordinary turnip tops can be cooked in the same way, but swede tops have a better flavour.

Sweet Corn
[Lat. *Zea mays rugosa saccharata*, Fr. *Maïs*]

Sweet corn was the staple food of the American Indians, and was adopted by the first European settlers to avoid starvation. It became one of the favourite American dishes, and its popularity has only recently spread to England. It needs a lot of sun to ripen, however, and can only be grown successfully in southern England, and in good summers. It has a very high content of both sugar and starch, and should therefore be avoided by those on diets. Where conditions are favourable, it is well worth growing, as it is one of those vegetables which lose much of their excellence soon after picking.

To prepare: The end of the stalk should be trimmed and most of the hairy coating removed. Only the soft inner covering should be left until after cooking. If cooked immediately after picking, corn-on-the-cob needs only 5–8 minutes in boiling water to become tender; the following day it will need 20–30 minutes. When very fresh, it can also be grilled, or baked in the oven.

To prepare corn off the cob, hold the cobs downwards on

to the table and slice the kernels off the cob with a sharp knife, as close to the cob as possible. This is easily done, and is far preferable to using frozen or tinned corn, which loses much of its sweet milky taste. When cooked off the cob, corn needs only a short cooking in a little lightly salted water, brought to the boil before adding the corn. A delicious chowder can be made from corn, also corn pudding, fritters, creamed corn, dishes of corn with eggs, or corn mixed with lima (or broad) beans to make succotash.

Sweet Potato
[Lat. *Convulvulus batatus*, Fr. *Patate douce*]

The sweet potato came originally from South America, and was the first form of potato to reach the British Isles. It is often mentioned in English cookery books of the sixteenth and seventeenth centuries, but is no longer generally popular in England. It has reappeared, however, in areas with a high immigrant population, especially from the West Indies where it forms a staple part of the diet. It is immensely popular in the southern States of America and is much liked all over the States. There are two types: the ordinary, or Jersey, sweet potato, and the yam. The former has a pale yellow flesh of a dry floury consistency, while the flesh of the yam is orange in colour and more oily. Both are treated in identical ways. The sweet potato is rich in vitamin C, and takes the place of the ordinary potato in the diet of most tropical countries.

To prepare: The potatoes should be well washed or scrubbed before cooking; in most cases they are peeled after cooking. They can be cooked very much like the ordinary potato: boiled, baked, fried, or made into a purée. To boil: cut in pieces if large, or leave whole. Cover with cold salted water and boil until soft. Drain well, add butter, salt and black pepper, or make into a purée. To bake: heat the oven to 400°, lay the scrubbed potatoes on the oven rack, and bake for 45 minutes to 1 hour, until soft when squeezed with a cloth or pierced with a skewer. Serve with butter, salt and black pepper. To fry: peel the potatoes and cut them in slices. Shallow fry in butter until soft, turning often. Season with salt and black pepper.

Tomato

[Lat. *Lycopersicum esculentum*, Fr. *Tomate*]

A native of South America, the tomato is strictly speaking a fruit, but as it is always treated as a vegetable, I am including it as such. Originally known as the 'love apple' – it was thought to have aphrodisiacal qualities – the tomato was introduced to England in the sixteenth century. It had the immediate appeal of a novelty, but its popularity later waned. It was not much used in the United States until the early nineteenth century, by which time it was again popular in England. Their flavour combines well with onions, leeks, garlic, herbs, aubergines, courgettes and marrow, while their colour lends a pleasing contrast to many pale dishes. A tomato sauce provides the perfect accompaniment to many vegetable dishes such as soufflés and timbales, stuffed green vegetables and all the farinaceous dishes like gnocchi, pancakes and noodles.

Tomatoes contain valuable minerals, and vitamins A and C. They are one of the few vegetables which do not suffer from canning; indeed a good canned tomato often has more flavour than a mediocre fresh one. They need a lot of heat to bring out their true flavour, which perhaps explains why the Italian plum-shaped tomato, sold extensively in tins, is so good. There are a few hardy varieties which can be grown out-of-doors in less hot climates, but on the whole they do better under glass in England. The type generally grown throughout England and the United States is the smooth-skinned round tomato, with a lot of juice. A far preferable variety is the one grown widely in France, particularly the South. Very large, with a rather ugly appearance, deeply ridged skin and a much drier flesh, it has an excellent flavour and is better for all dishes, especially for stuffing. A yellow variety that was popular in England before the war is rarely seen nowadays; there is also a tiny 'cherry' tomato that was much used as a garnish, with fruit not much bigger than marbles.

To prepare: Unless they are to be cooked in the oven or under the grill, tomatoes should always be skinned before cooking. This is quickly done by pouring boiling water over them and leaving for 1 minute, then plunging them into cold water. The skin will then slip off easily. They can be cooked in a multitude of ways: fried in butter, cut in half and grilled, baked in the oven either whole or sliced, steamed or stewed in their own juice.

Truffle
[Lat. *Tuberacei*, Fr. *Truffe*]

There are three main sorts of truffles, by far the most highly esteemed being the black truffle which is found in France, particularly in the area round Périgord. The truffle is a form of fungi, with some of the magical qualities of the wild mushroom, in that it has defied all attempts to cultivate it. The nearest approach to cultivation has been to make plantations of the trees they prefer to grow under in places where the soil is suitable, that is chalky, and hope for the best. They are notoriously difficult to find, and special dogs, and pigs, are used to hunt for them.

In the north of Italy there is a white truffle which is found in the autumn. It is quite different from the black, both in texture and flavour. It has a sweet nutty taste, like a cross between a nut and a mushroom, and has a hard consistency. Its uses are limited, as it is only ever eaten raw, usually as a garnish for a dish of noodles, a risotto, or a dish of scrambled eggs. It should be cut in the thinnest possible slices and scattered over the cooked dish.

In former times, truffles were found extensively in parts of Southern England, particularly in Hampshire, Sussex, Wiltshire and Kent. They were in fact a similar but inferior form of the French, or black, truffle; they were highly thought of in England, and one man kept a pack of truffle hounds and made his occupation from finding and selling truffles to the London markets. They grew best under beech trees, near the edges of woods, while in France they are generally found under young oak trees. Even the best French truffle has very little actual flavour of its own, but it has a curious quality of bringing out the flavour of other foods, particularly poultry and pâtés. It is almost always used in small quantities as a garnish, as it has great visual appeal. Its glossy black surface lends a very pleasing appearance to a ham mousse, for example. In England and the United States they can only be bought in tins, either whole, or the cheaper version which is the peelings. In Paris they can be bought fresh during the early winter. They are so extremely expensive now that they are rarely cooked as they used to be, as a dish in their own right. (They were poached in champagne, or a mixture of champagne and veal stock, for 10–15 minutes, and served wrapped in a napkin. Alternatively they were roasted in hot ashes for 35–45 minutes.)

Turnip
[Lat. *Brassica napus*, Fr. *Navet*]

Turnips have been cultivated since the earliest times, and it is hard to know where their actual country of origin was. There are many different varieties, but they fall into two main types: the round or slightly flattened turnip which is mainly grown in England and the United States, and the oval-shaped root, rather like a fat carrot, which is popular in France. I am very fond of the latter variety, and buy it whenever I can find it, as I have yet to find a 'woody' turnip of this type. However tiny the round ones are, they may still have that hard core which is impossible to make tender by cooking, if they have been incorrectly grown.

To prepare: Young turnips make delicious eating raw, as crudités; they have a sweet taste and crisp texture that is ideal for this purpose. They should be very thinly pared, cut in slices and chilled to be eaten at their best. To cook, they should be cut in halves, quarters or chunks according to their size. Like all root vegetables they should be covered with cold water, lightly salted, brought to the boil and cooked until tender. It is hard to give exact timing, as so much depends on the age of the turnip. After 10 minutes they should be tested frequently with a fine skewer. If allowed to cook for too long they will disintegrate into a watery mass. They should be well drained, then tossed in melting butter with freshly chopped parsley. They can also be made into a delicious purée, which must be well dried out, with butter and cream added, and carefully seasoned with salt and black pepper. They also make excellent purées mixed with other root vegetables, such as carrots, parsnips or swedes, or with potatoes. Turnips have an affinity for fat, and should always have a generaus lump of butter added. They are the classic accompaniment to foods with a high fat content, such as duck, mutton, etc.

266

Turnip tops, the young sprouting leaves, make a vegetable dish in their own right. They should be thrown into boiling salted water, cooked briskly for 8–10 minutes, drained, then chopped and returned to the pan with a knob of butter, salt and pepper.

Vegetable Marrow
[Lat. *Cucurbita pepo ovifera*, Fr. *Courge*]

Since the introduction of courgettes, which are in fact a miniature form of marrow, the marrow itself has become less popular in England than it was formerly. Enormous marrows are still grown, but mainly for shows and harvest festivals, while their popularity as a vegetable has been largely eclipsed by the newer smaller varieties. However they are very easily grown, and make an impressive sight when allowed to clamber over a compost heap in the corner of the garden – they should be planted low down on the mound, and allowed to climb up over it – which still endears them to many cottage gardeners.

To prepare : In the days of Mrs Beeton marrows were almost inevitably reduced to a watery mush by boiling, and served in a watery white sauce. They should never be boiled, as their liquid content is so high already; they should be peeled, cut in chunks, the seedy interior removed and the remaining flesh cooked in a lidded sauté pan with a lump of butter or other fat. Cook gently for about 10 minutes, stirring occasionally to prevent sticking; they will then be tender and make an excellent dish, carefully seasoned with salt and black pepper. They go well with tomatoes, and half a pound of skinned and roughly chopped tomatoes can with advantage be added halfway through the cooking. The combination of colours, the pale green with the red of the tomatoes, makes a very pretty dish.

They are ideal for stuffing if you choose one of a good shape that is not too enormous. Its skin should be peeled in strips, to give a striped effect; again it is prettiest and most delicious when served in conjunction with a tomato sauce. (For recipe, see p. 121.)

The flowers of the marrow can be made into an unusual dish, just as the flowers of the courgette. They are stuffed with a light mixture of rice and herbs, dipped in batter, and deep-fried. Alternatively, they can be fried in deep fat without the stuffing.

Watercress
[Lat. *Nasturtium officinale*, Fr. *Cresson*]

Watercress is a native plant of the British Isles, where it can be found widely growing in streams. It is now grown commercially in an improved variety with much larger leaves, and is available all the year round. It is too often used merely as a garnish, left uneaten on the plate after the steak has been consumed. This is sad, as it is not only delicious and adaptable, both as a salad vegetable and a cooked food, but it is also extremely rich in iron. It makes excellent sandwiches, a classic soup, and a pretty pale green sauce to serve over *oeufs mollets*. It looks extremely decorative mixed with paler green leaves in a salad, while adding its own slightly astringent flavour.

To prepare: Watercress should be cooked as spinach.

Yam

One of the two main types of sweet potato. See SWEET POTATO.

Zucchini

The Italian name, which has been adopted in the United States, for the courgette. See COURGETTE.

Herb Encyclopedia

Herbs are of immense importance in vegetable cookery, and anyone with any space at all, even a broad window-sill capable of accommodating some large pots, would be wise to grow at least a few during the summer months. It is hard to find anything more unusual in the shops than parsley or chives, and when one does they are ridiculously expensive. I have nine or ten favourties which I try to grow each year; some of them, like chervil and dill, are annuals, which means starting from scratch each spring; others, like tarragon, are delicate and often perish during a hard winter. With limited space I would concentrate on basil, chervil, chives, dill, marjoram, at least one variety of mint, two sorts of parsley, tarragon and thyme. These are the herbs that I find most useful, with their fresh, light tastes. The others, with more pungent aromas and a stronger flavour, like rosemary, bay and sage, I find I use only with meat or fish, and not often then.

I rarely use dried herbs and except where specified the recipes call for fresh ones. However, if you do wish to use dried herbs, remember that they are much stronger and should be used in smaller quantities.

Angelica
[Lat. *Angelica archangelica*, Fr. *Angélique*]

A native of the Alps, the roots of angelica were considered to have medicinal qualities, and were imported into England from Spain during the seventeenth century as a prevention against the plague. It was also thought to be a protection against evil spirits. In its native habitat it grows more than 4 feet high, with large deeply-indented leaves and yellow flowers. A white-flowered variety called 'sylvestris' grows wild in England. It can easily be grown from seed, which should be planted in July or August. It will not flower until the second year, after which it should be dug up and replanted, as it will run to seed. The stems are crystallized and used as a decoration for cakes; in some parts of Europe the leaves are eaten as a vegetable, while the roots are the part with the supposed medicinal qualities.

Anise
[Lat. *Pimpinella anisum*, Fr. *Anis*]

A native of Greece and Egypt, it is hard to say whether anise is technically a herb or a spice. It has been used in England since ancient times both medicinally and as a seasoning; the Romans made a spiced cake using it as one of the spices. It was also used to flavour bread and soups, and was supposed to cure headaches and indigestion. A pretty plant, it grows about a foot high with very fine leaves and flowers like fennel or dill. It grows easily in a warm sheltered spot.

Balm
[Lat. *Melissa officinalis*, Fr. *Mélisse citronelle*]

Also known as lemon balm, this plant has a refreshing scent and flavour. It is a native of southern Europe, and grows wild throughout the southern parts of the British Isles. It is a pretty bushy plant, with tiny leaves of bright green which release their exquisite lemon scent when crushed. It was formerly used as a stewing herb, as well as for making wine and an infusion for herb tea. It was supposed to bring joy and to comfort the spirit, as well as curing toothache and asthmatic illnesses. It was also recommended to students to help clear the brain and sharpen the memory. It has not many uses nowadays, unless for making a *tisane*, but should be included in a herb garden wherever possible, on account of its delicious scent and appearance.

Basil
[Lat. *Ocymum basilicum*, Fr. *Basilic*]

There are many different varieties of basil: the one to choose for culinary purposes is 'sweet basil'. This variety has a large broad leaf, as opposed to the tiny leaves of the 'bush basils'. It is a native of India, where the Hindus considered it to be a holy plant, and grew it near their temples to protect them from misfortune. In medieval England it was thought to have powers against witchcraft. As a pot-herb it was more highly prized by the French than the English, who used it primarily as a strewing herb, and for its magical qualities.

Coming as it does from a very hot country it is not easily cultivated in more temperate climates, but is very well worth the effort. It needs a lot of sun to develop its true flavour, and benefits from being grown under glass, or even inside a sunny window, at least during the early part of the summer. After many experiments I tend to keep it indoors until mid-July, when I move it to a sheltered sunny spot in the garden, or simply leave it in its pot out of doors. It benefits by being used, and should be picked frequently.

At the moment it is my favourite among herbs, and particularly so in relation to vegetable cookery. I find its strong but delicate aromatic flavour absolutely irresistible, and use it frequently throughout the summer. It has a special affinity with tomatoes and with all pasta dishes, cheese and eggs. It is the basic ingredient for the famous Provençal sauce *pistou*, or *pesto* as it is called in Italy, when it is pounded in a mortar with a combination of grilled tomatoes, pine kernels and Parmesan cheese according to the version used, and served with *Soupe au pistou*, or a dish of noodles, or best of all, a dish of mixed new vegetables, freshly boiled and still warm.

Bay
[Lat. *Laurus nobilis*, Fr. *Laurier*]

This is not strictly speaking a herb, but the leaf of the bay tree. However, ever since the French chose to include it in their classic bouquet garni, it has been treated as such. It has become one of the classic flavourings for many dishes – almost all casseroles of meat, poultry and game, fish *court-bouillons*, soups and stocks.

Bergamot
[Lat. *Mentha odorata*]

A variety of mint with lemon-scented leaves, this plant is also known as mentha citronata.

271

Borage
[Lat. *Borago officinalis*, Fr. *Bourrache*]

Native to Europe and North Africa, borage is a pretty plant
growing about 18 inches high with bright blue flowers in
May and June. It was thought by the Romans to be good
for the spirits, and was much used as a cure for depression
and melancholy. The leaves were also used as a pot-herb,
while the flowers were candied. Nowadays its only use is as
a garnish for Pimms and other wine cups.

Camomile
[Lat. *Anthemis nobilis*, Fr. *Camomille*]

A tiny low-growing plant with minute white flowers, camomile flourishes by being walked on, and is ideal for small
lawns or paths, for instance through a herb garden. It has
been used in this fashion in England for the last four hundred years. It should be rolled with a roller, and only needs
occasional clipping. Do not attempt to make a camomile
lawn in a shady place however; the plants will grow tall
and straggly, searching for the light. In France it is still used
to make a *tisane* with supposed medicinal qualities, as it has
been for many centuries.

Chervil
[Lat. *Scandix cerefolium*, Fr. *Cerfeuil*]

Chervil is a native of southern Europe, and was brought to
England by the Romans, who prized it highly. It is listed in
the earliest-known English cookery books as a necessary
part of the herb garden, to which much importance was
given. It is somewhat like parsley, but with a more delicate
flavour; also like parsley, it comes in two varieties, the flat-
leafed and the moss-curled. The latter is not often seen
nowadays, but is pretty as a garnish. I am particularly fond
of chervil, and try to grow it every summer as it is almost
impossible to find it in shops or nurseries. I like to use it
instead of parsley in many dishes; it is also good in a mixture
of herbs, as its flavour is not so strong as to dominate the
others, as do basil and tarragon.

Chives
[Lat. *Allium schoenoprasum*, Fr. *Ciboulette*]

A member of the onion family, the chive is a native of southern Europe. Together with parsley and mint, it is one of the few herbs still in common use in England and the United States today. Its main use is as a garnish, as it quickly loses its flavour when subjected to heat. The bright green tubular leaves make an attractive decoration for pale dishes, while the sharp onion flavour contrasts perfectly with bland creamy foods like vichyssoise. They should always be cut with scissors, rather than chopped with a knife, which spoils their shape and bruises them so that they turn black.

Clary
[Lat. *Salvia sclarea*, Fr. *Sauge sclarée*]

Clary is a form of sage nowadays only seen occasionally as a decorative plant. It was very popular in seventeenth-century England for making wine, for flavouring soups, and raw in salads. The leaves were also chopped and made into fritters, and eaten as a sweet dish. It is easily grown: the seeds should be sown in the spring and must be re-sown each year, as the plant dies after the seeds ripen. It grows to about 3 feet high, with spikes of mauvey-pink flowers.

Coriander
[Lat. *Coriandrum sativum*, Fr. *Coriandre*]

Coriander is usually thought of as a spice, for the seeds are much used in oriental cookery, but the young leaves can also be used in their fresh state. They are much used in Chinese cookery, where they are also called *hsiang-tsai*, or 'Chinese parsley', and in Indian cookery. When crushed they add a hot taste to food that is very popular in the East, where they are added to food as a seasoning after cooking. In medieval England coriander was grown in herb gardens; the seeds were used to flavour liqueurs, and as a preventive against gout.

Dill

[Lat. *Anethum graveolens*, Fr. *Aneth*]

Dill is an annual plant, native to southern Europe. In appearance much like fennel, it has very fine leaves and flat flower heads containing the seeds. It was formerly used in England as a pot-herb and in salads, but is now rarely seen, although it is much used in Austria, Hungary and Poland, as a sauce for boiled meat, and in conjunction with cucumbers. In Scandinavia it is cooked with boiled potatoes, which are sometimes served with a sprig of dill curled around them. It is easily grown, and I highly recommend it. It has a pleasant fresh taste that goes well with eggs and vegetable dishes, or as a flavouring for a cream sauce. It also combines well with mustard, and makes an excellent dish with poached chicken in a mustard and dill sauce. The seeds are used in pickling cucumbers; they can be bought in packets like celery seed and aniseed, but I prefer to use the fresh leaves.

Fennel

[Lat. *Foeniculum officinale*, Fr. *Fenouil*]

We are dealing here with the common, or garden, fennel, as opposed to the wild fennel which can be found growing wild in England and France, or the *finocchio*, or Florence fennel, which is cultivated for the sake of its swollen root base, especially popular in Italy. The common or garden variety is very similar to dill in appearance, with the same feathery leaves and flat flower heads, but has thicker stalks and a slightly bitter flavour. It is usually used with fish, either flambé as a flaming bed for grilled red mullet, or *loup de mer*, or in a sauce. In medieval times it was the most usual accompaniment to grilled mackerel, either alone, or combined with gooseberries. The seeds are used to flavour liqueurs. It was also used for soup, and salads, as a pickle, and as an infusion for herb tea.

Hyssop

[Lat. *Hyssopus officinalis* 'Fr. *Hyssope*]

Hyssop is an evergreen shrub with spikes of blue or pink flowers, according to the variety. It was formerly much used in England both as a stewing herb, and in salads. It has a fairly hot, pungent flavour that is no longer popular, and nowadays it is grown for decorative purposes rather than for cooking. It has a pleasant aromatic smell, and attracts bees.

Lovage
[Lat. *Levisticum officinalis*, Fr. *Livèche*]

Lovage can be found growing wild on the coasts of Scotland and north-eastern England; it was formerly much cultivated in herb gardens, but has fallen into disuse. It has a strong celery flavour, and can be used to advantage to flavour stews and meat dishes. Both the root and the seed can be used. It should be grown from seed planted in the late summer, and increased by root division in the spring.

Marigold
[Lat. *Calendula officinalis*, Fr. *Souci*]

Although no longer thought of as a herb, the marigold always used to be included in herb gardens, and was much used in the kitchen. The petals were added to salads, where they give a pleasing effect, and used as a flavouring for stews and casseroles. Dried marigold petals can still be bought from Culpeper House, also 'broth posies', which include marigolds along with parsley, thyme and bay leaves.

Marjoram
[Lat. *Origanum marjorana*, Fr. *Marjolaine*]

There are two varieties of marjoram, the 'sweet marjoram' or *marjoram officinalis*, which is the most common, and the 'French marjoram' or *origanum onites*. Much used in Italian and Greek cooking, where it is known as oregano, it has a delicious flavour that goes particularly well with tomatoes, especially in sauces for spaghetti and pizza, salads – in Greece a bowl of dried oregano is often handed as an accompaniment to a mixed salad with Feta cheese – fish and eggs. It is also good as a flavouring for minced-meat dishes, like meat loaf or meat balls, and in pâtés. It is easily grown as long as it is sown in a sunny position. It is a very aromatic plant, and should be grown from seed planted each spring.

Mint
[Lat. *Mentha*, Fr. *Menthe*]

There are many different varieties of mint, and if there is available space at least two or three varieties should be included in the herb or kitchen garden. The most commonly used is 'spearmint', or *mentha viridis*. This is the old-fashioned English variety, used for the classic dishes such as mint sauce. 'Applemint', or *mentha rotundifolia variegata*, is a particularly decorative variety with its variegated green and white leaves, while eau-de-cologne mint, or *mentha citrata*, should be grown for its delicious pineapple scent when crushed. Ginger mint, or *mentha gentilis*, also has variegated leaves and a warm gingery scent, while peppermint, or *mentha piperita vulgaris*, has the familiar peppermint smell. A useful variety for the kitchen is *mentha cordifolia*, which has a good flavour for sauces and salads.

In England and the United States mint is only used occasionally, as a sauce for roast lamb and as a flavouring for new potatoes and green peas, but in the Middle East it is the most commonly used herb in the kitchen. Most families dry their own mint, as they prefer to use it in its dried state for most dishes. It is used in far larger quantities there than we are accustomed to, for instance in *tabbouleh*, an Arabic salad entirely composed of parsley and mint. It is also frequently used as a flavouring for salads and sauces, and as a seasoning for grilled meat. It is almost too easy to grow, as the roots have a tendency to spread all over the garden. It is a good idea to plant it in a flower pot, or large tin can, so that the roots are contained, otherwise it will overrun the whole garden.

Parsley
[Lat. *Carum petroselinum*, Fr. *Persil*]

In England and the United States parsley is the most commonly used herb. Unfortunately it is more often used as a garnish rather than an actual food, although it is full of iron and other vitamins. There are three varieties: the flat-leafed, or 'French parsley', which is supposed to have the best flavour; the curly-leafed or common parsley, most popular as a garnish; and the 'Hamburg parsley', which is grown for the sake of its root, which has an excellent flavour for adding to soups and stews. I am very fond of all three, and like to grow them in large quantities. Parsley makes an attractive hedge for a herb or kitchen garden, or as a division between plantations.

In England it is most often used in parsley sauce, but in the Middle East it is eaten in large quantities in its own right, in salads and vegetable dishes. In France it has always been included in the classic bouquet garni, along with thyme, bay and a piece of celery, for flavouring casseroles, soups, sauces and *court-bouillons* for poaching fish. In the 1920s and 1930s parsley was often deep fried and served as a garnish, an elegant accompaniment to fried foods now rarely seen. It is easily grown, but exceedingly slow to germinate, taking seven or eight weeks for the plants to appear.

Rosemary
[Lat. *Rosmarinus officinalis*, Fr. *Romarin*]

A native of southern Europe, rosemary grows widely in the South of France, along the shores of the Mediterranean. It is a pretty evergreen plant, with little spiky leaves of greyish-green, and spikes of misty blue flowers. It has a pleasant smell, but for my taste its flavour is almost too strong for cooking. It would certainly overpower delicate foods, such as most vegetables, but can be delicious used in small quantities when roasting or grilling meat, a mature leg of lamb or mutton for instance; a sprig of rosemary is also sometimes used as a brush with which to marinate kebabs while grilling over charcoal, or on a barbecue.

Sage
[Lat. *Salvia officinalis*, Fr. *Sauge*]

Sage is another herb which I find has a flavour and scent too pervasive for frequent use, but it is a pretty plant, with its silver-grey leaves, and should always be included in the herb garden. There are several varieties, the common sage, the more unusual pineapple sage, with red flowers and a scent of pineapples, and at least two variegated varieties, one with golden variegated leaves, the other with red leaves.

Savory
[Lat. *Satureia hortensis*, Fr. *Sarriette*]

There are two distinct varieties of this plant: the summer savory, which grows from one central stem with the more delicate flavour, and the winter savory, which grows in a bushy shape, and is a stronger plant with a more pronounced flavour. I prefer the summer variety, although I only use it rarely. Both savories are the classic French accompaniment for dishes of beans, particularly broad beans, which are rarely eaten without a flavouring of summer savory. Summer savory is an annual, while the more robust winter savory will live through most winters.

Tansy
[Lat. *Tanacetum vulgare*, Fr. *Tanaisie*]

Tansy is a very pretty plant, growing about 3 feet high, with fern-like bright green leaves and yellow flowers. Its taste seems strangely bitter to us nowadays, but it was formerly much used, both as a flavouring for roast lamb, in the way we use mint, and in sweet cakes and puddings, when sugar was added to counteract its bitter taste. It was also used as an infusion for tea.

Tarragon
[Lat. *Artemisia dranunulus*, Fr. *Estragon*]

Although tarragon came originally from Siberia, the cultivated variety is a delicate plant which has to be nursed through severe winters if it is to survive. It is advisable to cut the stems down to ground level, and cover the plant with a litter of dry bracken or other protection. It is essential to get the right variety of tarragon, that is to say the true French tarragon, as this is the only one of any use in the kitchen. The other variety, although identical to the eye, has no flavour whatsoever. It is one of my favourites among herbs, with its very unusual and distinctive taste delicate enough to combine with other herbs, and equally delicious on its own. It is especially delicious with chicken, as in *poulet à l'estragon*, with eggs, in omelettes, in cream sauces, with fish, or in salads.

Thyme
[Lat. *Thymus vulgaris*, Fr. *Thym*]

A native of southern Europe, thyme is connected in most people's minds with the Mediterranean shores, with Greece and Provence, where it flourishes in the dry scrubby vegetation, and the great heat of the sun brings out its warm flavour and aromatic scent. There are many different varieties of this charming plant; some have tiny white flowers, others pink or mauve, while the leaves can be grey, golden or variegated. My favourite nursery stocks twenty-two different varieties, several of them the creeping thymes which can be used to excellent effect to make small carpets, or paths. For cooking the best variety is the common thyme, but there is also an interesting variety called *thymus citriodorus*, with an unusual lemon flavour, excellent with eggs and tomatoes.

Valerian
[Lat. *Valeriana officinalis*, Fr. *Valériane*]

Formerly grown as a pot-herb and for medicinal reasons, valerian is not much seen nowadays.

Suggested Autumn and Winter Menus

Minestrone/French beans with bacon, cucumbers
stewed in cream, baked tomatoes

Spinach pancakes with tomato sauce/Stuffed leaves of
Chinese cabbage, Middle Eastern aubergines, raw
mushroom salad

String bean vinaigrette, tomato salad, raw mushroom salad,
onion bread/Curried vegetables with eggs

Courgette fritters with skordalia/A dish of mixed spring
vegetables *or* mixed vegetable casserole, onion bread

Homus with *pitta*/Potato pancakes *or*
boxty, fennel *or* chicory mornay, grilled tomatoes

Cheese soufflés in artichokes/Celery rémoulade, spinach
and yoghurt salad, cold ratatouille with home-made bread

Wholemeal *or* buckwheat pancakes with spinach filling/
Eggs Provençale, a simple lettuce salad

Risi e bisi *or* carrot risotto, gratin of chicory, baked
tomatoes/Cucumber and watercress salad

Timbale vert *or* spinach soufflé with tomato sauce/
A simple vegetable stew, onion bread *or* pirog

Provençal *or* Solferino soup/Champ *or* colcannon,
braised root vegetables, grilled mushrooms

Suggested Spring and Summer Menus

Crudités (raw vegetables – carrots, young turnips, celery, radish) with aïolli *or* skordalia/Leeks mornay, corn pudding, baked *or* grilled tomatoes

Cold spinach soup/Stuffed cabbage leaves, fennel and tomato salad

Guacamole with tortillas (bought in tins) *or* wholemeal pancakes/Broccoli au gratin, baked onions, carrot purée

Green gnocchi/Stuffed eggs rémoulade, beetroot salad, cucumbers in sour cream

Cucumber and tomato ring *or* tomato and mushroom mousse/Timbale of green peas with cream cheese sauce

Aubergine omelette *or* scrambled eggs with red peppers/ Cucumber and cheese salad on lettuce leaves, tomato and onion salad, rice salad with herbs

Oeufs mollets (soft-boiled eggs) in watercress sauce/ Stuffed mushrooms, sorrel *or* lettuce and bacon salad, carrot salad

Piperade with home-made bread/Leeks vinaigrette, saffron rice with peas, broccoli salad
Stuffed eggs guacamole/Vegetable cous-cous

Cauliflower and egg vinaigrette/Beetroot fritters, green rice, courgettes poached with herbs

Metric Equivalents

$\frac{1}{4}$ oz =	7$\frac{1}{2}$ grammes		$\frac{1}{4}$ pt =	1·5 decilitres
$\frac{1}{2}$ oz =	15 grammes		$\frac{1}{2}$ pt =	3 decilitres
$\frac{3}{4}$ oz =	20 grammes		$\frac{3}{4}$ pt =	4 decilitres
1 oz =	30 grammes		1 pt =	6 decilitres
1$\frac{1}{2}$ oz =	45 grammes		1$\frac{1}{2}$ pt =	9 decilitres
2 oz =	60 grammes		2 pt (1 qt) =	1·2 litres
2$\frac{1}{2}$ oz =	72 grammes		2$\frac{1}{2}$ pt =	1·5 litres
3 oz =	80 grammes		3 pt =	1·8 litres
4 oz ($\frac{1}{4}$ lb) =	110 grammes		3$\frac{1}{2}$ pt =	2.1 litres
6 oz =	170 grammes		4 pt (2 qt) =	2·4 litres
8 oz ($\frac{1}{2}$ lb) =	220 grammes			
12 oz ($\frac{3}{4}$ lb) =	340 grammes			
1 lb =	450 grammes			
1$\frac{1}{2}$ lb =	670 grammes			
2 lb =	900 grammes			

Index

Index

292

297

299

300

All Sphere Books are available at your bookshop or newsagent, or can be ordered from the following address: Sphere Books, Cash Sales Department, P.O. Box 11, Falmouth, Cornwall.

Please send cheque or postal order (no currency), and allow 19p for postage and packing for the first book plus 9p per copy for each additional book ordered up to a maximum charge of 73p in U.K.

Customers in Eire and B.F.P.O. please allow 19p for postage and packing for the first book plus 9p per copy for the next 6 books, thereafter 3p per book.

Overseas customers please allow 20p for postage and packing for the first book and 10p per copy for each additional book.